CHANGING
VIOLENT
MEN

Sage Series on Violence Against Women

Series Editors

Claire M. Renzetti
St. Joseph's University

Jeffrey L. Edleson
University of Minnesota

In this series . . .

CHANGING VIOLENT MEN

R. Emerson Dobash
Russell P. Dobash
Kate Cavanagh
Ruth Lewis

Sage Series on Violence Against Women

Sage Publications, Inc.
International Educational and Professional Publisher
Thousand Oaks ▪ London ▪ New Delhi

For information:

Sage Publications, Inc.
2455 Teller Road
Thousand Oaks, California 91320
E-mail: order@sagepub.com

Sage Publications Ltd.
6 Bonhill Street
London EC2A 4PU
United Kingdom

Sage Publications India Pvt. Ltd.
M-32 Market
Greater Kailash I
New Delhi 110 048 India

Printed in the United States of America

Library of Congress Cataloging-in-Publication Data

Changing violent men / by R. Emerson Dobash ... [et al.].
    p. cm. — (Sage series on violence against women)
  Includes bibliographical references.
  ISBN 0-7619-0534-0 (alk. paper)
  ISBN 0-7619-0535-9 (alk. paper)
  1. Wife abuse—Great Britain—Prevention—Evaluation. 2. Abusive
men—Rehabilitation—Great Britain—Evaluation. 3. Abused
women—Services for—Great Britain—Evaluation. 4. Evaluation
research (Social action programs)—Great Britain. I. Dobash, R.
Emerson. II. Series.
  HV6626.23.G7 C45 1999
  362.82'927'0941—dc21
                                        99-6265

This book is printed on acid-free paper.

00   01   02   03   04   05   06   7   6   5   4   3   2   1

Acquiring Editor: C. Terry Hendrix
Production Editor: Sanford Robinson
Editorial Assistant: Patricia Zeman
Typesetter: Christina M. Hill
Indexer: Janet Perlman

Contents

In loving memory of Ike Emerson,
a kind and gentle man.

Acknowledgments

W e wish to thank the men and women who participated in the Violent Men Study and hope that the stories of their lives will help create more effective ways of working to eliminate violence against women in the home. We acknowledge the important efforts of the staff of the abuser programs—CHANGE and the Lothian Domestic Violence Probation Project (LDVPP)—in working to end men's violence against women partners by adding a vital and positive response to this serious problem and thank them for their cooperation with the research. The court personnel in Edinburgh and Central Region, Scotland, were generous in allowing us access to their records and helpful in assisting with our enquiries. We also thank the Women's Aid groups in Central Region. The Violent Men Study was funded by a grant from the Scottish Office and the Home Office, England, and we are particularly grateful to Lorna Smith, Joe Curran, Val Cox, and Colin Baxter. Dan Ellingworth made important contributions to the statistical analysis reported in Chapter 6.

Dobash and Dobash would also like to express their appreciation to the Rockefeller Foundation; the Harry Frank Guggenheim Foundation; the Centre for Interdisciplinary Research (ZIF); the University of Bielefeld, Germany; and the Volkswagen Foundation for supporting various colloquia that contributed to the theoretical and empirical work reported here.

1

Focusing on Men's Violence and the Process of Change

The problem of violence against women in the home was "discovered" in the early 1970s, along with "discoveries" of other forms of violence in the family, including the physical and sexual abuse of children and marital rape. Violence in the heart of the institution of the family was difficult for the public to comprehend or accept, and these forms of violence were often denied or minimized in a vain effort to preserve the image of the idyllic family. This, however, soon gave way as increasing numbers of those who had been victimized and remained silent broke their silence and came forward for assistance. Evidence from a variety of sources began to show the widespread existence of violence between intimates. Attention turned from questions of whether the problem of intimate violence actually existed to questions about its nature and extent, its causes, the efficacy of existing responses, and the possibility of creating new approaches to its solution.

Responding to Abused Women

For women who had been the victims of violence by intimate partners, shelters or refuges for "battered women" opened and were instantly filled despite almost universal claims that the problem did not exist in that neighborhood, area, or nation. At local and national levels, government bodies held hearings and passed legislation, mostly offer-

1

ing protection orders and emergency housing for women fleeing violence (Dobash & Dobash, 1979, 1992; Hague & Malos, 1993;
Schechter, 1982; Stubbs, 1994). There was active debate and policy
making at local and national levels of government during the early period of discovery in the 1970s, and this extended to the international
level in the 1990s. The World Bank recognized men's violence against
women as a significant economic problem because of health costs and
loss of labor, and it was similarly acknowledged by the World Health
Organization (Heise, 1994, 1996). The United Nations first recognized it as an issue of human rights at the 1993 International Conference on Human Rights in Vienna and addressed it in the "Declaration
on the Elimination of Violence Against Women" at Beijing in 1995
(Charlesworth & Chinkin, 1994; Klein et al., 1997; Stubbs, 1994,
pp. 226-231).

In this relatively short period of time, the issue of violence against
women in the home has been "discovered" worldwide and it is now
generally recognized as a problem of importance not only to the individuals concerned but also to society at large. Thousands of projects,
programs, policies, and practices have been developed worldwide.
Small groups, local communities, and nations are attempting to
address the problem by responding to those who suffer abuse and by
intervening with respect to its perpetrators. Taken together, these
efforts add up to much more than each of the separate parts. Each of
the thousands of shelters now dotting the world have not only made an
important contribution to the safety of abused women but also had an
impact on public awareness, legal systems, and public policy in their
own nations and across nations. It is difficult to speculate how many
local projects have been tried, how much time and money has been
spent, and how much change has been effected. It probably would not
be an exaggeration to say that the sheer volume of effort worldwide
ranges from substantial to phenomenal.

At the same time, a large and growing body of evidence has developed at local and national levels. Knowledge about the issue has come
from many different sources, including official records, local and
national surveys, and victim report studies, and from the years of experience of activists and professionals (see Dobash & Dobash, 1992,
pp. 251-284). Overall, the evidence from this wide variety of sources
shows that violence against women in the home is widespread, that it
affects the emotional and physical health of women and children, and
that it sometimes ends in death. In our earlier research, we found that
25% of all forms of violence processed through the justice system was

violence against a woman partner (Dobash & Dobash, 1979, p. 247). The pattern of violence against women partners varies somewhat from nation to nation and from official data to local and national surveys, but it seems to exist everywhere across the globe. In Britain, estimates from sample surveys range from 10% to 25% of women at some time during their life having been the victim of violence from a male partner (Mirrlees-Black, 1994; Mooney, 1994; Painter & Farrington, in press; Smith, 1989). Statistics Canada's 1995 national Violence Against Women Survey of 12,000 women found that 25% of married women experienced an incident of domestic violence at some time in their life (Johnson, 1996; Johnson & Sacco, 1995). A small, local community survey of women in Northern Ireland found a similar figure of 27% (cited in McWilliams & McKiernan, 1993, p. 5) and a national survey of 679 women in the Republic of Ireland found a figure of 18% (Kelleher, Kelleher, & O'Conner, 1995, p. 15). Numerous surveys in the United States show that a substantial number of American women have been the victims of such abuse at some time during their life (for an overview of evidence and debates, see Kurz, 1997). In Sweden in 1993, 14,000 cases of assaults on women by males known to them were reported to the police, 3,000 women are battered on a typical Saturday night, and a woman is killed every 10th day (Eduards, 1997, p. 120). It is acknowledged as a problem among Jews and Arabs in Israel (Haj-Yahia, 1996); across the populations of Australia, including aboriginal groups and later British, European, and Asian immigrants (Cook & Bessant, 1997; Stubbs, 1994); and as far afield as Ecuador, Papua New Guinea, and the countries of Africa (Counts, Brown, & Campbell, 1992). No location seems untouched.

"Domestic Violence" Is Asymmetrical

The pattern of domestic violence is asymmetrical. Overwhelmingly, it is men who use violence against women partners, not the obverse (Dobash, Dobash, Wilson, & Daly, 1992; Dobash & Dobash, 1992; Nazroo, 1995). That is not to say that no woman has ever been violent. Obviously, this is not true. The *main pattern* of violence among intimates, however, is one of violence perpetrated by men against women. Of course, individual cases of women's violence exist, but such cases do not alter the fact that the overall *pattern* of intimate violence is dominated by men as abusers and by women as the abused. Evidence also indicates that when women do use violence against a spouse or male partner, whether assault or homicide, it is often against the backdrop of a history of the man's use of violence against the woman (Counts, Brown, & Campbell, 1992; Daly & Wilson, 1988, 1990, 1992). To illustrate, it is difficult to identify dozens, hundreds, or thousands of cases where women systematically and severely beat and intimidate male partners over sustained periods of time while the men remain trapped and terrorized in the relationship, yet it is easy to identify thousands upon thousands of cases where men have abused women in this fashion. The former is rare, the latter is commonplace.

While many couples may have had an exchange of slaps or minor blows at some time, and this is unfortunate and regrettable, this does not necessarily constitute a pattern of systematic and sustained violence meant to harm, intimidate, terrorize, and brutalize. It is the latter and not the former that constitutes a violent relationship; it is the latter and not the former that inflicts high costs on victims and witnesses, including children; it is the latter and not the former in which the intent is that of intimidation, injury, and harm; it is the latter and not the former in which the consequences are likely to necessitate a host of interventions aimed at assisting the victim and dependent children; it is the latter and not the former that necessitates effective interventions aimed at stopping the perpetrator from repeated and escalating episodes of violence. While any and all conflicts between partners are regrettable, not all escalate to the type and level of violent relationships necessitating public or private concern or active intervention. The focus of attention here is on those relationships characterized by systematic or severe violence, by injuries, by fear, by intimidation, and by various forms of intervention.

Throughout much of the world, individuals, small groups, local communities, and the state have mobilized to provide sanctuaries for women who have been the victims of men's violence. To a lesser extent, efforts have been addressed at the primary *source* of the problem, the men who perpetrate this violence. The most frequently used legal sanctions have been fines, suspended sentences, and protection orders. These are important efforts that help protect many women and may deter some men. But they cannot stop this violence without the addition of more explicit efforts to address the violence itself and to work to change violent men. Programs for abusive men, first established in the United States and later in Canada, Australia, New Zealand, and Britain have focused explicitly on the actions and supporting attitudes of those who use violence and considered how they might be changed.

The Transformative Project

Taken together, all of these efforts form the parts of a social project that is intended to be transformative. With respect to the overall problem of men's violence to women, the transformative project is, of necessity, both broad and narrow in focus and both general and specific in nature. The transformative project contains at least three general arenas that must be effectively addressed in seeking a solution. It is simultaneously a project of personal transformation for those who use violence and for those who are its victims; it is a project of institutional transformation for organizations that provide assistance to victims of violence or intervene with respect to those who use violence; it is a project of social and cultural transformation of public orientations to this violence and tolerance of it. All three arenas (personal, institutional, and cultural) need to be clearly identified as constituent parts of the problem and thus of any set of responses or proposed solutions. To opt for an overall approach contained in only one of the three general arenas in which the problem is created and sustained is to opt for an approach that will inevitably fail as a transformative project. While this three-part vision of change may not be embodied in every specific intervention or response, all three parts must be present in the overall complement of responses that make up the wider transformative project the goal of which is the end of this form of violence.

If we are to consider what is to be done to eliminate this form of violence, we must begin with what is known about the nature of this violence and with some theoretical notions about why it occurs and how it is maintained. Adopting the theoretical idea of the three-part transformative project of change at personal, institutional, and cultural levels does not require that every specific innovation actively engage with all three arenas of change equally or at once. The focus of any specific intervention is usually more narrow and often concentrates on one of the three arenas of change. The three-part transformative project does require an awareness, however, of how any particular innovation or intervention that concentrates on only one of the arenas of change may have an effect on the others. For example, the police may develop a policy of "proarrest" or of "diversion." While such policies are focused primarily on the arena of institutional intervention, they may also have transformative effects in the arena of individual change as abusers feel more or less confident about their continued use of violence and as abused women feel more or less secure or willing to seek assistance from the police. At the same time, the specific policy may also have transformative effects in the wider social arena as the general public considers the symbolic messages of the relative importance of violence used against women compared to other forms of violence or crime. General messages of relative "rights" and "wrongs" and of tolerance or intolerance of violence against women are conveyed at a wider social level even when specific interventions remain more narrowly focused on direct action at the institutional or individual level. Thus, any specific intervention would be expected to have some effect, for better or for worse, on all three of the arenas of change in the wider transformative project even if the primary focus of that intervention is concentrated only on one of them. It is therefore important that all interventions and innovations are scrutinized for effects at all three of these levels of change. While this task is difficult and is never likely to be complete or completely accurate, it nonetheless deserves attention, if only to try to avoid some of the worst consequences of ignoring the varied and various effects of interventions that seek to end this violence.

While specific initiatives or interventions may gain the attention or approval of policymakers or the general public simply because they appeal at face value, it behooves policymakers, professionals, advocates, and taxpayers alike to seek information about their effectiveness before such interventions either receive wide-scale approval or are eliminated from the portfolio of approaches to be tried. Research evaluations help examine such innovations, address questions of effectiveness, and provide insight into processes of change. The issues are complex and do not come in the form of single or simplistic answers, but adequate research helps provide insight into the details of how specific interventions might work and why that might be so (see Pawson & Tilly, 1997; Schalock, 1995: Weiss & Jacobs, 1988). At the heart of any evaluation is the process of change. If it is adequate to the task, evaluation research must provide information about the various facets of the problem itself, the context in which the problem occurs, and the elements that might be changed. Individuals, their social relationships, and the social contexts in which they live all form constituent parts of the problem and shape possible solutions. Where possible, research evaluations should be attuned to the holistic nature of the problem and its context as specific interventions, responses, outcomes, and the processes of change are examined.

Bearing this in mind, our purpose in *Changing Violent Men* is to examine the effectiveness of various criminal justice responses to men who use violence against a woman partner and to place this in the wider context of change as discussed above. We shall examine the effectiveness of two court-mandated abuser programs compared to more traditional justice sanctions such as fines, probation, and others. In doing so, our aims are fourfold: (a) to provide detailed descriptions of the nature of violence to enable an understanding of the phenomenon needing intervention and change; (b) to consider interventions directed at violent men, particularly abuser programs, and examine how the intervention articulates with the violence it seeks to change; (c) to ask if violent men can change and therefore consider at a more fundamental level if the transformative project is possible and should be continued or if it is impossible and should be abandoned completely; and (d) to theorize about the process of personal change among those men who do change.

Our means of seeking answers to these questions is through the use of evaluation research, and we shall also examine this general method and consider some of the dilemmas presented by it. While all of this will be located in the context of a wider base of literature, we shall, for the purposes of detailed illustrations, use the methods and findings of the Violent Men Study, which we undertook as an evaluation of court-mandated abuser programs and other responses to violent men (Dobash, Dobash, Cavanagh, & Lewis, 1996). Both qualitative and quantitative data are used to delineate the patterns of violence and personal change and to give a voice to men and women speaking about their relationships, about the impact of various criminal justice interventions, and about changes in their lives.

The "Fit"

To seriously address the transformative project, those who would develop an intervention aimed at ending this violence (whether shelters for women, programs for abusers, or other responses) must scrutinize in detail the intervention itself and similarly examine the phenomenon of the violence and consider to what extent the one "fits" the elements of the other. Obviously, a beautifully designed and well-run program directed at eliminating tooth decay would not likely have much bearing on the phenomenon of violence against women in the home, and no one would expect it to. But simply designing a program that has something to do with abused women or batterers may be equally far from the mark unless the program is carefully tailored to what is known about the phenomenon of the violence it is meant to address. Thus, it is the task of innovators to carefully examine the nature and content of the intervention with a similarly careful analysis of the nature of the violence as they specify what is to be done and "mark" it relative to aspects of the violence identified as in need of change.

Evaluation researchers who would seriously consider the transformative project of change have three tasks. They must not only examine in detail what is known about the phenomenon that is the focus of change (e.g., violence) and consider in detail the intervention that is meant to effect that change (e.g., abuser programs), they must also design a research project that will capture this dynamic process. That is, the specific content of the *intervention* needs to fit the phenomenon of *violence* that is the focus of the intervention and, in turn, the *research* evaluation needs to be designed to fit both the intervention and the phenomenon of violence that is to be changed. This three-way fit moves across the three large landscapes of the phenomenon, the intervention, and the evaluation, that is, the violence, men's programs, and the research. If the research is to reach its full potential in contributing to the transformative project, the overall approach must be both theoretically informed and empirically examined. While each of the three aspects of the fit (violence, intervention, research design) could easily form a study in its own right, the purpose here is to combine them in a broader approach meant to inform the overall transformative process. While any specific study or intervention must, of necessity, be viewed as modest in the face of a social problem of the magnitude of violence and an agenda of social and personal change, the Violent Men Study builds on important work already done in each of these three arenas and seeks to link the three separate areas in an overall approach aimed at examining the dynamic nature of this process of change.

For this overall project, the specific nature of the intervention (abuser programs) must be theorized beyond the level of descriptive detail to serve as a template to "lay over" the phenomenon of violence that is the subject of the transformative project. In turn, the research evaluation needs to be designed to serve as a template to lay over both the intervention and the phenomenon of violence. It is perhaps a bit like taking a long pipe made of three sections joined together. For our purposes, the three sections fitted together are those of the violence, the intervention, and the research. Each of the three sections, however, is divided into internal segments (a bit like an orange when cut in half), which correspond to its component parts. For example, the phenomenon of violence may be composed of different elements such as "notions of power and control," "attitudes toward women," "notions of male authority," "specific forms of violent abuse," "other controlling behaviors," and the like. Similarly, the intervention (e.g., abuser programs) would have corresponding segments meant to fit with those elements of the violent behavior targeted for change. Finally, the various elements of the evaluation research must be designed so as to capture corresponding elements in the intervention and the phenomenon of violence to consider what, if any, effect might have been produced and to provide some understanding of why the outcome was or was not achieved.

While each of these three main sections is made up of its own constituent parts or segments, and those can be examined separately and in their own right, the segments of one section must at the same time correspond to those of the others, at least in a general sense if not in identical detail, if one is to link to the next in the overall process of change. That is, all of the three main sections (violence, intervention, evaluation) with their internal segments must be fitted together like a long pipe to make the transformative process. At that point, the degree to which the internal segments in each of the three main sections corresponds with those in the other two segments provides an indication of the fit across all three. If a viewer were to look through this long pipe with its three internally segmented sections joined together only to find that the internal segments of one section bore no resemblance to those of the others, nothing could be seen and nothing could flow. If, however, the internal segments of each of the three sections corresponds perfectly with those of the other sections, light could be seen all the way through the pipe, movement can take place across all three sections, something can happen. Obviously, it is the best fit between the segments of violence and intervention that provides greater prospects for change and the additional fit with the evaluation that provides an opportunity to gain better knowledge about this transformative process.

In summary, the degree of correspondence across the three separate sections (violence, intervention, and research evaluation) displays the overall transformative project. In theory, greater correspondence between the elements of the violence and the specific elements of the intervention should provide more opportunity for personal change in behavior and attitudes. Similarly, greater correspondence between the elements of the research evaluation and those of the intervention being studied (which is in turn matched to the violence) should provide greater insight into the effectiveness of the intervention in changing the violent behavior. While perfect correspondence across all three sections may be possible in theory, it is unlikely that such perfection will be achieved in reality. Nonetheless, increasing the degree of fit, or correspondence, across the three areas of violence, intervention, and evaluation should yield more effective results than would be possible with approaches that are neither aware of nor sensitive to the relationship of each to the other in this overall transformative process. A greater fit across each of the three sections should allow the sighting of more light through the tunnel. The basic imagery of the overall task is one of seeking to include all of the relevant facets in the transformative process and doing so in a way that allows each to inform the other and all to work in a more singular and focused fashion toward ending this form of violence.

That is the task we have set ourselves. In approaching this task, we begin with an overview of the violence that is the focus of change. We start with the voices of men who have abused a woman partner and listen to them speak about what they have done and why they have done it. Later, we shall add the voices of women to complete the picture and provide more details. We follow with an overview of the philosophy, content, and specific technologies of the court-mandated men's programs to provide a description of the intervention being evaluated in the Violent Men Study . We will then discuss evaluation research in general and the Violent Men Study in particular as we consider the fit between what was studied in the research, what was done in the intervention, and what effect the intervention might have had on the violence that is the subject of change and the wider transformative project.

2

Men Talking
About Violence

Men who are processed through the justice system or experience any other form of intervention, such as an abusers program, for violent behavior have usually perpetrated several violent events prior to the first formal intervention. Rarely does the first violent event begin the process of intervention for abusers or the help-seeking activities of its victims. The first assault is not usually reported to police, social workers, or medical staff. It is generally safe to assume that those receiving their first formal intervention are not there on the occasion of the first violent attack. Our own research and that of others indicates that numerous violent incidents occur prior to the first report to any formal agency and only a few incidents are ever reported (Bowker, 1983; Dobash & Dobash, 1979, pp. 161-222; Grace, 1995; Mullender, 1996, pp. 33-36; Worrall & Pease, 1986). That interventions are almost always directed at those with repeat experiences of violence and rarely at the first offender has consequences for the type of interventions likely to have an effect on a behavior that has usually become well established before any form of intervention begins.

Responses to violence from whatever source may serve several purposes at once: They reflect public or institutional perceptions of the seriousness of a particular event, serve as a barometer of public or professional concern about the problem in general, and show intent to deter subsequent violence by the perpetrator or to provide support and protection for its victims. While the specific focus here is on the effectiveness of interventions for batterers, this is conceived of as an integral part of an overall complement of interventions directed at abusers as well as those they abuse and must be placed in the wider context of changes in the community and social change directed at the more general acceptance or rejection of this particular form of violence.

Before considering the effectiveness of various responses to men who batter, we describe the violence they have used against their women partners. This overview is meant to provide a theoretical understanding of this form of violence that is empirically informed. This characterization of violence serves three purposes. It provides an understanding of the nature of the violence leading to and necessitating intervention and develops a foundation from which to examine the fit between the elements of the violence as articulated here and the elements of the intervention meant to alter this violence. In turn, this empirically informed conceptualization of violence is used to consider what elements appear to change among men who alter their violent and controlling behaviors. Overall, this provides a conceptual or theoretical basis from which to examine the possible effectiveness of different forms of intervention in eliminating violence and sustaining change over time. The initial articulation of the violence, including the context in which it occurs and the processes whereby it is rationalized and sustained, begins the three-part process of examining the fit between the phenomenon; the intervention meant to effect a change in the phenomenon; and the research evaluation meant to examine the nature, extent, and sustainability of changes in the phenomenon.

At this point, the voices of men are used almost exclusively to illustrate the general nature of their violence and intimidating behaviors; of the injuries they admit inflicting on women partners; and of associated attitudes about violence, women, wives, and relationships between men and women. It is unusual to hear the voices of men in this area of study as most research has concentrated solely on the voices of women who have been abused or, more commonly, contains the voice of neither abuser nor abused but only the voices of researchers, professionals, or activists. Later, we add the voices of women partners to reflect on the different accounts provided by men and by women and discuss some of the dilemmas posed for the researcher by these differences.

To examine the effectiveness of an intervention directed at violent men, it is essential first to examine their perceptions of the violence and their rationales for its use. Here, the voices of only a few women are used and only for the purpose of further elaborating the points made by the men. All comments are those of the men and women who participated in the Violent Men Study that will be discussed later. Here, we have taken the unorthodox step of presenting some of the qualitative data before introducing the research itself. Our intention is to provide a theoretically and empirically informed characterization of the phenomenon of violence that is the focus of the transformative project. This serves as a starting point for thinking about what is in need of change and how an intervention might address and deal with—fit—that phenomenon. Later, we turn explicitly to the particular methods used to study the violence and to evaluate the effectiveness of various responses to violent men.

The Violence

The violence used by men against their women partners ranges across a very wide spectrum from pushing and slapping to homicide. In a given relationship, the frequency of violent events may be regular and as frequent as several times a week or irregular and as infrequent as once a year. The consequences of the violence usually include physical injuries and negative psychological effects. The pattern of violence may change over time as men become more accustomed to its use, more insensitive to its consequences, and more emboldened by a lack of effective responses or intervention. While there is considerable diversity in the types and frequency of violence used by men against their women partners, there are, nonetheless, discernible patterns. It is these patterns that are of interest to and shape this discussion. The comments of violent men constitute a characterization of the nature of their violence and controlling behaviors and provide insight into thinking, language, and rationales that must be the focus of any intervention that attempts to stop such behavior.

The men are identified by membership in the group that was placed on probation and went through the reeducation program for abusers (identified as Men's Program) or in the group that received some other form of intervention in the justice system, for example, warning, fine, traditional probation, or prison (identified as Other Criminal Justice, or Other CJ). These identifiers become important when we compare the effectiveness of the different interventions but are also relevant here as they show the general similarity in the initial attitudes and behavior of men processed through the different forms of intervention.

Physical Attacks

Nature

Most violent events contain a combination of physical acts, and the 122 men interviewed in the Violent Men Study provided hundreds of accounts of their violence. The few accounts presented below not only illustrate the nature of attacks and injuries but also provide insight into some of the rationales used to justify the violence and to blame the woman for behavior enacted by the man. Slapping, pushing, punching, and kicking are commonly used by men when they attack a woman partner.

> She was that close, roaring and bawling at me, so I hit her. She tried to say the child saw it all and everything. It was a lot of lies. I just punched her in the face. Just the once. That's about it. She got up and ran out. She went to [the hospital], a hairline fracture she had. I don't know if it was her jaw or her cheekbone. (Man, Other CJ: 054)

> We had an argument and I grabbed her by the hair and I hit her and pushed her and that was it. She hit me over the head with her shoe. Then somebody phoned the police. (Man, Men's Program: 016)

> We argued about money that night and I punched and kicked her and she went down to her Gran's. I went down to her Gran's [because] I wanted to borrow her bank card [to return to the pub]. Her brother came to the door and he punched me and I didn't realize what I had done. I was angry because he punched me. You see I didn't realize what I had done. I knew I'd done something but I didn't realize it was as bad as it was, but it was bad. (Man, Men's Program: 053)

Although slapping, punching, and kicking are the most common forms of physical attack, head butting, forced sex, and other forms of attack are also used:

> *Can you remember the very first time you hit her?* Two years ago, it was, when I came from my work. It was on the Sunday afternoon about twelve [noon]. I came in and I told her I was going down to the pub to have a couple of drinks. She said to me, "Well, mind your time because you've not had anything to eat and your dinner will be ready at four o'clock," but I didn't come in till about half past twelve [midnight], and I was really bad drunk. I don't remember whether she was in her bed or up the stairs, but I tried to have sex with her, pushed myself a lot if you know what I mean, but she wasn't wanting it and I just started hitting her. *What sort of violence?* Head butt. *And did you force her to have sex?* No, I was trying to but she wouldn't so I just got

mad with her. *Injuries?* Broken nose and two black eyes. (Man, Men's Program: 038)

What was she doing? Screaming. She came to the point when she realized she was pushing somebody who really wanted to hurt and use violence. She never realized that she was messing about with something that she knew nothing about and she should have left me alone. . . . I'm bigger than her and I told her, "I've got enough running through my head at the moment without you hassling me," and then she pushed me. There just came a point where I snapped. *How serious?* Potentially, very. *Did you feel justified?* Now, no. There was no justification for me doing that whatsoever. I'd come to a point when I could take no more. I could take no more of [her]. *You felt justified?* Drunk-minded, yes. Sober-minded? I'd say it was total insanity. (Man, Other CJ: 023)

Household items may be used as instruments or weapons and walls and stairs are also hard objects into which the body might be pushed:

I says, "What's wrong with you?" And we just started arguing. I can't remember what the argument was about. I jumped up and said, "You think you're smart, huh?" And I picked up the [electric] fire and threw it through the window and I went to the bedroom and smashed our window. . . . When I walked out the door, I gave the door a kick and when I came back she was lying on the couch and her nose was bleeding and I said, "What's wrong with you?" It was when I was walking out, I kicked the door . . . in a temper. When I kicked the door, the door hinges went back and hit her in the face, bust her nose. I didn't mean it and she knows that herself, it was a pure accident. It was totally not meant. She knows that. She said, "Look, just leave me alone." I took a cloth and I tried to clean her face and she just told me to get out. *So you went to the police and they told you they wouldn't take you?* [The police officer] said, "It's Friday night, just go home." So I came back again and just caused a riot. I just went mental. (Man, Other CJ: 055)

I was in control enough because if I wasn't in control enough I would have battered her, do you know what I mean? I hit her, yes, but I didn't—I mean if that had been me in a fight in the pub then it would have been a completely different kettle of fish. If that had been a guy, I'd have been kicking and punching and pulling hair. I'd go on biting and doing whatever else I could, but I slapped her and I did toss the table at her, but then all I was trying to do was get her out of the room. I was in control enough not to go that far but the slap was a reaction. It was just a slap. I didn't say, "Right I'm going to hit you." She scratched me and it was almost instantaneous. [She] had a bash on her head where the table had bashed her head and that was all, and a bit of a sore face, but there was no black eye or anything. I had slapped her but nothing—not really badly. (Man, Other CJ: 056)

Sometimes, but not often, knives, hammers, fire pokers, and other instruments are used as weapons of attack, and strangling may also occur:

> *And then what happened after that?* We had a slanging match in the hall. I got into the bedroom and put [infant daughter] in her cot. She started crying and I picked her up and I was on the bed and she slapped me in the face so I slapped her back then she pulled my hair. Well, nobody pulls my hair or I just crack up. So she pulled my hair and the next thing I had her on the bed and I was trying to strangle her. Well, I wasn't trying to strangle her—but she was fighting back—but I had my hand round her throat and I had one hand trying to hold [daughter]. (Man, Men's Program: 036)

Although guns are more often used in countries such as the United States where they are widely available, the general absence of such weapons from homes in Britain means they are less likely to become the tools of attack or of self-defense. Domestic homicide occurs less frequently, and when it does occur it is more likely to be the outcome of the physical attack itself and may involve knives or household implements used as weapons, but not guns. As domestic homicide is not the topic of this research, it will not be discussed here. It should be noted, however, that for female victims of homicide, it is not uncommon to find a history of violence directed at them by a male partner, husband, ex-husband, boyfriend, or lover (Campbell, 1992; Daly & Wilson, 1988; Dobash & Dobash, 1979; Polk, 1994; Wallace, 1986). While it is important to remember that most violence against women in the home, like violence in other settings, rarely ends in homicide, it is also important to note that when women are killed it is usually by men who are intimates, there has often been a history of violence against the woman, and this is often known to the police or others.

Frequency

Physical attacks may occur with great frequency and regularity, sometimes as often as several times a week. Attacks may also be regular but infrequent—once or twice a year—or simply irregular and spasmodic. The violence sometimes increases in frequency and severity over time as it becomes a more routinized response to issues of disagreement or conflict. By the time the man and his violence come to the attention of the justice system and action begins to be taken, most men have been using violence for some time and have established a pattern of use. As stated earlier, rarely is a "first" offender before the police or courts for what is truly his first offense. Instead, men are repeat offenders long before the first call to the police is ever made.

> *How often would you say that you actually hit her?* Every week. *How long did that go on?* Months. (Man, Men's Program: 016)

Other Controlling Behavior

Men who use physical or sexual violence often use other forms of intimidating and controlling behavior and these acts are integral to the overall constellation of violence. The overall composite of violence, control, and intimidation may include shouting, pointing and shaking of fists, slamming doors, and destruction of the house or its contents, as well as physical threats against children and pets or the man's threats to take his own life if, for example, the woman leaves him or does not comply with his wishes.

General Intimidation

> It was the house that got it. The telly, anything got it because I knew she was quite house proud so I just took it out on the house. I couldn't get back at her any other way so I just took it out on the house. I don't even think it's violence. Well, it is, but it's not. Well, a lot of things [she] did made me annoyed and . . . I think it was my frustration, so I took it out on the furniture. I don't think that's violence towards [her], I actually hurt myself more than anything. *But at the same time it can be frightening for [her] can't it?* Oh, probably. *In a way it's like saying to her, "I can damage a sofa like this so I could do the same to you if you don't watch it."* Well, I don't look at it that way. *But she might?* Yes. I knew she didn't like me breaking any furniture or shouting and swearing, but she also knew that I never ever went near her. (Man, Other CJ: 047)

The same man was arrested, prosecuted, and found guilty of an offense involving destruction of property. His behavior frightened and intimidated his partner and their child although the incident did not involve a direct physical attack on the body of the woman concerned. In this case, however, protestations such as, "She knew that I never ever went near her," are probably not convincing or easily accepted by a partner as evidence that there is no intention to do harm to her person similar to the damage done to the house.

> She [estranged wife] wouldn't open the front door [after midnight] so
> I went in through the window and she was shouting and screaming. I
> smashed the window with an old bike that was laying out the back.
> The inside pane broke first and my hand followed through and I cut
> the tendons in my hand. I said, "I either come in the window or in the
> door." I says, "Are you going to open the front door because I want to
> know what's going on." (Man, Other CJ: 047)

Shouting and name calling are common and while such behaviors
may not be infrequent occurrences among couples in the heat of an
argument, they take on even greater significance in relationships where
violence has been used and is therefore known to be a possible or likely
outcome of a verbal dispute. Many controlling and intimidating behaviors are simply not recognized or acknowledged by the men as problematic, threatening, or frightening. For some men, this is part of the
process of minimization and denial of the overall constellation of violence. Such activities are removed from any notion of what constitutes
intimidation that might foreshadow a physical attack. Such behavior
thus remains acceptable to a man and is consequently even more difficult to eliminate from his repertoire.

> *The actual bodily harm, who was the victim?* That was my girlfriend,
> but I didn't punch her. That was the thing, I put my fist through her
> car windscreen but I didn't touch her. I just put my fist through her
> windscreen. *While she was there?* Yes. *How come you got [charged
> with] actual bodily harm if she had no injuries?* She got scratched by a
> bit of glass. (Man, Men's Program: 017)

Effects of Violence

Injuries

Punching and kicking often result in injuries, usually bruising, but
such attacks may also result in internal injuries, broken bones, and
bleeding where blows break the skin.

> I hit her on the face, that was it. I hit her in the face and there was a cut
> above her eye and her lip and she had a few bruises. Well, I can only
> remember three punches. One in the stomach and two in the face, but
> the wife says I hit her hell of hard and punched her quite a few times.
> *How did you feel after it happened?* Sick. I cleaned her up. Put her in
> the bathroom and cleaned her up. *Was there a lot of blood?* I think
> there was on the bed. She had to have three stitches in her head. *So
> you helped clean her up, and then?* Called the doctor out, but the doc-

tor wouldn't come out so we had to ring for an ambulance and, of course, the ambulance arrived and the police arrived with the ambulance. And the police arrested me. (Man, Men's Program: 017)

I've never been to court before about it, but I should have been. *How's that ?* Because I broke [her] jaw and they wouldn't charge me for it. Because she had no witnesses. [Her] jaw was broken and they saw it and everything, but they wouldn't charge me. They wouldn't charge me then, but they charged me [now] for a couple of bruises. (Man, Other CJ: 010)

Miscarriages and internal injuries, while less common than bruising and cuts, nonetheless do occur and are evident in the accounts of the women in this and other studies (Campbell et al., 1992; McFarlane, Parker, Soeken, & Bullock, 1992). References to such injuries appear very infrequently in the accounts provided by men. The following comment reveals a sense of regret after the event and once the full extent of the damage was known, but it also reveals a sense of justification for the violence at the time it was being inflicted.

Did she have any injuries? A ruptured bladder. *Do you think you were right to hit her?* Before it and during it, yes, but after it, no. Before it and during it—well, it was just to shut her up, but when I saw what the damage was, I never meant to do that deliberately. (Man, Men's Program: 019)

Visibility of Injuries

It should not be surprising if men and women differ in their accounts of injuries suffered during such attacks. For a variety of reasons, men may not wish to reveal that their attack has resulted in any injuries at all or may only acknowledge those injuries that are minor or are difficult to deny because they have received official attention by medical staff or been recorded by police. While men may wish to deny or diminish the injuries they know they have inflicted, they may also be unaware of some injuries that remain invisible to them. For example, a woman may be well aware that her elbow hurts for several days as a result of her arm being twisted up her back, that a tooth is loose, that she bit the inside of her mouth when punched, that her ribs or spine remain painful after a kick, but such injuries remain inaccessible to the man because there are no obvious or visible signs and he is unlikely to inquire about such injuries. Only if she tells him of every painful area or if medical treatment is absolutely necessary is there even a possibility that the full extent of injuries ever becomes accessible to the perpetrator of the injuries. It would be surprising, therefore, if men and women gave identical accounts of injuries sustained during a given violent event.

Even the most candid of men provide revelations only of injuries they can see or are willing to admit or that have been pressed into their consciousness through the comments of the women, medics, or police. Other injuries simply "do not count," "have not occurred," or "could not be that bad." Such responses highlight the need to include the accounts of women if the full extent of injuries is to be known and alerts us to the problems of relying solely on the accounts of injuries that are visible to or willingly admitted by perpetrators. Later, women's accounts of injuries will be used to expand on those presented here by the men. At this point, it is essential, however, to understand the type and level of violence acknowledged by the perpetrators, since this is the point at which intervention must begin.

The visibility of injuries is important. Cuts inside the mouth and bruises inside the hairline, while technically visible, are unlikely to be seen by casual observers or even the man himself. Bruising takes time to develop. Twisted and strained muscles and internal damage or bleeding are not seen. All may easily go unidentified and untreated if the woman does not seek medical attention. Similarly, police may deem no injury to have occurred unless blood, cuts, or burns can be seen at the time they arrive at the incident. The lack of immediate visibility of injuries can be a problem in the recognition and identification of abuse, particularly if injury is deemed necessary to establish that an attack has occurred. Bruising, strains, and other internal injuries are commonly associated with attacks such as kicking and punching, and their immediate or long-term invisibility is problematic for interventions relying on a mark, or signifier, of attack (Campbell et al., 1992). Even though many women seek help from doctors and nurses, there is still considerable reluctance to use medical staff and many women seeking assistance are under threat from the man should they reveal the source of the injuries. This adds to the invisibility of the violence by reducing the number of incidents reported to medical and other professions and thereby reducing the numbers that make their way into official records and statistics.

> *So she wasn't injured?* No, no. She never went to hospital anyhow.
> (Man, Men's Program: 016)

Some men try to make the injuries invisible by creating an illusion for observers:

> She is a bit [angry], but it's just back to normal except she's going
> about with a black eye, and it's not very nice and I'll ask her to wear
> sun-glasses, you know, to hide them. [She says she complies reluc-
> tantly to avoid further argument]. (Man, Other CJ: 058)

Violent men and others (e.g., family and friends) may attempt to make
the violence invisible by binding the woman to silence through notions
of loyalty to the family and its reputation or respect for family privacy,
which, in reality, means the man's privacy. Notions of privacy serve to
isolate women from contact with others and to reduce the probability
of intervention by others either in support of the woman or in response
to the man and his violence.

> Well, I've told her if we move to . . . she's not going to be telling the
> next door neighbor and the woman down the road and all the rest of
> it. I say . . . you don't have to go into the next door neighbor's houses
> and let them know how we live and all that. For there's no need for all
> the neighbors to know. *But why can't she speak to whoever she wants
> the same way as you do? It is her right to do as she pleases as a person.* I
> think what goes on in my family is nothing to do with anybody else in
> the street. . . . I don't want my neighbors to know what's going on.
> And she knows I don't want them to know, . . . so I tell her to shut up
> and that's it, she shuts up. (Man, Other CJ: 062)

Emotional Effects

It is not possible to endure repeated physical attack, to sustain
repeated injuries, and to live in an atmosphere of fear of repeat victimization without experiencing anxiety and emotional tension. While the
long-term effects of violence and permanent emotional damage cannot
be assumed, there can be little doubt that such an atmosphere causes
considerable stress, fear, anger, and resentment, and abused women
sometimes exhibit states of anxiety and a lowered sense of self-worth
resulting from abuse. In this and other studies, women sometimes
report a sense of the loss of themselves—of the person they used to
be—of feeling like someone who has been substantially reduced by the
humiliation, degradation of self, isolation, and continual threats that
often accompany the violence (Kennedy, 1992, pp. 86-87; Mullender,
1996, pp. 23-26; Smith, 1989, pp. 18-19; Stanko, 1985, p. 57). While
men may set out to "shape" the type of woman they wish their partner
to be and closely control her in that process, many men are indifferent
to this process or unaware that it exists. Again, the process of changing
the overall constellation of violence, including other intimidating and
controlling behaviors, needs to address this process of "creating the

wife" through restricting her autonomy, mobility, and independence and by attacking her sense of competence and self-worth.

> *How do you think she felt afterwards?* Terrified. Even though she was trying to fight back I knew she was terrified just by looking at her. Just the look on [her] face, I knew she was scared. (Man, Men's Program: 036)

> A couple of days later, my mind's still on it—I was loading a van and [she] passed by and I ran up to her to speak to her and I caught her [on the street] and when she turned round and saw me she just about died, she was that frightened. I was shocked. (Man, Men's Program: 053)

A woman concurs:

> *Has his violence changed your relationship in any significant way?* It feels as though it has made me more insecure. (Woman, Men's Program: 1116)

One British study of women at risk of suffering depression found that one third had experienced violence from a male partner and many women speak of feeling worthless or depressed because of violence (Andrews & Brown, 1988). While it may not be surprising that repeated violent attacks within one's own home lead to states of fear, anxiety, and depression among the victimized, one might ask if those who perpetrate the violence and create an atmosphere of fear are aware of its emotional effects. Do the men realize or care how the women feel, how much fear they create, or what the effects are on children? Like invisible physical injuries, emotional damage is also invisible unless, of course, there is an awareness of the signs of fear, anxiety, stress, and depression. Such awareness requires a level of concern and a willingness to be attuned to the condition of others. The accounts of many men reveal a lack of such awareness and an apparent insensitivity to the emotional effects of violence on the woman or the relationship. Some men even fail to comprehend the point of such a question:

> *How do you think she feels about the violence?* Well, she must feel something for me or she wouldn't put up with it. (Man, Other CJ: 058)

> *Would you say that your violent behavior is damaging the relationship at all?* No! Well it's no big deal. I'm not saying that I'm not as bad as the next one, but I know people who've actually beat up a woman like

they've beat up a guy, with kicking in the head. I'd never do that to a girl. (Man, Other CJ: 003)

When men do comprehend that their violence may have some effect on the woman and her sense of self-worth and well-being, this is often tempered by the notion that any cessation in the violence will automatically bring an immediate and permanent end to her fear and anxiety, that there will be no lingering effects. The men's appreciation is also tempered by the notion that it is the woman's responsibility to leave the relationship if she is being harmed and thus the responsibility to change lies with her and not him.

> *Would you say that your violent behavior is actually damaging your relationship with your wife?* In the past it has. *Is it doing that just now?* No. I've never been violent to her for months now. (Man, Men's Programs: 019)

She knew what I was like. She shouldn't have been around. She should have left me. She knew what I was like at that point and she had a choice. It's like if you had a dog who every time you took it out it would go and bite people, then if you walked up to that dog and it bit you, it would be your own fault. (Man, Other CJ: 045)

Obviously, any intervention directed at stopping this violence would need to address the problem that men do not see it as a problem; do not believe that it truly harms others; imagine that there are no effects beyond immediate injuries; and harbor the notion that once the violence stops everything is immediately solved, all is forgotten, everything is repaired. This bears many similarities to notions held by men who rape women or sexually abuse children (Waterhouse, Dobash, & Carnie, 1994; Williams & Finkelhor, 1990).

Whether the effects of violence are physical or emotional, they are costly in material and psychological terms not only to the woman who has been abused but also to the children who directly witness the violence or simply live in an atmosphere of conflict and tension. They are also costly to the man who himself lives in a state of heightened tension, anger, and aggression and who may eventually lose the woman, children, and home that he may value although his immediate behavior would seem to indicate otherwise. These are also issues about which the man may not be aware and which may need to be built explicitly into an intervention directed at dealing with the entire complement of attitudes and orientations associated with the continued use of violence. We shall return later to the costs of violence.

Sources of Conflict

The circumstances in which men choose to use violence reveal a great deal about rationalizations, minimization, and legitimation of violence; about relationships between men and women; and about orientations to intimate partners. The specific sources of conflict form the bedrock of men's rationales for using violence and must, therefore, be understood and addressed in any serious response to its elimination. In earlier research, we found four general conditions under which violence was likely to occur: (a) as a response to sexual jealousy and possessiveness, (b) as a method of enforcing demands for domestic service, (c) as a means of establishing or maintaining male authority, and (d) as a prerogative of male authority and privilege (Dobash & Dobash, 1979, pp. 98-103, 1984). These overlapping and interlocking issues constitute the usual sources of conflict and arguments leading to violent events. As such, they form risk factors in need of close attention by any intervention designed to reduce or eliminate such behavior.

Jealousy and Possessiveness

> (re: former boyfriend) She once told me that she had held hands with another boy. I went seriously mad about that. (Man, Other CJ: 045)

> *Has jealousy changed your relationship?* Yes. . . . I might be wrong but I thought she was seeing somebody. . . . *You said earlier that she used to go out more. . . . Why does she go out less often now?* I suspected her about maybe a year ago. I suspected she was seeing somebody else and she was denying it. Now she knows I don't like her going out. My idea is that she's going out to meet this bloke or whoever it is. *So she's reduced her social life because of what you thought about her?* Yes. *Would you say that you have a jealous nature?* Yes. *Does your wife have a jealous nature?* No. (Man, Other CJ: 062)

His partner confirms his views and reflects on how it affects her life, her friendships, and her freedom of movement:

> *Has jealousy affected your relationship or changed it in any way?* Yes. I hate it, I hate it when he goes on all the time when I go out with my pal [a woman] because [he thinks] I meet a new fella. *Has he always done that?* Yes. *He's always been jealous?* Yes. There isn't one minute when he doesn't moan. He just goes on and on even when I've just gone down to my pal's. He looks at the watch and the clock, and times me, how long it takes me to get something from my pal's. I'm really restricted to the house. Really I can't go out when I want to. . . .

He doesn't like my friends. Half of them are not married, they're divorced or separated and he doesn't like them. (Woman, Other CJ: 1062)

Many men reiterate the theme of jealousy:

Are you jealous at all? Yes. *Did that affect your relationship?* Yes. I accused her of doing things she was not doing. *Why?* Just because I did not want to lose her. *Was there any particular theme to that argument before you hit her?* Jealousy. (Man, Other CJ: 081)

What about jealousy? Did that change your relationship? Yes, I'm quite jealous and so is she. (Man, Men's Programs: 144)

A woman notes the effect of jealousy and possessiveness on everyday life:

I mean, a guy just had to look at me the wrong way and he'd say to me, "Do you know him?" There was one night we were out and this guy, and all he was asking me was . . . where to go for a disco that night and, well, I used to frequent the discos in [the area] and I knew where they were and I was petrified because I was standing at the bar waiting to be served and [my partner] was sitting down and I was frightened that he saw the guys talking to me. (Woman, Men's Programs: 1126)

Social Activities and Isolation

Do you argue about [her] going out with friends? Well, it's not really an argument—she just gets told to shut up [laughs]. (Man, Other CJ: 007)

Jealousy, or more broadly, male sexual proprietariness (Daly & Wilson, 1988) are associated not only with the man's fear, real or imagined, of sexual infidelity but also with his desire to exclude the woman from what the man defines as his exclusive circle of male friends. This may take the form of his sense of possession of "his" rather than "their" friends and may also serve the purpose of ensuring that the woman has no opportunity to have any form of contact with other men even if that contact is made in the man's presence and thus under his scrutiny or supervision. A woman speaks about this:

He disagrees about my friends more than I disagree about his. I get on good with his friends, but he thinks I get on too good with them. Like when they come to visit, he thinks I should go out of the house. He doesn't think I should be here. He thinks they come down to see him and they don't want to see me. We've had arguments about it and I say, "Right, I'll ask them," and I have asked them, I say, "Listen, you don't mind me being here when you come to visit, do you?" and they went, "No, because we come to visit you as much as we come to visit him," because we get on well. *It sounds as if he's a bit jealous of the way you can get on with his friends.* It is. He doesn't like me getting on with them and talking about all the things that they get up to. They come and tell me what they get up to and what they've been doing and stuff like that and he doesn't think that's right. He thinks they should be sitting with him and I shouldn't be anywhere near them, whereas his friends don't see it like that. It's just him and they've told him that as well. (Woman, Other CJ: 1055)

Domestic Work and Domestic Service

Men expect and demand domestic service throughout the day and night. They want what they want when they want it and that even includes the expectation that a woman time her labor so that a man does not have his rest disturbed by her work.

> *Can you tell me if there's anything in particular that you can think of that you have disagreements about?* Classic example, housework. I like to have a long lie in on a Saturday morning if I'm not working, because I can't usually lie in longer than about seven or half past seven, and that causes disagreements [because she cares for the children and does the housework]. (Man, Men's Programs: 041)

> *What kinds of things do you have disagreements about usually?* Money, housework, my dinner not being made. (Man, Other CJ: 055)

This man's partner comments at length about conflicts over domestic work:

> *What kinds of things do you argue about?* Silly things. *When you do argue with each other, what usually happens? What do you do?* The thing that annoys me, he walks in with working boots on. . . . I say, "For God's sake, take them off." [He says] "I'll not take them off, they're not dirty," but I feel they are dirty—he's been out at work at a building site all day so they're obviously dirty. Then maybe the kids will come in, he'll say, "Get your shoes off at the door," so he's actually contradicted himself. He's walked through the hall and living room and he's telling the children to take their shoes off at the door. Now that can cause a row. I say, "You just walked through yourself, what are you telling them to take them off at the door for?" "You shut up, you're being stupid." I wasn't being stupid, it was him who was

being stupid and he goes up to the room and there's a peach carpet on the floor and he walks over it then he takes his clothes off and bits of stone and plaster are all over the place—that annoys me and [he says] "Oh shut up, you," "Oh, you shut up," but then I'm away down the stairs and that's it. (Woman, Men's Programs: 1041)

Male Authority

I was wanting to show her [by using violence] who was the boss. (Man, Men's Programs: 038)

Men who are violent toward their partner do not believe a woman has the right to argue, negotiate, or debate, and such behavior is deemed both a nuisance and a threat to their authority. Violence is commonly used to silence debate, to reassert male authority, and to deny women a voice in the affairs of daily life:

How does she try to stop you being violent to her? Shuts her mouth. She used to carry on the arguments and I wanted to let it drop but she'd carry it on and that's when I ended up, I would turn round and hit her. *Can you understand why she needed to continue with the argument?* Not a bit. (Man, Men's Programs: 017)

Why did you hit her? Because she knows how to wind me up, basically. Sometimes she doesn't take "no" for an answer. Sometimes she'll go on and on and on about different things. (Man, Other CJ: 006)

Do you think there is anything [she] could or should do to stop you being violent? I've battered her that many times, she should know when to stop her crap. She knows when I get annoyed because I sit and clench my teeth. Why do I hit her? I don't know. Sometimes she just really nips my head. And it doesn't matter what I say, she won't shut up. (Man, Other CJ: 007)

When you think back to when you actually hit her, can you think what you were hoping to get? Well, it was just actually to get her to shut up. (Man, Men's Programs: 019)

Has she ever tried to stop you being violent to her? . . . One of the things you mentioned earlier was that she stopped arguing. Yes, but that's about all she's done. It's the times when I tell her to shut up because like when I'm having her nag, nag—I feel it building up inside me to do something and that's when I tell her to stop. It's either stop or just take what comes. Well, like after an argument, as far as I'm concerned I've won the argument whether I have or I haven't, if you know what I mean. An argument is you disagree with what I'm saying or I disagree with what you're saying, but in the end, I'll win that argument. (Man, Other CJ: 062)

Male authority in the household can extend to all things, even the sense of ownership and control of the use of electricity or domestic water. A woman describes an instance:

> *Did you make tea or coffee after an argument?* I'm not allowed to put the kettle on. *Why not?* I'm not even allowed to use the phone when we're having an argument. If I went near that phone I got battered. I was just to sit there like a wee silly lassie and do nothing. "You're not using that, that's my electricity." "That's my kettle." And then there's one instance he said to me, "You're not using the water." I says, "It's not yours, it belongs to the Region, not you." (Woman, Men's Programs: 1126)

The specific sites of conflict center around the routines of daily life. Money, children, relatives, daily activities in the house, mobility outside the house, the use of time, the consumption of alcohol, sex, and the use of material resources are common arenas of disagreement between men and women and the source of conflict leading to violence.

Money

> I suppose I might have [felt justified] the last time because we argued about money and I thought [she] had spent too much but in the end she hadn't. (Man, Men's Programs: 053)

> He always blames me for spending it all. *What does he think you spend it on?* Well, unless he's there to see what the money has been spent on, then it's been squandered. He's got to have proof of how much things were. (Woman, Other CJ: 1055)

Children

Children may become involved in a variety of ways, either because they are threatened or physically abused (not common in this study), because they enter a violent encounter attempting to protect or defend their mother, or because they become a source of conflict when a man sees them as limiting the amount of attention he receives from the woman or as a restriction on his freedom.

> I think the only time we nearly came to blows when I've been sober was over the kids. (Man, Other CJ: 023)

> *What effect, if any, did the kids have on the relationship?* Well, it's tied us down. (Man, Men's Programs: 114)

Well, before the kids came along we used to go out at night, perhaps twice a week out for a drink, now we do not go out and our sex life has changed. (Man, Men's Programs: 126)

[re: arguments about children] I think they [kids] should get more discipline. I think she should lock them in their room rather than smack their bum, but she thinks that causes a problem being locked in a room. But I wouldn't agree with that. It was the only thing that taught me when I was young. Well, if I was bad I got locked in my room, the only thing that would teach me a lesson, a smack or that wouldn't bother me. I'd just go and do the same thing, but if I got locked in my room, I would be better. (Man, Men's Programs: 144)

Women also reflect on the effect of children on the man and the relationship:

To begin with we had no kids. Then we only had the one, which was good. I felt after that—two, three kids—that was it. I felt there were too many. *Too many. Why do you say that?* [He] was the kind of person—like when I was pregnant, "Oh great!" He'd have done anything for you. When you had the baby, oh the hospital visits were fantastic! After that, the first two or three months was alright. After that, disaster. He just couldn't cope with it. He couldn't cope with a baby. He could have been gone away for the first year of the three children's lives and come back when they were walking and talking and all that sort of thing. He just couldn't handle the responsibility. (Woman, Men's Programs: 1041)

Alcohol

Alcohol is particularly complex as it represents several problems at once. There is, of course, the disinhibiting effects of alcohol and drugs, which clearly affect judgment and distort perceptions (Reiss & Roth, 1993; Sumner & Parker, 1995). Drugs and alcohol also provide a social and cultural context in which violence may be more likely to be used or sources of disagreement may more readily be defined as sufficiently serious to "warrant" the use of extreme measures, including violence (Dobash & Dobash, 1979, p. 247, 1984, p. 273; Mullender, 1996, pp. 42-44; Ptacek, 1988, p. 144). The consumption of such substances also constitutes a drain on the domestic economy and men and women often compete for limited amounts of money to be used either for men's entertainment at the pub or for food, rent, and children's clothing. For those who consume alcohol in bars or pubs, there is also the possibility of conflict over the amount of time spent at home with members of the family versus that spent away from the home. In all these respects, alcohol can become a complex source of conflict between men and women. First, a man reflects on the effects of alcohol and plays down its significance:

> You see them here [other men]. They don't work but they've always got a can of Pilsner or a can of lager in their hand and they get drunk and go barmy. (Man, Men's Programs: 036)

Then, a couple reflect on the negative effects of alcohol on themselves and on their relationship:

> I used to spend a lot of money on drink and we argued about it. (Man, Other CJ: 081)

> Whenever he got drunk I got rather scared. (Woman, Other CJ: 1081)

In some ways, alcohol provides an explanation that seems less threatening to both the man and the women as the violence can be viewed as caused by this external force, the resolution of which will result in an end to the violence. Armed with such an explanation, men need not view themselves as violent or see their relationship as such, and women are able to do the same. Externalizing the cause of the problem makes it seem less embedded in the person and more amenable to a simple change that does not involve addressing the violence itself.

> If I was to stop drinking, [she] would never have a black eye. It's only been with alcohol, that's all it is. (Man, Other CJ: 058)

Sex and Sexual Service

Another arena of conflict and argument that may lead to violence is that of sexual relations, which some men view as another type of domestic service. Sometimes this may even go to such lengths that it can only be described as marital rape (Campbell, 1989; Finkelhor & Yllö, 1985; Russell, 1982).

> Well, he was just under the impression whenever he wanted it he would get it and that he could not understand that I was tired and things. (Woman, Other CJ: 1081)

> We argue less than we used to, but I mean, the basis, the whole thing all happened because of [her] attitude towards sex. That was the bottom line. (Man, Other CJ: 023)

> Well, if she'd let me do it [have sex] I wouldn't have punched her. (Man, Men's Programs: 038)

Some women talk about how repeated violence diminishes or elimi-
nates their desire to have sex with the man who uses violence against
them:

> *You say your relationship is very bad just now, what has changed your*
> *relationship over the years?* I hate having sex with him? . . . I don't
> want to sleep with him [now]. . . . I'm quite happy when I'm not get-
> ting it and he doesn't understand that, and then he goes on, "You
> must be getting it from somewhere." (Woman, Other CJ: 1062)

The Context of Violence

It is important to note that men and women do not necessarily
agree on what constitutes violence. The men we interviewed sometimes refused to define their behavior as violence or denied that it constituted violence. The men's programs evaluated in the Violent Men
Study aimed to assist men to rethink violence, to reconsider their defi-
nitions and the thresholds of behavior that might be deemed violent.

Men are violent to their women partners in a wider context of family, friends, and the general cultural and institutional settings in which
such behavior and accompanying attitudes are more or less condemned or condoned. The messages and responses are often mixed
and ambivalent, showing support for men's authority over wives,
boundaries of "appropriate" behavior for women in the role of a wife,
and more or less tolerance for the use of violence under certain circumstances and within notional limits. Sanctions for the use of violence are
often weak or nonexistent and men incur few if any costs for its use. If
violence is learned behavior, then it may be learned in these and other
contexts. If the attitudes toward women—particularly wives—are relevant, they also may be learned and supported in numerous contexts.
Behavior and attitudes are learned and sustained in the spheres of
friends, relatives, the community, the justice system, the popular
media, and other arenas that form the overall contexts in which individuals live and make the decisions that constitute daily life.

Supporting Violence and Associated Attitudes

Personal and Cultural Contexts—Mixed Messages

In various personal and cultural contexts, some messages reinforce
notions of men's authority over women and husbands' authority over

wives. Some messages support or ignore the use of violence as a means of achieving what is desired or of punishing real or perceived transgressions; some reject the use of violence and refute the conditions under which it is justified. There is no clear or single message. Both the man who wishes to justify his violence and the man who wishes to eliminate such behavior must maneuver through this maze of mixed messages. The responses of the justice system do, of course, constitute one source of message and form a part of this maze. Messages may, of course, be ignored. Messages may also be ambiguous, mixed, or misinterpreted as they are differentially taken on board by men and incorporated into the overall corpus of notions used to sustain or eliminate violent behavior.

The differing nature of these messages is revealed in the comments of violent men reflecting on their perception of the world around them in relation to the acceptability of violence and to a set of orientations to women in general and to wives in particular. The following incident of violence toward a sister illustrates how men are deemed to be in control of female members of their family and how violence may be used as an enforcer of that authority:

> My father was going away to Australia to see his sister and he asked me to look after my sister, and she had only just started work. She'd just got this job. I was coming in at twelve o'clock at night and there she is drunk with two guys sitting there. So I went, "Right you've got work in the morning. Get to your bed now," I said, "and you two can bugger off." The two guys got stroppy and, of course, I said just get out the house and [was] quite happy to hammer them. Fair enough, I'd had a drink but then my sister started on me saying I wasn't to run her life and everything like that and I said to her, "Look, Dad told me to look after you and that's what I'm doing." And, of course, she started and I just turned round and slapped her round the face. (Man, Men's Program: 017)

In some male environments, attitudes toward women may be old fashioned and stark (Hey, 1986):

> *What do your friends think of women then?* That they're here for one thing and that's it. *Do you not think that men's attitudes towards women are changing?* Not in the pub that I go to. (Man, Men's Program: 016)

Many men feel comfortable, or at least not terribly uncomfortable, with their use of violent behavior against their woman partner. Many seem to exist in a cultural context in which such behavior is ignored or minimized and the use of violence incurs few if any costs. Violence may thus be assumed to be acceptable or at least not terribly important. Some men live in a context where violence is common and they view it as acceptable under certain circumstances. They can articulate when violence might be used, how much violence is appropriate, and what constitutes the wrongdoing of a woman vis-à-vis a husband or male partner.

> *How acceptable do you think it is today in society generally for a man to hit a woman?* There's that much of it going about that it's accepted. I mean round about this area it happens all the time. I would say it's acceptable. (Man, Men's Program: 036)

The same man reflects further and articulates the complexity of mixed messages and contradictory behavior:

> *What do you think of men who hit women?* This is contradictory but I would say that I totally disagree with it. If I saw somebody walloping her in the street, I'd wallop him, but I mean I've done it myself. *Why was it okay for you?* It wasn't okay for me, but I did it. (Man, Men's Program: 036)

Justifications for Violence—Blaming the Victim

Men interviewed in the Violent Men Study offered a range of justifications for their use of violence: She talks too much—she talks too little; she argues—she refuses to argue; she is too materialistic—she is too spiritual; she wants to go out to work—she wants to stay home; she stands against him in protecting the interests of the children; she likes to drink too much—is against drinking; and the list goes on. They have a reason and, anyway, the violence "isn't that bad." Self-justification, minimization, and victim blaming are recurring features of men's discussions of their use of violence:

> *Have you ever wanted to stop being violent?* I wouldn't really say I'm violent. I've been given reason to be violent. I'm not just violent for the sake of it. (Man, Other CJ: 047)

> I was sometimes justified in hitting [her]. I never hurt her badly physically—I never cut her or beat her senseless. She'd always push and push until there was really no alternative [to hitting]. (Man, Other CJ: 045)

> Right, there is violence and I mean I'm not the type that ties them up and does this and stops giving them money and doesn't feed the kids.

There's guys like that, I know that, but there's also women that just take the piss out of [belittle] guys. (Man, Other CJ: 054)

Rejecting Violence While Supporting Violence

Condemnation of men hitting women is generally voiced but often followed by exculpatory statements relative to the specific circumstances in which violence may be used and deemed legitimate:

What do you think of men who hit women? I don't agree with it but it all depends. It depends what the circumstances are. Unless you're fully aware of the circumstances, you don't really have the right to criticize. I suppose it's not alright for a man to hit a woman, but I mean there are certain circumstances when it's inevitable—it's going to happen. Well, I hit [her] for a reason. (Man, Other CJ: 006)

When do you think that it's okay for a man to hit a woman? Never. *Do you think that there are any people in this society that think that it is okay?* No. I don't think so. Well, I don't know. *Why do you think men do it?* What? Bang women? I don't know. I know why I did it, I was pushed to it. (Man, Other CJ: 054)

When do you think it's okay for a man to hit a woman? I don't like it. A slap, yes, now and again, if it's needed. *What do you mean "needed"?* If you're sitting in a pub with all your pals and she comes in and gives you a load of cheek. To put her in her place verbally, and if verbally doesn't work, physically. (Man, Other CJ: 007)

I think what is good enough for one is good enough for the other. Women are screaming for equality everywhere, the same job, the same opportunities, but when it comes to the kids men get 10% of what the women do [referring to custody]. It's not right to scalp [beat] her but in saying that there are times and places. Women do a lot they shouldn't do. (Man, Other CJ: 005)

Of course, hitting a woman and turning her black and blue is bad but there's some women are just bloody rotten. There's a lot of bad women out in that world. (Man, Other CJ: 058)

The comments of these men reflect the difference between ideals and practice. They articulate the general notion that violence against a woman is wrong and at the same time rationalize the use of violence under specific circumstances. As we shall see later, this presents a dilemma for the researcher, who needs to capture both these realities, and for the designers of interventions, which need to move beyond the socially acceptable or socially desirable stance that violence is wrong to the lived reality that it is acceptable when the woman engages in some behavior judged by the man to be undesirable or unacceptable to him and others in his circle of friends. Similar patterns of thinking and action are also apparent among men who rape women or sexually abuse children.

Violence Is Functional and Purposeful—
It Works Yet It Fails

While many men claim a lack of knowledge and control with respect to their use of violence—it is a mystery; it just happens—some do articulate what they want to obtain through its use and reflect on whether they have been successful in achieving that end. In this sense, violence is functional even when those who perpetrate it may not be aware of what they hope to achieve through its use. While often successful in achieving short-term aims, violence may also be costly in ways that are less likely to be contemplated in advance. Thus, violence may work to achieve specific, immediate purposes, yet it may also fail as partners and children become alienated from the abuser and may eventually leave him.

> It [using violence] was the thing I could do and she couldn't, the one way the situation could be controlled to my liking. (Man, Other CJ: 045)

> *Would you say you were successful in getting what you wanted, did it work?* Yes, I definitely got her attention, but I think if she had answered the door when I threatened to smash the window there wouldn't have been any smashing and then I would have been home and there would have been no trouble. (Man, Other CJ: 047)

Sometimes violence works, sometimes it does not. The following man both succeeded and failed in achieving his declared aims:

> *Did you feel justified in hitting her?* I did [because] she wouldn't let me see my daughter. *What did you hope to get by hitting her then?* To teach her a lesson. [And I succeeded] Because I get to see my [infant] daughter now. *When you hit her, what did you hope to get?* I wanted to get [her teenage daughter] out of the house. *Did you succeed?* No. (Man, Men's Program: 016)

Collective and Cumulative Amnesia

Another strong and almost universal characteristic of men who use violence against intimates (and this is also true for those who commit incest, sexually abuse children, or rape adult women) is the strong will to forget, the refusal to speak of the past, the desire to move forward in their quest to become a changed person or to move on to a new life with a new woman without detailed reference to the violent behavior that necessitated a change (see Waterhouse et al., 1994). The desire to draw a line through the past before it has been mentioned, to forget about it and expect others to do the same, is meant to avoid focusing on the behavior that caused harm and offense to others and is that which is in need of change. It becomes part of the process of focusing elsewhere, on the behavior of the woman or others; on the circumstances of daily life; on childhood neglects, fear, and harms; or on other issues that are more easily addressed as causes or explanations of violence and particularly ones that place the responsibility elsewhere. This allows men to escape the process of addressing the nature of their violent behavior, its harmful consequences for others, and their responsibility for choosing to use such behavior. It is doubtful if one needs to change a behavior for which others are responsible; a behavior that does no real harm; or a behavior that has not been identified or articulated and thus has no real shape, form, or consequences. Again, it would appear that interventions designed to assist men to eliminate violence must ensure that the violence is brought clearly into vision and is not allowed to recede from view before the work has begun. If the man is to take the process of personal change seriously, it will inevitably be painful, since it is not possible to truly recognize the pain and harm done to others and to take full responsibility for inflicting that pain and harm without at the same time feeling distress at causing such harm (Tavuchis, 1991). This may help explain why it is almost universal that such men do not wish to talk about their violence, want to forget about it completely and immediately, and want others to do the same. This will to forget, this selective inattention, is an integral part of the continuation of violence (as are minimization and blaming others) and must therefore be addressed in any serious attempt to eliminate it. We return to this when we examine the interventions and again when we consider the ways in which men change.

The context in which violence against women continues to be seen by some as an acceptable response to women's real and imagined transgressions is one in which the behavior may be practiced with few impediments to the person and little sense of shame, guilt, or a felt need to stop. Interventions directed at violent men and their behavior enter this context of mixed and contradictory messages and responses that may serve to assist or impede the task of reducing or eliminating violence. In turn, the responses themselves not only serve as enforcers or deterrents but also form a part of the expanding body of messages received by violent men. Since any intervention will be placed in the context of a network of immediate friends and acquaintances who may reinforce new attitudes and forms of behavior or support the old, its effectiveness will to some extent be influenced by these circumstances. Similarly, the overall community or society in which the perpetrator lives may to a greater or lesser degree tolerate or reject the use of violence against women and thus provide an atmosphere in which he either behaves with impunity or must conceal his deviance and possibly incur costs should his violence be detected. The ever-widening contexts of immediate friends and kin as well as community and society are thus an ever-present part of the process of personal change.

3

Intervention for Change
Responding to Violent Men

How do you think violence by men against women can be stopped?
That's the million-dollar question. (Violent Man)

Physically abusive men have largely remained out of sight and
beyond reach as initial responses rightly focused on the safety of
abused women and their children, and their safety must continue as a
fundamental part of any meaningful response to this problem. The
provision of refuge has forever changed the circumstances of women
who seek sanctuary and protection. Shelters often provide a vital first
step for women who seek to escape a violent episode or renegotiate a
violent relationship into one of nonviolence. For those who seek to
leave a violent man, shelters may provide a final step in the abusive
relationship and a first step in beginning a new life. Whether used or
not, shelters serve as a symbol of safety, provide a tool in negotiations
with a violent partner, and constitute a reminder that abuse is taken
seriously by members of the community. The fact that alternative
accommodation exists may also serve as a deterrent to some men who
strive to isolate the women they abuse from any form of external assistance to ensure that the women have no alternative to remaining with
them despite their continued violence. But is this enough? Can shelters
for women serve as the single source of deterrence to men's violence
and thereby secure women's safety?

At a theoretical level, *all* women can be safe only if *all* women
escape from *all* men who are violent or if *all* violent men can be trans-

formed into peaceful partners. Both options may seem utopian or Orwellian, and neither is likely to be completely achieved. In the best of all worlds, all male violence will be eliminated, the safety and well-being of all women will be secure, and the need for refuges and escape routes will thereby be eliminated. In the worst of all worlds, the violence will go unchecked, tolerated in society as it apparently is in some kinship societies (Chagnon, 1983; Descola, 1996, pp. 182-200). Such social conditions "turn up the volume" on violence by tolerating, and at times supporting, its existence. In such a world, the best option is to make universal provision of safe and secure sanctuaries available for *all* women, since most will need to flee from the majority of the population of men, who are violent and deemed beyond concern, control, or effective intervention.

As neither the universal elimination of all violence nor universal escape seem likely in the near future, can either be approximated in a more modest agenda of reducing the number of violent men in the population and increasing the safety of an ever-larger number of women? Would such an agenda represent a retreat from the ideal position of a total and unequivocal rejection of violence against women in favor of some acceptance on pragmatic grounds of lesser forms of violence to be tolerated by fewer women? Of course not. The goal remains the same as the process of change begins at the starting point inherited as a social legacy from the past. Even the more modest agenda of turning down the volume of violence for increasing numbers of men and turning up the volume of safety for increasing numbers of women is not only a small undertaking, it is a necessary and inevitable part of the pathway to the elimination of *all* violence against women. The route to any ideal goal is through real social and personal processes, and this particular agenda of social change has been under way for some years and has already made important progress toward the ultimate goal, although a long journey still remains ahead.

Since the 1970s, a growing number of women's groups and victim organizations have been providing safe havens for the victims of violence in the United States, Britain, Australia, New Zealand, European and Scandinavian countries, and other parts of the world, and there is also a growing response to addressing the violence at its source by responding to the perpetrators of the violence. This has mostly occurred within the justice system and has sometimes included programs that focus explicitly on abusers, their violent behavior, and their need to change. Like Janus, attention must be turned in two directions at once, toward the woman who is abused and toward the man who perpetrates the abuse. To fail to address the abuser is to fail to address the abuse itself, the risk of repetition, and the question of how it might be stopped. Ignoring the perpetrator and failing to focus clearly and explicitly on him and his violence leaves these questions unaddressed and thereby increases the likelihood that the violence will be repeated in an unending cycle. This repetition is tragic for those who live with violence and disturbing for those who work toward its end. Must this violence continue?

The Justice System

Turning to men and their violence, one might ask if a necessary and sufficient approach lies solely in the traditional responses of the justice system: arrest; charge; prosecution; and sanction through fines, probation, or prison. Is it sufficient simply to make these sanctions work more effectively? In fact, domestic violence has been the focus of a number of criminal justice innovations in many countries during the past two decades. Innovations have included enhanced police awareness of domestic violence through improved training; the strengthening of civil injunctions, sometimes including the power of exclusion from the home and the provision for arrest when breached; improved support for the victims of violence through specialized units in the police and courts (Grace, 1995); and an emphasis on arrest, prosecution, and justice-based programs designed to deal with the offending behavior (Dobash & Dobash, 1992). There have been many such developments in the United States (Fields, 1994; Schneider, 1992a, 1992b) and Canada (Buzawa & Buzawa, 1992; Johnson, 1996, pp. 209-222) and fewer in countries such as Britain (Barron, 1990; Hague & Malos, 1993; Morran & Wilson, 1994; Wright, 1995), Australia (Francis, 1995; McGregor & Hopkins, 1991; Seddon, 1993; Stubbs, 1994), and New Zealand (Busch, 1994) but, overall, there has been a growing move to improve the responses of the justice system, particularly of the police, by providing support for those who have been abused and responding more effectively to the perpetrators of abuse. But what might constitute an effective response within the justice system?

Protection Orders

Research conducted in England in the 1980s found that despite new policies and practices only a small proportion of calls to police (2% in one study) result in arrest and prosecution (Edwards, 1986).

The most frequently used intervention was a form of protection order—injunction—which tended to increase in use nationally once its relevance had been identified and stressed (Edwards, 1989). Several English studies investigating the use of these civil remedies provide insight into their effectiveness, finding that the enforcement of injunctions and the use of powers of arrest were often inconsistent and inefficient (Barron, 1990; Edwards, 1989; Faragher, 1985; Homer, Leonard, & Taylor, 1985). These studies revealed that police officers sometimes failed to serve injunctions on abusive men, continued to tell women that the problem was a private matter, and were reluctant to act. Women reported continued violence and intimidation despite the existence of exclusion and nonmolestation orders; only a minority of women judged them useful (Barron, 1990).

Evidence from the United States and the Violent Men Study (see Chapter 5) indicates that under certain circumstances injunctions can be useful (Chaudhuri & Daly, 1992; Finn & Colson, 1990; Grau, Fagan, & Wexler, 1985; Horton, Simonidis, & Simonidis, 1987; Ptacek, 1995). For example, a study of three U.S. cities revealed that around three quarters of women interviewed immediately after obtaining an injunction reported positive short-term effects (Keilitz, Hannaford, & Efkeman, 1996). After 6 months, even higher proportions of women (80%-93%) reported significant life improvements and a reduction in abuse as a result of using an injunction. The North American research indicates that injunctions can be effective in jurisdictions where the judiciary provides clear and explicit admonitions regarding violence and harassment and other justice personnel are prepared to enforce these messages. The willingness to apply sanctions when men breach a civil order is also important. While British investigations into the use and effectiveness of injunctions provide important evidence and show minimal effects, it could be that recent legislative changes have improved the effectiveness of injunctions and, in any case, research on effectiveness could be strengthened by including comparison groups. Although evidence from England does suggest that most women do not find injunctions useful, it seems important to know how this might compare with doing nothing, with arrest only, or with arrest followed by some other form of intervention.

Why Not Just Arrest?

In some areas in the United States, pressure from women's groups and justice officials has resulted in the introduction of strong proarrest or mandatory arrest policies. In these jurisdictions, police are required to arrest under the presumption of "probable cause" where secondary evidence indicates an assault has occurred. In Canada and the United States, proarrest or mandatory arrest policies have sometimes been linked to men's programs designed to alter the beliefs and behavior of abusers. Arrest appears to be a more common response in the United States and Canada and less common in Britain, New Zealand, and Australia, although recent British research seems to suggest that arrest may now be more likely than it was in the 1980s (Lees, 1998). But does arrest on its own stop subsequent violence? Findings from the first National Institute of Justice (NIJ) arrest experiment in Minneapolis seemed to indicate that arrest on its own without any subsequent response (e.g., prosecution and sentencing) might be relatively more effective in reducing subsequent violence than other types of police response (Berk & Newton, 1985; Sherman & Berk, 1984). Subsequent NIJ replications of this study in five cities present a more mixed picture (see Berk, Campbell, Klap, & Western, 1992). The basic question of whether arrest on its own would have the effect of deterring violence was originally answered "yes"; and then followed by answers such as "maybe," provided the man is white, employed, and committed to the relationship; and, finally, "Things might get even worse" for men without some or all of these characteristics (see Berk et al., 1992; Dutton, 1995; Pate & Hamilton, 1992; Sherman & Smith, 1992). Interestingly, other research not included in this NIJ program and focusing on women's sense of well-being showed much less equivocal results. Women included in these studies offered very positive evaluations of police intervention and supported the use of arrest (Jaffe, Wolfe, Telford, & Austin, 1986; Langan & Innes, 1986).

On the basis of the results of the Minnesota study, Sherman (1992) suggests, counterintuitively, that the men for whom arrest is least likely to work (i.e., the most criminalistic and presumably habituated) should simply not be arrested. Critics might say exactly the opposite. That is, the men most likely to repeat the offense are precisely those in greatest need of a concerted and focused response to the violence that includes arrest but goes beyond it to address the problem of its repeated use. The debate about the effectiveness of arrest centers on the effectiveness of this single, straightforward, and relatively simple intervention as a stand-alone response to violent behavior that is complex, often routinized, and likely to have a history of repeat victimization before the first call is ever made to the police. Repeat victimization, mostly unreported to the police, may also involve several calls to the police before the first arrest is ever made and many subsequent calls before a second or third arrest is made (Worrall & Pease, 1986). While Berk and his colleagues (1992, p. 701) have stated, "The weight of evidence suggests that doing 'something' is better than doing 'nothing,'" the question of *what* to do is still very much alive.

Many men who eventually come into contact with the criminal justice system have an extensive history of physical violence to their partner; few have an extensive history of arrest for such violence. Thus, even if arrest alone served as a deterrent to subsequent violence, most men are not arrested for the vast majority of acts of violence they perpetrate. There is also the very obvious problem in the arrest studies of the assumption that only those men who are subsequently arrested by police have "failed," that is, used subsequent violence. This assumption is very doubtful, as shall be seen in our own findings comparing men's self-reports of subsequent violence with those of their partners and with police reports during a one-year follow-up after an arrest. Even more central to the research reported in Changing Violent Men is the unarticulated or unproblematized notion embedded in the arrest studies that arrest without any subsequent action can actually stop violent behavior; this is highly problematic. In the United States a great deal of very sophisticated statistical analysis has gone into considering the effect of arrest as a "one-stop" intervention, and this will no doubt provide insight into who, if anyone, might be stopped with this quick, half measure from the justice system. If, however, the cessation of violence is the aim of such intervention, the findings presented later suggest that the task is much more difficult. This is unlikely to be achieved by a single act (arrest), even one that might be seen as costly to the man (rational theory of deterrence) or results in him being watched and monitored (social control theory of deterrence) (Williams & Hawkins, 1989). While our findings show that the notions of cost and of surveillance seem to be important to men who do change their violent behavior, they are certainly not the only factors, nor are they brought about through arrest alone. This will become clearer as we present the content of programs for abusers in this chapter and later the findings about those men who do change their violent and controlling behaviors after an intervention from the justice system.

Programs for Abusers

Volunteer or Criminal-Justice Based?

Abusers often agree to participate in men's programs for purely instrumental reasons, such as wanting a partner to return home or in an attempt to avoid prosecution, and many drop out as soon as that immediate objective has been achieved. This is a problem for all abuser programs but a particular one for those who recruit only men who volunteer to attend rather than those mandated to attend by the justice system with its authority to ensure completion of the order and ability to sanction those who drop out or return to using violence. While some men do volunteer to join a program in search of personal change, the overwhelming majority do not. For the most part, violent men do not define themselves as having a problem and do not voluntarily seek to change their behavior. Men's programs based on voluntary entrance experience several fundamental difficulties: The vast majority of violent men do not come forward; those who come forward because a partner has left or they face an appearance in court often drop out of a voluntary program as soon as the immediate crisis has passed; men find it very difficult to fully engage in the challenging process of taking responsibility for their violence and resist doing so if at all possible. Most batterer programs in the United States have a 40% to 60% dropout rate in the first 3 months (DeMaris, 1989; Gondolf, 1991; Pirog-Good & Stets, 1986), and as few as 10% of men referred to programs may actually complete them (Gondolf & Foster, 1991). In addition, evidence suggests the dropouts are those most likely to have committed the more severe forms of violence and to reoffend (Gondolf, 1997). They are the ones Sherman (1992) suggests removing from the attention of the justice system.

Men who volunteer can and do leave programs if the task is too challenging and thus the tension for voluntary programs is either to work with the very small number of truly dedicated men or retain the less dedicated with a curriculum that is less challenging in an attempt to reduce attrition. This also includes those anger management programs that fail to address the central question of why the man is angry and the appropriateness of that anger and couple counseling or family therapy that remove the man and his violence from the central focus and all too often eventually move to a position in which the victim of violence becomes the focus of attention (often because the man has left the program) and is eventually made responsible for the violence or the reformation of the offender (see Dobash & Dobash, 1992, pp. 213-240). Justice-based programs for violent men help address many of the difficulties in retaining men in voluntary programs while at the same time pursuing a challenging approach to the violence itself and to the men's need to change. Probation orders that require men to attend a program form a crucial part of such an intervention. While not without problems of retention, the justice-based approach has been found to be one of the most effective means of recruiting and retaining a substantial number of violent men in programs designed to deal exclusively with them and their behavior (Edleson, 1990; Hamm & Kite, 1991; Pence & Paymar, 1993).

The police play a vital role in responding to the violence, first as an essential 24-hour service to those needing protection but also as a vital element in communicating to the men, women, and children directly involved and to the community at large that this form of violence, like all others, is illegal and will not be ignored or condoned by the agency of the state responsible for enforcing laws about issues deemed to be right or wrong. The responses of the police and the remainder of the justice system, including lawyers and judges, convey important symbolic messages to the entire society at the same time as they provide very real, material responses to the perpetrators and victims of violence. Both the symbolic and the material responses of the justice system are thus essential in an overall effort to respond directly to the perpetrators and victims of violence and play a vital role in conveying at a wider social level the clear commitment to the unequivocal rejection of this and other forms of violence. They play a crucial role in turning down the volume of violence in a general sense by representing an intolerance of violence in one of the social institutions of central importance in setting normative social standards.

To assume that the justice system can be left out of any concerted effort to end domestic violence is to doom that effort to fail. If, in other contexts, violence is wrong and will be treated as such, then a diminished response to violence against women in the home can only be interpreted by perpetrators, victims, and the community as meaning that it is somehow less wrong and more likely to be tolerated, leaving all to believe that it will neither be clearly rejected nor responded to with vigor. This stance has a long historical legacy in legal systems throughout the world (Dobash & Dobash, 1979; Pleck, 1987) and it is all too common even today to find a willingness among legislators and criminal justice personnel to retreat to this position even when examples of good practice now exist. In addition, some feminist academics and abolitionists propose that the legal system may be beyond effective use or redemption (Masters & Smith, 1998; Smart, 1989, 1995; Snider, 1990; for a critique of this position, see Dobash & Dobash, 1992, pp. 210-212). Given this legacy, it is not surprising that diversion schemes often include violence against women as one of the few if not the only form of violence deemed appropriate for exclusion from the full attention of the justice system while other forms of crime and other forms of violence are seemingly defined as more important to that institution and thus continue, for better or for worse, to receive the full attention of the formal system charged with responsibility for such affairs. This continues to be a contested arena, but it is unlikely that the perpetrators of violence against women remain unaffected by their own understanding, often based on direct personal experience, of what is and is not acceptable in this area of law and of what will and will not be tolerated by the enforcers of law. This surely constitutes one of the learning environments in which men measure the acceptability of their violent behavior and consider the costs to themselves of its continuation. At an individual level, the justice system may provide the necessary lever to encourage a man to embark on the process of personal transformation and facilitate meaningful program participation. The men's programs evaluated in the Violent Men Study were explicitly based in the justice system so that this vital organization might constitute a central part of the overall response to the perpetrators of violence against women.

In the United States and Canada, court-mandated and voluntary programs for abusers are fairly widespread (Edleson & Syers, 1990; Edleson & Tolman, 1992; Eisikovits & Edleson, 1989; Gondolf, 1991; Saunders & Azar 1989) and are developing in Britain (Morran & Wilson, 1994, 1997), New Zealand, and elsewhere. The programs evaluated in the Violent Men Study were, at the time of the research, the only two justice-based programs for abusers in Britain and were defined as experimental in nature rather than elements of the overall complement of criminal justice responses.

There are very few dedicated programs (voluntary or court mandated) in Europe and Britain. In 1994, a telephone survey of possible British programs discovered only a score of initiatives that were either partly or exclusively working with men who battered; very few were working with men referred by the courts (Scourfield & Dobash, 1999). A parliamentary committee has, however, recognized the importance of responding to the perpetrators of violence and supported the introduction of programs for abusers in prisons: "We recommend the establishment, and wide dissemination, of programmes in prison which first encourage men to recognise their violent behavior towards women and then to change it" (Parliament, House of Commons, 1993, para 74). Some prison staff also recognize that the prison environment is one in which men express extremely negative orientations to women and see it as a context in which the violence, coercion, and intimidation of partners might be addressed (CHANGE, *Annual Report*, 1993-1994).

The development of justice-based programs for physically and sexually violent offenders varies across different countries, and innovations continue at an uneven pace. In the United States, early model programs for abusers include EMERGE, the first dedicated program for physically abusive men, which began in Boston in 1977; Man Alive in Marin County, California; and the Domestic Abuse Intervention Program (DAIP), commonly called the Duluth model, of Minnesota (Adams, 1988; Pence & Paymar, 1993; Ptacek, 1988; Sinclair, 1989). All provide examples of best practice based on years of experience of working with abusers. While only the Duluth program began by working with court-mandated offenders, all three programs now work with such men. These programs have served as models for the development of other programs in North America and been modified for use elsewhere. Since the programs evaluated in this study were strongly influenced by these programs, particularly the Duluth model, we present a general overview here. This overview of the philosophy, content, and specific technologies of the men's programs is presented to provide a description of this type of intervention, to offer some insight into its theoretical underpinnings, and to serve as a backdrop for discussion of the two justice-based programs evaluated here.

As stated in Chapter 1, the specific content of abuser programs needs to fit the phenomenon of violence they are intended to alter and, in turn, the research designed to evaluate the effectiveness of that intervention must be geared to the violence and the intervention. To reiterate our conception of the implementation and evaluation of the overall transformative process: There must be a three-way fit that includes a consideration of the phenomenon, the intervention, and the evaluation (i.e., the violence, men's programs, and research), and this effort must be both theoretically driven and empirically informed and examined.

Model Programs for Abusers

The Domestic Abuse Intervention Project (DAIP) constitutes an example of a community-based program for violent men and serves as a backdrop to the discussion of the programs in this study. The Duluth model, as it has come to be known, was created in 1980 in Duluth, Minnesota, a city with a population of about 100,000 and a police department of about 100 uniformed officers (Pence & Paymar, 1993). The relatively small size of the city, an established pattern of progressive community action, and skilled feminist activists were important factors in producing what is generally acknowledged to be one of the most successful community-based justice projects for violent men anywhere in the world. Beginning from a base in the battered women's movement and building through local financial support, the profeminist project works to achieve several goals:

- Reduce the screening out and diversion of cases of violence in the home from the justice system
- Shift responsibility for the violence away from the victim and onto the state and the assailant
- Impose and enforce increasingly harsh legal sanctions on the abusers who fail to stop
- Create policies and practices that provide specific deterrence for individuals and general deterrence for the wider community
- Provide a proactive response for victims to increase support, protection, and the victims' use of criminal justice interventions
- Achieve these aims by improving interagency communication and cooperation "to secure a consistent and uniform response" (Pence, 1983; Pence & Paymar, 1985)

A major strategy of the Duluth project is to *protect women* by reducing men's violence through a reeducational program aimed at convincing offenders that they are responsible for their violent behavior and for its elimination. The method for achieving this goal is to treat the violence as a crime and ensure effective processing and sanctioning by the justice system in ways that focus on the elimination of future violence rather than on punishment for a given offense. From the outset of the project, police training, the support of the chief of police, and new practice guidelines all formed part of the strategy for responding to abusers and thereby providing protection for abused women (Buel, 1988, pp. 213-226; Dobash & Dobash, 1992, pp. 180-183; Stanko, 1989, pp. 46-69).

Duluth takes a proactive approach to engaging the victim and offers assistance and support should the case be pursued through the courts. Legal advocates assist victims in their resolve to press charges, help them prepare for court hearings, provide the prosecution with information concerning the case, assist in gathering evidence, and accompany victims to court (Pence, 1989; Pence & Shepard, 1988). During the early stages of development, this resulted in a greater use of civil protection orders as well as criminal sanctions.

Men convicted of assault on their partner are required to attend 12 weeks of counseling sessions followed by 12 weeks of Batterers Anonymous meetings, where their attendance is monitored and reported to probation officers. Three unexcused absences and they are returned to court, where, depending on the seriousness of their behavior, they may have a jail sentence imposed or be mandated to continue in the Batterers Anonymous group. Over the course of its existence, the Duluth project has made significant progress in shifting the focus of criminal justice intervention from the victim to the assailant, establishing meaningful consequences for violent abusers, and reducing the frustrations and dissatisfactions of members of the justice system. There has been an important shift in perspective. Rather than seeing violence in the family as merely a "domestic" problem arising from pathological individuals or dysfunctional families, battering is now seen as a criminal offense. The violence is also seen not simply as the acts of the sick, deranged, or poor but as attempts by normal men to establish and maintain control in their relationships with their women partners. The lessons from Duluth have been widely disseminated and influenced the two programs evaluated in the Violent Men Study.

The Research Sites

CHANGE and the Lothian
Domestic Violence Probation Project

Here, we describe in some detail the philosophy, organization, and operation of the two Scottish, justice-based abuser programs, CHANGE and the Lothian Domestic Violence Probation Project (LDVPP), as they operated during the period of research. Their general philosophy, aims, and specific approaches or technologies are examined to delineate the nature of the intervention meant to eliminate the violence (i.e., the fit between the phenomenon and the intervention) and the intervention as the object of the research evaluation (i.e., the fit between the intervention and the research). More information about how the programs were established and managed and even greater detail about their workings during the period of study are available elsewhere (see Dobash et al., 1996; Morran & Wilson, 1997).

Both programs adopted a model of reeducation for men found guilty of an offense involving the use of violence against a woman partner and identified themselves as profeminist in content. The programs were attended as a condition of probation orders for a period of not less than 6 months. Both programs used a cognitive-behavioral approach to personal change while at the same time emphasizing that the violence is part of a wider social context that cannot be ignored. Both generally worked with men in groups meeting on a weekly basis. Both preferred to have both a man and a woman facilitating the groups and both worked with their local shelter group, albeit in ways that evolved during the period of research. The main difference between the two groups was that CHANGE operated in the community as a voluntary organization while the LDVPP served as a probation service in a statutory organization (social work department).

CHANGE began to be actively discussed in 1986 when a small, informal group including Women's Aid, a prominent sheriff (judge), social workers, researchers, and a solicitor (attorney) formed a steering group to develop an innovative approach to abusers. After 3 years of effort, funding was secured in 1989 through the Urban Programme and the local social work department. The LDVPP opened in 1990, spearheaded by a local government women's committee. It was established in the social work department (which operates the probation service) with funds earmarked solely for criminal justice services for offenders. Both programs drew on models from the United States, particularly Duluth and Man Alive. In addition, the two programs had contact with one another as they developed their general philosophy and the specific content of the interventions.

Fundamental Principles

Both programs hold the position that a man's violence stems from the unequal relationship between men and women in marriage and in society and view it as part of a set of relationships that include power and control over women in intimate relations. Abusive behavior is defined as learned and intentional rather than the consequence of individual pathology or solely caused by stress, alcohol or substance abuse, or "dysfunctional" relationships (CHANGE, *Annual Report,* 1991-1992). The violence is deemed to be intentional behavior, a tactic or resource used in the attempt to control and dominate, rather than irrational or emotional ventilation beyond the control or comprehension of the perpetrator (see Cantoni, 1981). If violence is intentional behavior chosen to serve some purpose, even if only vaguely articulated, then men may be deemed to be responsible for their choices and actions and accountable to others for what they choose to do. Thus, the violence itself and the process involved in its use become fundamental foci of the programs and this cannot be diminished or ignored in the context of the intervention. The starting point involves men's agency and thus the responsibility for their own behavior and for the harm inflicted on others (see Tavuchis, 1991). Rather than being ignored, past violence is remembered so that it may play a vital part in the reformative process.

The violence is articulated rather than left hidden in silence so that the attitudes attached to its use might be exposed and considered and the processes associated with the choosing of violent behavior are revealed as integral elements of the transformative process. Thus, the past is linked to the present and to the prospect of a transformed future. Men are not allowed to forget their violence and its effect on others, nor are they forever crystallized by those acts; instead, they are defined as active, learning subjects who must become the central agents in their own transformation if such transformation is to occur.

The process begins with a "retributive" starting point meant to lead to one that is reparative and reformative (see Dobash et al., 1995; Duff, 1986). Making amends and remedying wrongs are fundamental aspects of this process as the programs seek to engage the men as active participants in their own transformation. Communication is two-way, involving dialogue, persuasion, and challenge (see Ptacek, 1988). Feelings of responsibility, shame, and guilt are starting points in the process of self-reflection meant to end with personal change rather than end points whose sole purpose is punishment or revenge. Such a direct and focused approach is inevitably challenging to the man. Looking backward at the violence, intimidation, and associated attitudes while attempting to invoke a sense of responsibility for their use and their impact on others is of necessity both painful and challenging; looking forward to the process of personal change continues to be challenging but is also positive in terms of the possible outcome. Both are essential in the process of personal transformation. Gaining insight into one's actions and motivations is meant to enhance empathy with others, and gaining new skills and techniques is meant to form the foundation of new ways of thinking and acting.

Challenging work focuses directly on violent behavior and associated acts, orientations, motivations, and intentions. The behavior, its consequences, and responsibility for its use, while central to the program, are not addressed in a combative manner, but in a style we have characterized as "respectfully retributive." Borrowed from Martin Luther King, Jr.'s conception of appropriate responses to those who perpetrated racist violence, the idea is that the individual is treated with respect as a person while at the same time required to focus on *his* acts, which are defined as unacceptable and for which he is responsible. In this sense, acts such as racial or gender-based violence are neither ignored nor excused. In the process of being reprehended, one must look back at what was wrong and harmful to others as a necessary part of moving forward to the elimination of such behavior. In a similar way, it has been deemed important that the holocaust must not be forgotten, lest history be repeated. Although the men are challenged and reprehended about their violent behavior, this is undertaken in a way that is respectful of them as individuals and oriented to positive personal change and a better future for them and for those whom they have harmed. In this way, recognition and acceptance of past behavior becomes an integral part of the transformative process.

Process of Referral and Entering the Program

All the men who were accepted as possible candidates for participation in these programs had been charged with an offense involving violence against their partner. Prior to program acceptance, separate interviews were held with the man and his partner to assess the man's suitability. At a basic level, the men had to acknowledge that they had been violent to their partner and had to indicate that they were willing to participate on the program. Without this minimal level of cooperation, the programs had nothing with which to work. A man who maintains that he has not been violent has nothing to change and one without a minimal willingness to participate will not attend or will not participate. Men with alcohol or substance abuse problems were referred to other agencies for assistance before the violence could be addressed. Both men and women received separate leaflets with basic information about the program and expectations of the men. The materials clearly stated that the man is responsible for his own behavior and must work and learn to make personal changes. Before beginning the program, men signed before witnesses an "agreement to participate," making clear that participation is a condition of probation and that attendance and active participation are necessary to successful completion. This served not only as an important part of the sentencing process but also emphasized the importance of the man's willingness to enter a process of personal change.

The leaflets for both men and women stressed that violence was the problem on which the programs would focus. Expectations about attendance were made clear; it was stressed that there was no promise to keep the relationship together; alcohol abuse was rejected as a "cause" of violence (with the acknowledgment that those with such problems need assistance from another agency); and it was indicated that failure to attend constituted a breach of the probation order. Information given to the men at this point included items such as

What can I learn?
The program can help you to understand why you have been violent or abusive to your partner. It looks at the kinds of excuses you may have used to explain your violence and how you can learn to live without being violent in the future. What you learn is up to you and how seriously you want to change. The program offers no guarantees and it is important that both you and your partner know this.

What if I don't think the violence is all my fault?
It is usually easier to blame someone or something else for things we do that we are ashamed of. No matter what kind of excuses you come up with they are just excuses. In the end it is you who makes the choice to be violent or not to be violent. By blaming other people or other things you are simply giving yourself permission to go on being violent. Only by taking responsibility for yourself and your actions can you take the first step towards stopping your violence. (CHANGE, *Information Leaflet for Men,* n.d.)

Information provided for women stressed that the court was considering placing her partner on the program because of his violence and emphasized that the program was for men only and focused on his violence and how it might be stopped. Materials further stressed that she was not responsible for his violent behavior; that her safety could not be guaranteed; and that it was important that she continue with her personal safety plans, which might include protection orders and the use of police, friends, and the women's shelter. Information for the woman included items such as

How will I know if the programme will help me?
CHANGE cannot guarantee that the programme will stop your partner being violent. That is up to him.
We will try to keep you informed of his participation in the programme and also if he is suspended for any reason.
You are not responsible for the violence nor for stopping it. You should always put your own safety first. (CHANGE, *Information Leaflet for Women,* n.d.)

Main Aims

Program materials delineated the main aims as focusing on the violence, attitudes, and new skills and monitoring the progress both of the men and of the programs. The CHANGE project was designed with a wider scope than the LDVPP, including the delivery of the abuser program along with training and consultancy to other professionals working in the area, encouraging an interagency approach to the problem, and working at the community level to raise the profile of this issue through publications and conferences. With respect to the men's program, the four main goals of CHANGE included (a) to develop self-awareness, (b) to challenge attitudes and beliefs, (c) to build skills, and (d) to monitor progress. The LDVPP set five similar objectives for men: (a) understanding acts and belief systems, (b) increasing willingness to change actions, (c) increasing understanding of the causes of violence, (d) providing practical information about changing abusive behavior, and (e) encouraging men to become accountable to others.

The curriculum for the men attending the weekly sessions was designed to deliver specific aspects of these more abstract and general goals. The example presented below illustrates some specific aspects of the approaches taken by the programs as they worked toward the achievement of these more abstract goals. The main aims are delineated and the weekly curriculum is presented not only to illustrate the specific nature of the program delivered to the men in this study but also by way of considering the fit between the content of the programs for abusers and the phenomenon of violence and, as we shall see later, the fit between this form of intervention and the research designed to consider its effectiveness. As the general curriculum of the two programs was quite similar at the time of the study, only one example is presented here (Table 3.1). The weekly curriculum of both programs is presented (Tables 3.2 and 3.3) to illustrate the similarity between the two programs, which will become more relevant with respect to the research design as both programs are combined to form the experimental group for comparison with other responses in the justice system.

Techniques and Challenges

Throughout these sessions, attention was paid to other forms of controlling and intimidating behavior and to the specific means of working to effect personal change. The range of specific techniques used included

- Reenacting or "dissecting" specific violent events in terms of associated thoughts and actions
- Using videos and vignettes depicting violent events and conflicts in marital relations to increase participants' self-awareness

Table 3.1 CHANGE Program Outline and Main Aims

1. *Focus on violent/offending behaviour*
   - defining violence and abuse
   - exploring men's excuses & explanations
   - demystifying violence—
   - "blind rages"
   - violence as choice/intentional
   - recognising patterns of past violence
   - recognising Denial, Minimisation, Blame
   - recognising effects of violence on partner/children
   - the "gains" and losses of violence

2. *Focus on attitudes and beliefs*
   - that violence to partners is:
       acceptable
       natural
       not serious
       woman's responsibility
   - about women and "women's roles"
   - "rights" re: authority and services
   - men's "need" to be in control
   - "appropriate" behaviour (jealousy)
   - fear of loss of power

3. *Developing knowledge/ skills/ strategies to avoid further violence*
   - learning the consequences of past violence
   - re-examining beliefs/attitudes/excuses
   - taking more responsibility for self and behaviour
   - recognising and acknowledging emotions
   - recognising escalation
   - learning to take Time Outs responsibly
   - practising alternative ways of behaving
   - examining "faulty thinking"/"self talk"
   - learning the basics of better communication
   - accepting others' rights

4. *Accountability—monitoring men's progress*
   - maintaining individual records
   - maintaining group progress records
   - assessing men's "self reports"
   - partner checks and partner contact
   - contact with Women's Aid/Probation
   - social work feedback and review

5. *Accountability—monitoring programmes*
   - programme "integrity"
   - suitability and non-suitability factors
   - decision making
   - staffing—safety/supervision/support

SOURCE: CHANGE (1994); for details see Morran and Wilson (1997).

Table 3.2 Content of Weekly Sessions—CHANGE

- DEFINING VIOLENCE
- DISCUSSING THE ROOTS OF VIOLENT BEHAVIOUR
- RECOGNISING THE GAINS AND LOSSES OF VIOLENCE AND ABUSE
- FIRST "CASE STUDY"—JOE AND HELEN
- BELIEFS EXERCISE (SELF ASSESSMENT)
- BREAKING DOWN THE VIOLENT EVENT
- SIGNALS
- RECOGNISING ANGER AND MOODS
- MAKING PERSONAL SAFETY PLANS
- MAKING AND TAKING A TIME OUT PLAN
- TAKING RESPONSIBILITY FOR AREAS OF PERSONAL CHANGE
- PREVIOUS PROMISES TO CHANGE AND WHY THEY HAVE GONE WRONG
- CASE STUDY
- THE VIOLENT EVENT
- THE POWER AND CONTROL WHEEL AND THE EQUALITY WHEEL
- INTIMIDATION AND BEING INTIMIDATED
- LEARNING THE BASICS OF COMMUNICATION AND NEGOTIATION
- SELF ASSESSMENT
- "SELF TALK"
- REVISION

SOURCE: CHANGE, Program Materials (n.d.).

Table 3.3 Content of Main Sessions—Lothian Domestic Violence Probation Project

Three to five weeks are given to each major section.

GROUP SESSIONS

- POWER AND CONTROL WHEEL
- MINIMISING, DENYING AND BLAMING
- USING CHILDREN
- USING MALE PRIVILEGE
- USING ECONOMIC ABUSE
- USING ISOLATION
- USING EMOTIONAL ABUSE
- USING INTIMIDATION
- USING COERCION AND THREATS/PHYSICAL VIOLENCE (5 WEEKS)

SOURCE: Lothian Domestic Violence Probation Project, Program Materials (n.d.).

- Teaching cognitive techniques for recognizing the sequence of events and the nature of emotions associated with the onset of violence
- Using continuous forms of self-assessment and monitoring such as maintaining weekly anger and control logs as a means of reinforcing group work
- Using didactic methods to enhance offenders' understandings of the nature of violent behavior to women and its social and cultural supports
- Practicing new behavior through role playing
- Other methods, such as brainstorming, small group exercises, and feedback sessions

These and other techniques were used throughout the structured program.

The challenging nature of the approach to this work is reflected the LDVPP's articulation of the role of the group worker in presenting the curriculum to the groups:

- To keep the group focused on issues of Violence, Abuse, Control and Change
- To facilitate reflective critical thinking in the group
- To maintain an atmosphere that challenges rather than colludes
- To provide new information and teach non-controlling relationship skills
- To facilitate an open and respectful Group Process (LDVPP, *Role of the Group Worker*, n.d.)

The specific goals of personal change for the men were also outlined in the information sent to women partners. At periodic points during the man's participation on the programs, women partners were sent information about specific aspects of the program and what was expected of the man. This was meant to keep the partners informed and help ensure that the men did not mislead them about the program to serve their own purposes. It was stressed that the women should continue with their own safety plans and should not continue the relationship hoping for a miracle cure simply because the man attended. The excerpts in Table 3.4 illustrate the nature and content of information sent to women partners.

The nature, focus, and content of the men's programs as outlined above informed the design of the research meant to evaluate the effectiveness of this form of intervention. The focus of the programs was on violence as intentional, as a means to obtain and maintain power and control, as functional even though it has long-term costs, as a part of an overall nexus of behavior and attitudes that support the violence and

Table 3.4 Information Sheets for Women

Sheet 1 (excerpts)

During his time on the programme, your partner is expected to work to end all these forms of abuse; . . . The first step to stopping his violence lies in his taking full responsibility for the times in the past when he has been violent or abusive to you; . . . There are three sorts of excuses he will need to learn to recognise and reject: denial, minimisation and blame; . . . He has also been asked to think about what makes for a healthy relationship and to compare that with the effects that violence has on the person being hit. . . .

Sheet 2 (excerpts)

During this part of the programme we are working to increase your partner's understanding that his violence to you is not a "mystery" or something over which he has no control. Sometimes men tell us that the violence happens so fast they are unaware of what they are doing until it is over. This is often because their use of violence has become a habit. They need to understand the habit or pattern that they have learned and to change it; . . . he is asked to identify the kinds of "early warning signals" and the "violence pattern"; . . . asked to develop a "Time-out Plan"; . . . He must look at the attitudes, expectations and beliefs by which he has justified his use of violence and abuse in the first place.

Sheet 3 (excerpts)

During this stage of the programme your partner will have had to look in detail at the times he has used violence to you. He will also have examined previous attempts he has made to change, why they didn't work and how that looked from your point of view. The programme works with men towards an understanding that their use of violence, be it physical or otherwise, is intentional. Far from being a big "mystery" it involves choice and is used by men in order to establish and maintain power and control in a relationship.

Sheet 4 (excerpts)

learning empathy; . . . learning to communicate better, particularly learning that trust is something you have to earn; learning to negotiate/compromise over issues; We have also stressed to him that completing the men's programme is a beginning. He will have been encouraged to think about what he has learned about himself and what he still needs to work on in order to live non-violently; . . . examine his expectation of authority and services; . . . If he can come to see that he does not need to remain powerful, that it hurts you, and him: that it loses him love, trust and respect . . . then it is less likely he will use violence; . . . The process of "power sharing" or living as equals is one he must work at . . .

SOURCE: CHANGE, *Information for Women*, Sheets 1-4 (n.d.).

the particular treatment of women in their position as wives and in a wider context of men's views and orientations to themselves and the women in their lives. The research described in the next chapter was designed to consider the effectiveness of these programs compared to other forms of intervention used by the justice system. To undertake this task, it was necessary to design research that fits the intervention meant to effect a change in violent behavior. It is to that task that we shall now turn.

4

Methods for Evaluating
Programs for Violent Men

While research evaluations should be designed to fit the intervention being examined and the intervention should be structured to fit the issue or problem being addressed, a perfect fit across all three of these arenas is unlikely. The researcher is, nonetheless, confronted with the task of designing the best fit possible. What is to be studied, who is to be studied, and how they are to be studied are standard issues addressed in designing any research and they are made all the more demanding by the necessity of studying both the social phenomenon and the intervention in a single study. Here, the overall task is to examine the connection between theoretical ideas and empirical evidence about the phenomenon of the violence, the principles and practices of abuser programs oriented to personal change, and the research designed to examine the effectiveness of the intervention in eliminating subsequent violence. The focus of this chapter is on research designs and includes general issues regarding evaluation research, specific issues pertinent to evaluating abuser programs, and a delineation of the research undertaken in the Violent Men Study. We consider the problems and limitations associated with conducting valid evaluations and describe the Violent Men Study in terms of the overall research design, the sample of men and women, and the data collection instruments used at three time periods.

Violence and Personal Change

The process of designing the Violent Men Study began with an empirically informed theory about the dynamics of violence between men and women and a detailed specification of the intervention directed at personal change. While the phenomenon of violence and the nature and philosophy of abuser programs have been discussed earlier, it is essential to stress that they provide the foundation for making decisions about the design of the research and the data to be collected. Briefly, violence against women partners occurs in a context of intimate domination in which men have greater power and authority over women. From this position, men expect to be given sexual and domestic services and to have ultimate authority in the relationship, particularly in disputes or conflicts of interest, and believe they have the right to judge the woman's behavior and punish "wrongdoing" by various means, including violence. What constitutes the wrongdoing of a wife has a long historical legacy in most cultural and legal systems and includes real or imagined sexual infidelities, neglect of household duties, and presumed disobedience or disrespect to the authority of husbands. More specifically, these include issues of sexual jealousy and possessiveness; demands about domestic work including cooking, cleaning, and child care; and expectations of the respectful treatment of the man, including a limitation on the woman's ability to negotiate or debate about contested issues. The notion of "nagging" establishes such negotiation as inappropriate and unacceptable (see Dobash & Dobash, 1984).

Anthropological, historical, and contemporary evidence reveals that violence against women in intimate relationships is functional; it is used to maintain authority, to punish "wrongdoing," to coerce and force compliance, and to "mold" women to the demands of men. The process of personal transformation envisaged in the men's programs under study is one in which men must learn to reject violent behavior that has been useful to them in the past and to change the attitudes and beliefs that are associated with such actions. Violent and abusive men must begin by admitting that they have in fact perpetrated acts of violence for which they are responsible and are to be held accountable. When successful, the process of personal change is one in which the individual moves toward an acceptance of responsibility for his own behavior, a recognition of the costs to himself, and an awareness of the harm done to others. He must begin to seek personal change and be willing to continue the difficult work of learning new behaviors and attitudes. In this way, men are meant to shift from authoritarian relationships enforced through punitive and coercive measures to ones based on greater mutuality and trust in which violence is seen as inappropriate and unacceptable. Specific skills or techniques are learned as a means of managing oneself, of communicating with and listening to others, and of negotiating and settling disputes without violence. Such transformations are not easily achieved and it is important for all who embark on this enterprise (violent men, women partners, program staff, and evaluation researchers) to recognize that this is a formidable task (see Jennings, 1990).

Having theorized the violence and the process of personal change contained in the intervention, we need to reflect both in the research design meant to evaluate the effectiveness of the intervention. Criminal justice programs for offenders have long been the subject of assessment and judgment. At least since the mid-19th century, the efficacy of various interventions has been of interest to reformers, academics, community groups, and the public. The 19th century saw the creation of the penitentiary as a grand experiment in reforming wayward men and women (Dobash, Dobash, & Gutteridge, 1986; Foucault, 1977; Ignatieff, 1978). Since then, the penal terrain has been littered with grand and not-so-grand experiments aimed at transforming individuals, and the 1960s and 1970s witnessed an explosion of psychologically informed programs for offenders. Particularly in progressive areas of North America and Scandinavia, imprisoned offenders were subjected to a barrage of individual and group forms of psychodynamic therapies intended to cure their troubled personalities. By the end of the 1970s, commentators were declaring that these interventions were failures and that "nothing worked" (Martinson, 1974).

In the context of a conservative pessimism about liberal treatment programs, the prevailing mood of radical rejection of the supposed net-widening aspects of such treatment ideals, and a postmodern pessimism about the potential of the human sciences, stagnation and bleak judgments prevailed. Prisons embracing the rehabilitative ideal were judged no better at changing offenders than those enforcing more punitive and restrictive forms of confinement. Community treatment fared little better and was judged to have minimal impact on reoffending. In turn, these evaluations and bleak assessments were themselves subjected to scrutiny (Gender & Ross, 1987). Gradually, those who created and operated various programs for offenders and the researchers who evaluated them began to question such uniformly negative judgments and to suggest, instead, that certain types of interventions might have a positive effect on certain types of offenders. There is now a growing consensus that certain types of offender programs can be effective, but there is also agreement that all programs should be subjected to stringent evaluations to establish what does and does not work and to examine why that might be so. Unfortunately, such evaluations of programs for violent offenders are still relatively rare (Van Voorhis, Cullen, & Applegate, 1995).

Programs for all types of offenders have proliferated in the past decade, including those for men who perpetrate violence against a woman partner. Some are based on principles that are more traditional and psychodynamic while others are profeminist and cognitive-behavioral. For some, the abusers are mandated by the courts to attend, while others include men who join voluntarily in the search to reform themselves. Some lack clarity in goals, objectives, and coherence and offer unstructured or poorly articulated forms of intervention while others have explicit objectives and aims and are relatively clear about the type of individual best suited for the form of intervention being offered. Evaluators have great difficulty assessing programs unless they have explicit objectives and aims and a clearly articulated content that is, in fact, delivered to the abusers and can be known to the evaluators (Van Voorhis et al., 1995). Most profeminist, cognitive-behavioral programs for abusers have developed explicit objectives and clearly articulated program structures. Similarly, both of the men's programs in the Violent Men Study had clearly articulated goals and objectives as well as very specific structures and content, as illustrated in the previous chapter. In these programs, theoretical ideals and research knowledge were linked to the structure and content of the program, and specific techniques were clearly aimed at changing violent behavior and the orientations of abusers. Clearly articulated aims and objectives make it possible to begin the process of creating valid evaluations of such programs.

One of the initial problems confronting all evaluations is the decision about the type of evaluation to be conducted. The preferred option for most investigators and program sponsors is an *outcome* evaluation designed to assess whether the particular program works better than doing nothing or better than some other type of intervention. The main aim of the Violent Men Study was to compare court-ordered abuser programs with other forms of criminal justice response (fine, warning, probation, or prison) in their effect on subsequent violence, injuries, and controlling behavior and the beliefs that support and sustain such behaviors.

Issues in Evaluation Research

Attempting to conduct valid evaluation research is a sobering experience. Unlike ethnographic and other forms of research, where it is possible to be more flexible, conducting a valid evaluation requires adherence to a fairly rigid, preestablished design. Evaluation research has a long history in many disciplines, and procedures established in medical research are often proposed for social investigations (Sherman, 1992). Evaluation research in the social sciences, however, sometimes fails to consider the issue or phenomenon meant to be addressed by the intervention (e.g., violence and controlling behavior) and instead focuses on questions such as client or staff satisfaction with the delivery of the intervention and on outcome measures that are limited to the assessment of course completion by clients. Such issues cannot be considered relevant to an assessment of the impact on the problem of violence that brought the person to the program in the first place. While staff satisfaction and program completion are certainly important, they are more properly defined as monitoring and do not provide evidence for judging the effects of the intervention on the phenomenon of concern. The essential task is to construct a research design and develop measurement tools that can directly address more demanding questions about the effect of the intervention on, for example, violence and controlling behavior. It is also important to attempt to identify those aspects of the intervention that appear to be most successful in changing behavior and orientations and to seek to establish their sustainability over a period of time.

Randomized Designs

Randomized designs are sometimes proposed as the best or only method of answering the more demanding questions identified above. The practice of using a randomized design to evaluate the outcome of an intervention requires allocation on the basis of chance of some individuals to a *treatment* group and others to a *control* group (for a classic statement, see Campbell & Stanley, 1963). This approach requires the assumption that all potentially relevant variables, apart from the intervention itself, will have been dealt with through the procedure of randomly allocating individuals to different groups. The aim of randomization is to deal with potentially contaminating variables (such as differences in class, education, ethnicity, and histories of violence) that might themselves affect the outcome, thus ensuring that only the intervention is being examined for possible effects. The ideal of this model assumes that randomization of subjects is successfully achieved and that it provides an equalization of experimental and control groups prior to the beginning of the experiment. The assumption of preexperimental equalization is rarely, if ever, checked by the researchers, although this could easily be done. Instead, it is assumed that the method of random assignment has effectively canceled out any preexisting differences between the groups so that any observed effects found after the intervention can be assumed to be a result of the intervention and not of some preexisting condition such as differences in age, unemployment, or other factors. In this area, for example, observed outcomes would be presumed to be the result of the intervention or treatment, for example, abuser program, fine, or imprisonment, rather than other factors such as age, employment, or marital status. Despite the ideal of this approach, true randomized designs are rare in the natural settings studied by social researchers and, in reality, such evaluators always face a host of pragmatic and ethical dilemmas even if they choose to ignore them.

Despite the many obstacles, a few randomized designs have been used in the study of violence between intimate partners. For example, in the 1980s the National Institute of Justice (NIJ) used randomized designs in a number of experimental field trials assessing the effects of arrest as a stand-alone intervention for subsequent incidents of violence. The first of these was the much discussed and debated Minnesota arrest study (Sherman & Berk, 1984). Police officers were supposed to randomly assign cases to one of three possible outcomes: arrest, offering advice, and recommending that one or both partners leave the house to cool off (Sherman, 1992). While the results of this study do not concern us here, it should be noted that the research indicated that arrest was much more likely than the other interventions to reduce subsequent police interventions (Sherman & Berk, 1984). In an attempt to replicate this study, the NIJ conducted five additional field experiments using randomized designs. These studies produced much more equivocal results, with some indicating that arrest made a difference and others finding no such effect (Berk et al., 1992; Garner, Fagan, & Maxwell, 1995). While results of these studies and the supposed effect of arrest have been much debated (Buzawa & Buzawa, 1992), of concern here are the problems and limitations associated with randomized field designs.

The arrest studies failed to use or build on existing theoretical and empirical knowledge about the phenomenon of violence against women. Only in retrospect was deterrence theory used to "explain" the potential impact of arrest on subsequent violence; for the most part, there was no consideration of the limits of what might be expected or achieved through the use of arrest on its own as the single and final form of intervention meant to stop men from repeating their violence (Sherman 1992). A close engagement with existing research on the phenomenon of violence against women and an awareness of the documented pragmatic knowledge of activists working in this area would have led to considerable skepticism about what might be expected from the use of arrest on its own as a deterrent of subsequent violence. This body of research and pragmatic knowledge strongly suggests that many men who use violence against a women partner become habituated to its use and have committed numerous acts of violence by the time of the first contact with the police. In light of such evidence and the findings of more broadly based context specific studies, it would have been useful to consider arrest as well as other responses used by the justice system. None of the arrest studies was designed to investigate wider issues about criminal justice, such as the potential impact of prosecution and sentencing, the subsequent predicament of the men and women, and the nature of messages conveyed to men and women by police officers (see Hart, 1993; Stark, 1993; Zorza & Woods, 1994). The arrest studies also demonstrate that randomized designs are notoriously difficult to maintain in the field. In the Minnesota study, approximately 20% of the cases were not assigned to the appropriate random category. In addition, the entire experiment seemingly rested on the decisions of a small number of police officers (see Berk, Smyth, & Sherman, 1988) and their willingness to act at all times as researchers adhering to the strict rules about which intervention was to be assigned to each case rather than in their customary role as police officers using their judgment and discretion about each case as a guide to the action taken.

Ethics and Randomized Designs

Ethical issues are important to all forms of research, but randomized designs present particular problems. The question of the ethics associated with assigning individuals to various groups on the basis of chance has been widely debated in medical and health research and has recently been hotly contested in research trials using various treatment modalities for HIV (Bowling, 1995, 1997). In randomized designs, questions arise regarding the responsibility of researchers to inform those involved that they will be subject to random decisions pertaining to their future life, including experiments that may affect their health, safety, and well-being. Informing participants that they are involved in a study and of the possible implications for themselves and others who are directly or indirectly involved is a fundamental principle of ethical research. In addition to informing participants about their inclusion in the experimental trial and of the possible consequences of participation, the researcher must also seek their informed consent to participate.

Those researching this form of violence face some important issues regarding informed consent. First, from whom should consent be sought: the perpetrator, the victim, or both? Indeed, it could be argued that because domestic violence is of concern to the wider community that other stakeholders (women's groups, criminal justice, health care and social services) should also be involved in some way in the deliberations regarding the use of experimental trials, random assignment of different forms of intervention, and informed consent. Yet discussions of these issues do not appear in the literature in this area of study. They are missing even from the widely discussed arrest studies. It may be that ethical protocols are such an integral part of studies sponsored by the NIJ that researchers do not consider it necessary to discuss such issues when publishing their findings. If so, it would be helpful if they were discussed when outlining research designs and in final reports, since such protocols may not be widely known to those outside that community. If, as we believe, such protocols do not exist or are not adhered to, this raises serious concerns about such research since randomized designs may deny individuals access to services simply on the basis of chance decisions (for a discussion of the ethical dilemmas in evaluations of programs for sex offenders, see Marshall, Laws, & Barbee, 1990). This is particularly important as research using randomized designs is now being conducted on programs for abusers, yet discussions of these ethical problems are not apparent.

Under the auspices of the NIJ, the Victim Services Agency of New York City is conducting a 2-year evaluation of a community- and criminal justice-based project that includes a treatment program for men who use violence against a woman partner. The project appears to be a worthy one, modeled on the Duluth program, and the researchers are making a valiant effort to conduct a valid evaluation. Davis and Taylor (1995) report, however, that they have had extraordinary problems implementing their randomized design. Many of the potential participants are never sentenced because their cases are dismissed at an early stage, many men are unwilling to plead guilty (a requirement for assignment to the program), and some cases assigned to the men's program do not actually result in treatment. Because of these and other problems, the initial design specifying random assignment at the presentencing stage had to be abandoned. The modified design does not make random assignments at this early stage in the process but only after "all parties have agreed to the program [participation]" (Davis & Taylor, 1995, p. 12). This study is instructive in a number of ways. It shows how difficult it is to implement a truly randomized design in a field experiment and, as with the arrest studies, it seems to ignore the issue of informed consent. Ignoring the issue of informed consent is particularly problematic in a study where "all parties," presumably including women partners who have been victimized, must agree to program participation prior to random allocation. It seems relevant to ask what, if any, explicit or tacit promises have been made to the men or women once they reach this stage? What compromises have victims made, and what expectations are built into these processes? It is important to worry about such procedures relative to the interests of the entire community, victims, victim advocates, perpetrators, criminal justice personnel, and researchers and to enter into a dialogue regarding the appropriateness of randomized designs in the area of domestic violence. In doing so, it would be pertinent to consider examples of research designs that have not used randomized designs because of ethical concerns (see below and Hamm & Kite, 1991).

Evaluating Programs for Violent Men

Existing Evaluations

Randomized designs do not usually feature in the existing evaluations of programs for violent men. Yet, there have been a number of attempts to assess the impact of participation in an abuser program, and several reviews have summarized the results and limitations of some of the Canadian and U.S. studies (Burns, Meredith, & Paquette, 1991; Eisikovits & Edleson, 1989; Gondolf, 1997). While generally concluding that it seems safe to assume that program participation has some impact on subsequent violent behavior, the same reviews cite a multitude of problems threatening the validity of most of these evaluations (see Bersani, Chen, & Denton, 1988; Chen et al., 1989; Dutton, 1986; Edleson & Grusznski, 1988; Edleson & Syers, 1991; Gondolf, 1988b, 1997; Hamm & Kite, 1991; Saunders & Hanusa 1986; Tolman & Bennett, 1990). The main limitations of these evaluations include self-assessment by program staff; lack of control or comparison groups; small sample sizes at the initial stages of the research (usually about 50 respondents); lack of a pretest or posttests; high rates of attrition during the program and in posttest follow-ups (with dropout rates between 60% and 80%); very short or nonstandardized periods of follow-up; inadequate measures of outcome, including rearrests or men's self-reports as the sole indicator of change; and, finally, a failure to routinely include women's reports of changes in the abusive behavior of partners.

Most of these problems exist in all forms of evaluation research, but an additional problem in this particular domain is the potential impact of a "separation effect." If men and women who were originally included in the sample divorce or separate during the follow-up period yet continue to be included in the analysis, this may yield spurious results since such women *may* no longer be at risk of future violence if they have no contact with the violent man during the period of follow-up. Considerable clarification is required on this point as some separated or divorced women do remain at risk either through arrangements for contact visits with children or because men continue to stalk or harass them despite divorce or separation.

Another problem is the paucity of comparisons of different types of interventions (e.g., treatment focused on violence, punishment for violence, no response). Most of the existing evaluations are restricted solely to reporting that Treatment X is better than Treatment Y (Edleson & Gruszinski 1988; Saunders, 1996). These studies, while valuable, are, in fact, an assessment of one type of treatment compared to another type of treatment. To assess the effectiveness of treatment per se, it is necessary to compare treatment with other responses such as punishment or doing nothing. Then it is possible to judge the relative success of these categorically different types of response. In the Violent Men Study, we compared court-mandated treatment programs for abusers with other responses in the justice system that do not focus on the violence and do not constitute any form of treatment but more closely represent some form of punishment (e.g., fine, prison). Thus, this study constitutes a comparison of different *types* of responses to violent behavior and in so doing joins a very few other evaluations that have attempted to compare the impact of court-mandated treatment programs with other forms of criminal justice intervention (Chen et al., 1989; Hamm & Kite, 1991).

Program Integrity

Creating and implementing an adequate and practical research design is only one of the problems facing the evaluator. Another challenge is that of the implementation and operation of the intervention being studied, known as program integrity. Monitoring the implementation and operation of programs under study should be an integral part of the evaluation because they sometimes do not deliver the program outlined in their stated aims and structure but instead become transformed for reasons of changes in philosophy or personnel or because of the pragmatics of practice. Other interventions may fail to meet their stated aims and objectives because the treatment is inappropriate for the problem. On this point, Van Voorhis and her colleagues (1995) conclude that negative outcomes may create the impression that "nothing worked" when they sometimes reflect the fact that "nothing happened" (p. 20). Energetic dedicated staff, efficient referral procedures, seemingly useful programs, and ambitious treatment targets may come to nothing. Well-designed interventions may fail not because of internal problems associated with the project but because the program does not fit its external environment or meet the needs of its users. If the program does not receive clients or if it exists in a malevolent or indifferent environment, this would be expected to have a negative effect on its operation.

Evaluation researchers need to assess and monitor the nature of the program being studied to provide at least a minimal characterization of the nature of the intervention that may produce some form of outcome or effect. More detailed characterizations are necessary to consider more closely the relationship between the content of the program and what does and does not work. Internal change in a project, such as high staff turnover and radical shifts in philosophy, may seriously affect the nature of the treatment on offer. If, for example, a program starts life with staff dedicated to a certain form of intervention (e.g., psychodynamic) and changes in staff or philosophy bring about a shift to a different approach (e.g., cognitive-behavioral), this will mean that the researcher is evaluating two different programs and valid comparisons become impossible. Thus, frequent contact with the program(s) under investigation should form an integral part of the evaluation.

The Violent Men Study

The Violent Men Study was designed to extend the work of existing evaluations and to answer three general questions: (a) How effective are court-mandated abuser programs at eliminating violence used by men against a woman partner? (b) How effective are court-mandated abuser programs compared to court sanctions? and (c) Are observed changes sustainable over time? An ancillary task was to consider the general and specific mechanisms that might account for any observed changes in behavior or beliefs. Numerous other issues were addressed, including the safety of women partners and of women researchers, how best to interview abusers and victims, how best to measure violence and other related behaviors, and how to capture changes over time. In essence, the evaluation compared the effects of two court-mandated abuser programs with those of other sanctions used by the courts (e.g., fine, probation, and prison) to examine their effectiveness in eliminating violence and thereby enhancing the safety and well-being of abused women. In its broadest sense, the study was designed to assess the impact of a range of criminal justice sanctions on subsequent violent and controlling behaviors and accompanying attitudes and beliefs—what we have termed the constellation of violence.

Research Design

Two naturally occurring comparison groups were established, the "Men's Program Group" (men who were sentenced to and completed one of the abuser programs as a condition of probation) and the "Other Criminal Justice Group (Other CJ)" (men receiving another form of sanction from the courts). To compare the two groups, violent men and women partners were studied at three points in time, using in-depth interviews at Time 1 (immediately following the imposition of a court sanction) and postal questionnaires at Time 2 (3 months after initial contact) and Time 3 (12 months after initial contact). This quasi-experimental approach is sometimes referred to as a "nonequivalent control group" design (see Campbell & Stanley, 1963; Chen et al., 1989). The research design is set out in Table 4.1.

For both pragmatic and ethical reasons, a randomized design was not used in the Violent Men Study. Ethically, we were concerned about allocating on the roll of the dice cases involving violence in ongoing relationships where there is an obvious risk of subsequent violence. It was also judged to be too difficult, if not impossible, to develop an ethically appropriate procedure for obtaining informed consent from both offenders and victims to participate in an experiment with an unknown outcome. On a practical level, early discussions with prosecutors and judges and the funders of the evaluation convinced us that we would encounter considerable resistance from judges to the use of a randomized design both because of their ethical concerns and because of their belief that their own professional selection of a sanction would be better for all concerned (man, woman, justice system, and community)

Table 4.1 Violent Men Study—Research Design

	Time 1 Interview		Time 2 Postal Questionnaire		Time 3	
			(3 Months)		(12 Months)	
Intervention	Men	Women	Men	Women	Men	Women
Men's Programs	Å	Å	β	β	Ω	Ω
Other Criminal Justice	Å	Å	β	β	Ω	Ω

than one determined by the researchers' roll of the dice. We were also aware of the enormous problems experienced by other researchers in their attempts to maintain such designs in the field.

There are, of course, limitations associated with the design adopted in the Violent Men Study. This design cannot deal with potential selection bias that might have occurred through decisions made by those in the justice system. It may be, for example, that the sentencing practices of Scottish sheriffs (judges) resulted in two very different groups and, as such, men in the Men's Program group differed in significant ways from those in the Other CJ group. The method for dealing with this potential bias was to conduct ex post facto matching whereby the two groups were compared on a number of variables using data gathered at Time 1 to assess whether there were initial differences between the two groups that might have an effect on the subsequent outcome at the two follow-up stages. More than 30 relevant variables were examined across the two groups in considering whether they were basically similar or different before the start of the research. Relevant variables included basic demographic characteristic, histories of violence, and others. This will be discussed in more detail later; it is sufficient to note here that the groups were basically similar.

The Sample

The two comparison groups were created by drawing cases of all men sentenced for an offense involving violence against their partner in the two courts located in the locality of the abuser programs. They were identified throughout the course of the fieldwork through monthly scrutiny of all pending cases in the relevant courts. As there is no specific offense of "domestic assault," all pending cases had to be examined. Those involving violence in marital and marriagelike relationships were identified from information such as names and addresses of the offenders and victims, the nature of the charge, and details of the offense. The cases included misdemeanors as well as those that elsewhere might be defined as felonies involving very serious injuries.

Given the research design, the aim of sampling was to obtain respondents that reflected the different *types* of sentences (fines, prisons, and men's programs, etc.) rather than a sample that reflected the proportion of men receiving each of the different types of sentences. As the focus of the research was an evaluation of the effects of different types of sentences, it was essential to ensure that the sample included respondents from each of the relevant sentencing categories for purposes of comparison across the two groups. Our aim was not to obtain a sample composed of respondents reflecting the proportion of those sentenced to the different categories, as current sentencing practices would have yielded a sample composed mostly of men who had received fines and very few who had been sentenced to men's programs. One of the main aims was to obtain as many men sentenced to programs as possible to accumulate a reasonable number of cases in this group for the purposes of comparison with the group composed of other criminal justice sanctions.

Many of the cases found in the court records could not be included in the sampling universe because the record contained no address or the men could not be traced from the address given.[1] Excluding those cases lacking pertinent information resulted in a universe of 313 cases from court records (84 Men's Program cases and 229 Other CJ cases). At Time 1, the sample comprised 256 (122 men and 134 women partners); included among them were 95 couples. Of these 256 men and women, the Men's Program group comprised 51 men and 47 women and the Other CJ group contained 71 men and 97 women. All of the men and women participating in the Violent Men Study were white and from Scottish, English, or Irish parentage and, as such, were representative of the vast majority of the court cases examined in the two jurisdictions in the study.

By contrast to many longitudinal studies conducted on men's programs, this study did not experience exceptional problems in tracing respondents, although a few could not be found because they had moved or otherwise could not be contacted. The rates of questionnaire return at follow-up, particularly at Time 2, are quite good for a study on such a sensitive issue (Ribisl et al., 1996). At Time 2, 80% of men and 83% of women in the Men's Program group and 72% of men and 77% of women in the Other CJ group returned a questionnaire (calculated as a proportion of those interviewed at Time 1). These are more than acceptable rates of return for postal questionnaires, particularly in a longitudinal study examining such a sensitive subject. The rates of return at Time 3, while lower, are still respectable. Sixty percent of women with partners in the Men's Program group and 57% of women in the Other CJ group returned questionnaires one year after they were interviewed. The rates for men in both groups are lower: 57% of Men's Program men and 49% of Other CJ men returned a questionnaire at Time 3. These rates of return possibly reflect the excellent rapport established through interview at Time 1 and the small financial inducements offered at each stage of the research.

Gathering Data Relevant to the Research Questions

What sort of evidence could be used to assess the theoretically specified "constellation of violence" and changes in subsequent behavior and orientations of the violent men? Self-reports of the men and criminal justice records of rearrest and subsequent prosecution are not reliable indicators of the actual level of violent acts subsequently committed by men, and criminal justice records can tell us nothing about associated beliefs or acts of intimidation, harassment, and other forms of controlling behavior. While criminal justice reports are used in the Violent Men Study to assess subsequent prosecutions and the accounts of the men are used to assess their reports of changes in their own behavior, it was crucial to include the accounts of women partners as an additional and essential indicator of men's violence and any changes that might occur in the men's behavior and in the quality of life of both partners.

At Time 1, in-depth interviews with the women and the men were used to investigate a wide range of issues focusing on the constellation of violence (violence, injuries, and controlling behavior) and the wider interpersonal, marital, and institutional contexts in which violence begins and continues. The in-depth investigation at Time 1 provided a multidimensional baseline for assessing changes over time. At Time 2 (3-month follow-up) and Time 3 (12-month follow-up), the men and the women were sent postal questionnaires that included questions aimed at assessing changes in the criterion behaviors as well as measures of beliefs and orientations assessed at Time 1. While more information might have been obtained from face-to-face interviews at all three time periods, this is an extremely costly and time-consuming method to undertake on three separate occasions. While telephone surveys are commonly used in North America, where telephone ownership is almost universal, many of the potential participants in this study were unlikely to have a telephone in their home and would thus have been eliminated from the follow-up stages of the research. The postal questionnaire was appropriate for this study, as it was more likely to sustain the integrity of the research design by retaining at follow-up those respondents interviewed at Time 1 (see Dillman, 1978, for a detailed consideration of postal questionnaires).

The methods adopted for this study are within the long-standing traditions of evaluation research, and the overall methodology uses the context-specific approach adopted in our previous research (Dobash & Dobash, 1979, 1983; see also Dutton, 1996; Pawson & Tilly, 1997). The context-specific method (not usually named as such) is often used in anthropological and ethnographic studies and in sociological studies using in-depth interviews where the specific focus of investigation is located in the broader contexts in which it occurs. In this tradition, wider cultural, historical, and social processes are deemed to be important aspects of the context in which the phenomenon occurs and in which it must be understood and explained. When we first articulated the context-specific approach, the intention was to outline a methodology that embedded theoretical proposals and empirical knowledge in wide historical, cultural, social, institutional, and interpersonal contexts (Dobash & Dobash, 1979, 1983). This approach is neither slave to the quantitative tradition of logical positivism nor captive to the qualitative style of the interpretive school, wherein subjects' accounts are given precedence over all other forms of analysis. Both quantitative and qualitative methods are seen as complementary and there is an attempt to integrate theoretical ideas with empirical research in an overall contextual analysis. There is a growing use of "context" in research, and it has recently been proposed as an integral aspect of assessing and validating competing research claims (Longino, 1993).

The Constellation of Violence

Measuring Violence, Injuries, Controlling Behaviors, and Associated Beliefs

The in-depth interviews conducted at Time 1 used the context-specific approach and a form of event analysis as information was gathered about a wide variety of issues relating to the backgrounds of the men and women, the nature and levels of violence and other aggressive and controlling behavior, broader aspects of the relationship, and the use of third parties and formal agencies such as police and health care and social services. In addition, specific violent events were examined in detail. While this procedure provided extensive information about violent incidents and the changing contexts in which they occur, we also developed standardized, summary measures with which to make direct comparisons across the three time periods. The Conflict Tactics Scale has been used in some studies, but it was judged inappropriate for this investigation because of its limitations (Dobash & Dobash, 1992; Pagelow, 1985; Römkens, 1997; Yllö, 1993). Three indices were created to measure the "constellation of violence," including violent acts, injuries, and various forms of controlling behavior.

The Violence Assessment Index (VAI) includes 26 different acts ranging from aggressive threats and physical restraint to punching, kicking, and the use of a weapon (see Table 4.2). Women were also given the opportunity to specify any other violent acts that may have occurred. In contrast to most existing approaches, the specific form of attack was "connected" to the part of the body to which it was directed, reasoning that a punch in the face (Item C) would be experienced differently from a punch on the body (Item H). At the initial interview at Time 1, the VAI was used with the men and the women to assess the occurrence and frequency of use of the specific acts of violence throughout the entire relationship (ever prevalence); throughout a typical year; during the one-year period prior to the interview; and during two specific violent events, the first violent event and the last violent event that led to arrest and eventual inclusion in the study.

Until relatively recently, a significant problem in most approaches to the assessment of this form of violence has been a failure to document the consequences of violent acts, that is, injuries. By contrast, the Injury Assessment Index (IAI) (Table 4.3) developed for this study includes 21 specific injuries. After completing the IAI, the women were also given an opportunity to specify any other injuries that may have occurred. The injuries included in the index range from bruising of the body to lost hair, fractures, cuts, and internal injuries. Similar to the VAI, the IAI was used at the initial interview at Time 1 to assess the prevalence and frequency of occurrence of specific injuries sustained throughout the entire relationship; throughout a typical year; throughout the one-year period prior to the interview; and during two particular violent events, the first violent event and the last violent event that led to the man's arrest and eventual inclusion in the study.

Table 4.2 Violence Assessment Index (VAI)

Questions at follow-up after 3 months and 12 months:

- For the man: Thinking of ALL the incidents that may have happened in the last [x months], please tell me how many times [you] have done each of the following?
- For the woman: Thinking of ALL the incidents that may have happened in the last [x months], please tell me how many times [he] did each of the following?

Number of times

A ___ Restrained her from moving or leaving the room

B ___ Choked her or held your hand over her mouth

C ___ Punched her in the face

D ___ Forced her to do something against her will

E ___ Slapped her on the face, body, arms or legs

F ___ Pushed, grabbed or shoved her

G ___ Threatened to kill yourself

H ___ Punched her on the body, arms or legs

I ___ Used an object to hurt her

J ___ Kicked or punched her in stomach when pregnant

K ___ Threw things at her or about the room

L ___ Demanded sex when she didn't want it

M ___ Punched or kicked the walls or furniture

N ___ Threatened to hit the kids

O ___ Shouted at or threatened the kids

P ___ Forced her to have sex or some kind of sexual activity

Q ___ Tried to strangle, smother or drown her

R ___ Kicked her on the body, arms or legs

S ___ Shouted and screamed at her

T ___ Threatened her with an object or weapon

U ___ Kicked her in the face

V ___ Swore at her or called her names

W ___ Threatened to kill her

X ___ Twisted her arm

Y ___ Dragged her or pulled her by her hair

Z ___ Threatened her with your fist, hand or foot

NOTE: Wording modified throughout for men and women respondents. Shown here for men.

Table 4.3 Injury Assessment Index (IAI)

Questions at follow-up after 3 months and 12 months:

- For the man: Thinking of ALL the incidents that may have happened in the last [x months], please tell me how many times [you] have done each of the following?
- For the woman: Thinking of ALL the incidents that may have happened in the last [x months], please tell me how many times [he] did each of the following?

Number of times

A ___ Cut/s on her face

B ___ Bruise/s on her body

C ___ Burn/s anywhere on body

D ___ Lost hair/ pulled out

E ___ Broken arm or leg

F ___ Cut/s on her arms or legs

G ___ Bruise/s on her face

H ___ Miscarriage

I ___ Blackout or unconsciousness

J ___ Bruise/s on her arms or legs

K ___ Cut/s anywhere on her body

L ___ Black eye/s

M ___ Internal injury

N ___ Lost or broken teeth

O ___ Sickness or vomiting

P ___ Bleeding on any part of face

Q ___ Broken ribs

R ___ Bleeding on body, arms or legs

S ___ Split lip

T ___ Sprained wrist or ankle

U ___ Broken nose, jaw or cheekbone

NOTE: Wording modified throughout for men and women respondents. Shown here for men.

Men who perpetrate violence against an intimate partner usually engage in a range of other aggressive, controlling, and coercive acts as a part of the overall constellation of violence, and the abuser programs aim to address this constellation of behaviors as well as the values and beliefs that generate and rationalize the violence. The Controlling Behaviors Index (CBI) (Table 4.4) was used to assess this behavior. The

Table 4.4 Controlling Behaviors Index (CBI)

- For the man: In the last [x months] how often have [you] done the following things to [your partner] which means [she] must be careful?
- For the woman: In the last [x months] how often has [he] done the following things to [you] which means [you] must be careful?

	Never	Rarely	Sometimes	Often	Very Often
A. Threaten *[her/you]	O	O	O	O	O
B. Shout at her	O	O	O	O	O
C. Swear at her	O	O	O	O	O
D. Shout at the children	O	O	O	O	O
E. Threaten to hurt the children	O	O	O	O	O
F. Call her names	O	O	O	O	O
G. Question her about her activities	O	O	O	O	O
H. Check her movements	O	O	O	O	O
I. Have a certain mood/look	O	O	O	O	O
J. Try to provoke an argument	O	O	O	O	O
K. Criticise her	O	O	O	O	O
L. Criticise her family/friends	O	O	O	O	O
M. Put her down in front of others	O	O	O	O	O
N. Deliberately keep her short of money	O	O	O	O	O
O. Make her feel sexually inadequate	O	O	O	O	O
P. Point at her [threateningly]	O	O	O	O	O
Q. Make to hit without doing so	O	O	O	O	O
R. Restrict her social life	O	O	O	O	O
S. Use kids in argument against her	O	O	O	O	O
T. Threaten to hurt the pet	O	O	O	O	O
U. Nag her	O	O	O	O	O

NOTE: Wording modified throughout for men and women respondents. Shown here for men.

CBI includes 21 specific acts such as verbal forms of intimidation and coercion, including "swear at her" and "question her about her activities" and more indirect acts such as "put her down in front of others" and physical moves such as "make to hit." Again, this index was used in a similar fashion to the indices for violence and injuries. The women and the men were asked about the use of these behaviors in the relationship and in the context of specific violent events. The CBI was introduced to ensure that the respondent was clear that the questions were referring to the use of such behaviors in the context of violence and threats to safety rather than similar behavior in other contexts where they may have other meanings and, as such, do not represent aggressive threats or intimidation (e.g., point at someone for the purpose of emphasis rather than as an act of intimidation). The questions were introduced with the wording, " . . . how often have you done the following things to your partner *which means she must be careful?.*" For a discussion of the importance of the context of introducing the subject of violence in interviews and its effect on the validity of the data, see Johnson and Sacco (1995) on the Statistics Canada survey of Violence Against Women and Tajeda & Thoennes (1998) on the National Violence Against Women Survey sponsored by the National Institute of Justice and Centers for Disease Control and Prevention.

Using the Indices

The indices were used in the interviews after the men and women had responded to open-ended questions about the occurrence of violence during the relationship or during specific violent events. While the open-ended questions about specific violent events usually yielded lengthy and detailed accounts from the women, the men's accounts were often scant and contained a minimum of detail (see Dobash et al, 1996). The indices were useful in obtaining comparable information from both men and women and were invaluable in eliciting additional information from the men. They were administered using a cue card system (see Bowling, 1995, for the use of this method in health research). For example, instead of the men being asked if they had "punched their partner in the face," they were given a cue card containing a list of all of the items on the index, which were identified by a letter. The interviewer read out the letter corresponding to a given act and asked if it had been committed. Thus, both the respondent and the interviewer avoided using the words associated with a particular type of violence. This enabled the men to admit to acts and injuries that they had not revealed in response to open-ended questions. While this technique obtained additional information from men who might have been reluctant to reveal the extent of their violent behavior, it also yielded additional information from abused women, who sometimes recounted violence and injuries they had thought "did not count."

In practice, the cue card technique worked extremely well in the interviews at obtaining additional data, particularly from men. This is illustrated in the following example, which begins with the man's response to an open-ended question about a particular violent event, which was immediately followed by the cue card technique, which yielded a great deal of additional information about the nature of the assault and injuries inflicted:

> *Can you remember what happened the last time that you assaulted her?*
> Just hit her—there had been an argument.
>
> *Can you remember what happened?*
> Just started to argue and I just lashed out. I think I picked something up and hit her.
>
> *Can you remember anything else?*
> The police came and took me away.

Using the cue card technique to administer the VAI, the same man speaking about the same event was able to recount more violent acts and more injuries. Using this technique, he revealed that he had

- Restrained his partner
- Thrown something at her
- Threatened her
- Punched her in the face
- Called her names
- Hit her with his fist and a metal bar
- Shouted, screamed, swore at her
- Threatened to kill her
- Slapped, pushed, and grabbed her

Using the same technique to administer the IAI, he also acknowledged inflicting additional injuries, including

- A cut and bleeding face
- Bruised body and face
- Nausea
- Knocking her unconscious

Measuring the Quality of Life for
Men and Women

In addition to measuring the constellation of violence, it is also important to measure changes in the quality of life that might be expected if violence is eliminated. One of the aims of the abuser programs is to enhance the safety, security, and well-being of women as a consequence of an end of men's violence against them. We expected that women would feel safer and happier, albeit still cautious, if the man ceased to use violence and controlling behaviors. Positive changes in her quality of life would be unlikely if he simply reduced his violence and replaced it with threats and intimidation that might stand in its place and serve as a reminder that violence could return at any moment. Similarly, violence might be reduced if a pattern of fewer attacks with more severe injuries was replaced by one of more frequent attacks with less severe injuries, but such a change would not be expected to be followed by positive changes in the quality of life. Thus, we proposed that the overall constellation of violence, including violence and injuries and controlling behavior, would need to change in a positive direction to have an effect on women's sense of safety and well-being. Similarly, a reduction in men's violence and controlling behavior might bring about an improvement in their own sense of self-worth, and this would not be expected to occur if the men simply substituted acts of terror for acts of violence. To reflect on these and other issues relating to positive changes in the relationships included in the Violent Men Study, two additional indices were constructed covering changes in the quality of life over the 12 months of follow-up. Table 4.5 shows the Quality of Life Index (QLI) for men and Table 4.6 shows the QLI for women.

Data Collection

Time 1: Interviews

During the course of the fieldwork for the Violent Men Study, we contacted all the women and men it was possible to contact in each of the two target groups. For each valid case identified through the court records, the man and his partner were sent an initial letter explaining the research and inviting them to participate. No further contact was made with those who refused to participate for whatever reason.

Table 4.5 Quality of Life Index (QLI) for Men

Listed below are a number of things about you and your partner which might have changed since I interviewed you [about a year ago]. Please read them and tick one box for each statement.

	More	*Less*	*Same*
I am happy	O	O	O
I do housework	O	O	O
I am aware of my partner's feelings	O	O	O
I understand my partner	O	O	O
I am relaxed	O	O	O
I feel angry with my partner	O	O	O
My partner understands me	O	O	O
I enjoy the company of my children	O	O	O
I am possessive/jealous of my partner	O	O	O
I understand myself	O	O	O
I discuss things with my partner	O	O	O
I am interested in my partner's life	O	O	O
I am able to see things from my partner's point of view	O	O	O
My partner is frightened of me	O	O	O
I restrict my partner's life	O	O	O
My partner and I can laugh together	O	O	O
I am likely to use physical violence against my partner	O	O	O
My partner is happy	O	O	O
I look after the children	O	O	O
I like spending time with my partner	O	O	O
My partner feels able to argue with me	O	O	O
I get on with other people	O	O	O
I take responsibility for my violence towards my part	O	O	O
I am selfish	O	O	O
I control my temper	O	O	O
I see violence as a solution to problems with my partner	O	O	O
I control my drinking	O	O	O
I respect myself	O	O	O
I think about my violent and abusive behavior	O	O	O
I want to stop my violence	O	O	O
I threaten my partner	O	O	O
I use physical violence against my partner	O	O	O

Table 4.6 Quality of Life Index (QLI) for Women

Listed below are a number of things about you and your partner which might have changed since I interviewed you [about a year ago]. Please read them and tick one box for each statement.

	More	Less	Same
I am happy	O	O	O
My partner is aware of my feelings	O	O	O
My partner understands me	O	O	O
I am relaxed	O	O	O
I feel angry with my partner	O	O	O
I discuss things with my partner	O	O	O
My partner is able to see things from my point of view	O	O	O
I am frightened of my partner	O	O	O
My partner restricts my life	O	O	O
My partner and I can laugh together	O	O	O
My partner is likely to use physical violence against me	O	O	O
My partner is happy	O	O	O
I like spending time with my partner	O	O	O
My partner respects me	O	O	O
I am likely to use physical violence towards my partner	O	O	O
My partner is selfish	O	O	O
I feel able to argue with my partner	O	O	O
My partner takes responsibility for his violence towards me	O	O	O
My partner controls his temper	O	O	O
My partner wants to stop his violence	O	O	O
My partner controls his drinking	O	O	O
I respect myself	O	O	O
My partner sees violence as a solution to problems with me	O	O	O
I threaten my partner	O	O	O
My partner uses physical violence against me	O	O	O

Those who did not respond to the initial correspondence were sent further correspondence and contacted personally to establish their willingness to participate. Women who indicated that they did not wish to be included in the study or that they did not want their partner to be contacted because of concerns about their personal safety were excluded, as were their partners. All initial contacts with men and women were made separately.

Interviews were usually lengthy, typically lasting 1 to $1\frac{1}{2}$ hours for men and 2 to 3 hours for women. Interviews with women sometimes extended over 2 days and took as long as 7 hours. All but a few were carried out in the homes of the participants. While we always sought to interview men and women separately and when their partner was not at home, this was not always possible, and a few interviews were held when partners were present in the residence. In all situations, we sought to be sensitive to the woman's sense of safety and security, and if she felt uneasy about the time and location of the interview it was rearranged. If a woman indicated that she felt an interview would threaten her security, we withdrew. Fortunately, women did not usually feel threatened by the prospect of an interview. If asked, we offered advice, within the limits of our knowledge. The interviews contain a wealth of qualitative and quantitative information. While all of the interviews were tape-recorded, limitations of resources meant that only a representative sample of around one half were either fully or partially transcribed.

Time 2 and Time 3:
Postal Questionnaires

The two postal questionnaires used at follow-up were intended to assess changes in the behavior and orientations of men and the predicament of women at two periods of time. A fundamental issue was the extent and nature of contact women had with the men who had abused them. If these men and women had separated and were no longer engaged in any sort of relationship, then reports of "no further violence" might simply mean "no further contact" between the man and woman rather than some change in his violent behavior. We assessed this separation effect by asking the women to provide details of their living arrangements. If they were separated from the man who had assaulted them, we asked them to indicate how much contact they had during the two follow-up periods. Collection of this information was crucial in establishing whether a particular woman had actually been at risk of violence from the man who had assaulted her during the period of follow-up. Equally, it could not be assumed that separation or divorce meant no subsequent contact, as contact often occurs in relation to the visitation of children or for other reasons.

Once it was established that a woman was living with or had contact with her partner, we then assessed the current levels of violence, injury, intimidation, and controlling behavior. The women and the men were asked how many incidents of violence had occurred in the period under scrutiny and to provide details of the violence and coercive behaviors they had experienced by completing the three indices (VAI, IAI, and CBI) already used to establish the baseline at Time 1. They were also asked to give their views on *why* they thought the violence had increased or decreased and to consider how the particular criminal justice sanction (e.g., men's program or fine, etc.) experienced by the man had affected subsequent levels of violence, injuries, and controlling behaviors. Assessing specific changes in the level and type of violence was of course crucial to the evaluation. Also of importance were changes in the relationship and the level and seriousness of conflict between the men and women.

At all three stages of the research, the women and the men were asked to indicate the current levels of conflict in their relationship and to assess how well they were getting on with their partners—had the relationship deteriorated or improved during the follow-up period? As violence against women in the home is often preceded by aggressive conflicts and arguments, it follows that interventions should aim to alter the nature and intensity of these conflicts. It seems that all intimate relationships involve conflict, and a complete cessation of conflict is an unrealistic goal. It could be argued that successful programs might increase men's and women's ability to argue safely. If men are less violent and learn new methods of communication, they may be better equipped to argue without becoming violent and women should feel more secure when disagreeing with a partner. The effectiveness of the abuser programs should be reflected in the indicators of subsequent violence, injuries, and controlling behavior and also in the measures of quality of life for women and for men.

While the questionnaires used at Times 2 and 3 were nearly identical, the Quality of Life Index (QLI) was added only at Time 3. In contrast to the other three indices, which assess changes in the negative aspects of the relationship—violence, injuries, and controlling behaviors—the QLI has the potential to capture changes in positive behaviors and orientations such as, "I like spending time with my partner" and "My partner is able to see things from my point of view." By asking whether these aspects of the relationships had improved, remained the same, or deteriorated during the 12-month period of follow-up, it was possible to make assessments of positive changes for both women and men.

Note

1. Systematic inspection of court records during the course of the research resulted in the identification of 933 cases involving violence between intimate partners. Only three of these involved women being charged with an offense. To consider possible differences between the court cases included in the study and those that could not be included, we conducted a comparative analysis of three types of cases: those initially identified in the court records that could not be traced and therefore could not be included in the sampling universe, those that could be traced and were included in the sampling universe, and those for which an interview was eventually conducted. Because of the limited information on the excluded cases, the analysis was only based on the man's age and the number and nature of current offenses before the court. For these variables, no statistically significant differences were found between cases initially identified in the court records, those that were included in the sampling universe, and those that were finally included in the achieved sample. In this respect, there was no indication that those cases included in the study differed in significant ways from those that were not included (see Dobash et al., 1996, pp. 25-26).

5

The Context
of Intervention

Violence and
Violent Relationships

Before presenting the results of the Violent Men Study, we consider the context and history of violence and conflict in the relationships of the men and women included in the study. The nature of the violence and the context associated with it, particularly previous attempts to deal with the violence and its consequences, provide an essential backdrop to the violent incident that led to the man's conviction and subsequent inclusion in this study. Primarily through the voices of the women, we consider the nature of violence against women; the women's previous attempts to deal with violent men; and their efforts to use others, including the social services and the legal system, in these attempts. This provides the background necessary for understanding what is to be changed and the difficulty of effecting change.

The Relationships

Slightly over half of the women in the study (55%) were in state-sanctioned marriages and the remainder were in cohabiting relationships. Whether married or cohabiting, the relationships were of considerable duration. Fewer than 10% of the couples had been together for less than 2 years and about 30% composed each of three categories (2 to 5 years, 5 to 10 years, and over 10 years). About half of the women had two children and the remainder had three or more. In 40% of the families, the men were stepfather to some or all of the children.

Conflict and arguments were a recurring feature of these relationships. The vast majority of the women indicated that arguments were a recurrent aspect of their ordinary life, often occurring on a weekly basis. The women's accounts of the sources of conflict generally parallel those of the men presented in previous chapters and centered on familiar aspects of relationships. When asked to describe the usual sources of argument and conflict that occurred between the couple and may or may not have ended in violence, the women cited money (28%), alcohol (23%), trivial issues regarding domestic life (29%), children (13%), jealousy (12%), and the man going out (4%) as the major issues of dispute.

> *What kind of things do you have arguments about?* Money, his drinking. Like if something comes up he will not discuss it with me and talk. He says what is going to happen about it; I don't like that, my back goes up then. It should be discussed rather than him making the final decision. (Woman, Men's Program: 1116)

> I would do my utmost to avoid the subject [of past relationships]. I would change the subject or divert round about it as far away as possible, but he kept coming back to it all the time and it was just to provoke it [arguments]. (Woman, Other CJ: 1089)

> *Did you have arguments about housework?* No, I did it. *The times that you had an argument was there any particular theme that cropped up?* No, just anything. Any topic he chose. (Woman, Other CJ: 1064)

In addition to reporting that the man's consumption of alcohol was a source of argument leading to violent incidents or involved in such incidents, about half of the women said that it was a general problem affecting the overall relationship.

Eight out of ten women said that once started, arguments usually ended in violence. All spoke of the fear of violence and aggression as an important aspect of arguments with their partner and most spoke at length about how the relationship had transformed their life from one of relative independence to one constrained by the demands of their partner.

Since you've been with him, has your social life changed in any way?
Yes. Dramatically. We used to be out all the time. Even when we first
started going out together I was out all the time with my friends. It's
just sort of dwindled away. (Woman, Other CJ: 1055)

He would force me to stay in the house. He would force me to change
the way I looked, change the way I was, I mean totally change.
(Woman, Men's Program: 1126)

How often do you go out socially? Never. I never go out socially. I go
along the road to see my sister-in-law, but that's rare. . . . It's just now
and then. *Why don't you go out?* Just because he doesn't like it or because I have [baby]. (Woman, Other CJ: 1055)

He didn't want me to have anybody. . . . He always brought my family
down and he'd of loved me just to cut off from my family altogether,
cause there was a time I went through a bad patch with my mum and
we didn't speak for awhile . . . and then I started to get back on talking
terms—he didn't like that. He wanted me like to himself and nobody
else was gonna have me. I wasn't allowed [to speak to] my parents.
Even if I phoned them I waited until he went out. He didn't like me
seeing them. (Woman, Men's Program: 1126)

Apart from visiting relatives and neighbors, the majority of the women
said they were only able to go out socially once or twice a year, and a
quarter said they never had a night out. Seventy percent of the men
objected or strongly objected to their partner going out. By contrast,
the men experienced few restrictions on their social life from their
partner. Three quarters of them went out at least once a week.

Previous Violence, Injuries, and
Controlling Behavior

Persistent violence, injuries, and controlling acts were common
features of the vast majority of these relationships. Using the three indices, the Violence Assessment Index (VAI), the Injury Assessment Index
(IAI), and the Controlling Behavior Index (CBI), the women provided
information about the single occurrence of a specific type of act or
injury throughout the relationship (prevalence). They also told us how
frequently a particular act or injury occurred during a typical year of
the relationship. Frequent acts are those that occurred on five or more
occasions during a typical year. Figures A.1 to A.3 in Appendix A present details of the results; here we provide a summary.

Almost all the women reported that on a least one occasion
their partner pushed/grabbed (96%) or restrained (91%) them (see

Figure A.1, Appendix A). Other potentially more serious acts were perpetrated on the vast majority of women on at least one occasion: 87%
were slapped on the face, 80% were kicked on the body, 79% were
punched on the body, 78% were punched in the face, and 75% were
choked. Many women reported other serious acts of violence, including being punched or kicked in the stomach when pregnant (43%) and
kicked in the face (43%). The men commonly threatened the women
with violence (78%) or threatened to kill them (65%). The women also
told us of the men demanding (39%) or forcing (26%) them to have sex
at least once during the relationship.

Forced sex and violence during pregnancy were not frequent
occurrences in most of these relationships, however: 4% of the women
reported frequent acts of violence during pregnancy and 10% told us
that their partner frequently forced them to engage in sexual relations.
By contrast, well over half of the women reported a wide range of violent acts that did occur on a frequent basis: pushed and grabbed (69%),
slapped on the face (69%), restrained (58%). Many also reported frequent incidents of being punched on the face (35%) or body (48%),
dragged by their hair (36%), threatened with violence (44%) or death
(24%), or choked (25%).

Not surprising, injuries are a recurring consequence of this violence (see Figure A.2, Appendix A). Almost all of the women reported
bruising, often extensive, on at least one occasion: bruised body
(91%), face (86%), limbs (84%). Other injuries were prominent in the
women's reports. From two thirds to one half reported split lips and
cuts and lacerations of the face, as well as hair pulled out and nausea or
vomiting as a consequence of the violence. Forty percent of the women
told us they had been knocked unconscious on at least one occasion;
and 10% to 25% reported broken teeth and fractures of bones in the
face or limbs. Internal injuries and miscarriages were reported by only
a few women, 14% and 8%, respectively. The most frequently inflicted
injuries are bruising of the body (59%), limbs (54%), and face (35%).
Considerable proportions of the women also reported having their
hair pulled out (32%), nausea (20%), and bleeding faces (18%) as frequent outcomes of their partner's violence. None of the women
reported frequently suffering broken bones or teeth, internal injuries,
burns, and miscarriages, although many did experience these injuries
on at least one occasion.

As indicated in earlier chapters, existing research has shown that
violence against women in the home is usually associated with other
controlling and intimidating behavior. Beginning with the question,
"Did he [partner] ever do any of the following in a way which you

knew meant you had to be careful?" the women in the Violent Men
Study were asked to respond to the list of 21 items included on the
Controlling Behavior Index (CBI). The women reported a wide range
of intimidating and coercive acts, and most of these occurred on a frequent basis (more than five times in a typical year) in the relationship
(Figure A.3, Appendix A). All of the women told us their partner had
shouted and sworn at them at least once during the relationship, and
three quarters said that these acts occurred on a frequent basis. The
men were also likely to have called the woman demeaning names
(91%), threatened her (83%), engaged in intimidating looks (89%),
and criticized her or her family (83%). Around three quarters of the
men on at least one occasion had provoked an argument, questioned
the woman in an aggressive manner, nagged her, or feigned to hit her.
About one half of the women reported that these behaviors—from calling women demeaning names to feigning to hit them—occurred on a
frequent basis. Many of the women also reported at least one incident
of their partner's attempting to use children in arguments (75%), pointing in an aggressive manner (72%), putting her down (60%), restricting her movements (51%), threatening to hurt a pet (45%), telling her
that she was sexually inadequate (43%), and deliberately keeping her
short of money (43%). Many of these acts were reported by a considerable number of the women to have occurred on a frequent basis.

The results of the use of the CBI reveal that aggressive and intimidating acts are a recurring feature of these relationships. Some women
reported that the men continuously used controlling and coercive acts
as an integral aspect of the relationship. Not surprising, 91% of the
women assessed these acts as serious. Similar judgments were made
about the violence. When asked to assess the seriousness of the violence they experienced throughout their relationships, most of the
women judged it as serious (37%) or very serious (49%). Only 13%
thought the violence was not very serious. It is clear from these results
that as a group the women included in this study were living with men
who perpetrated a considerable amount of injurious violence along
with other aggressive and intimidating acts and that this constellation
of violence formed a significant feature of their relationships and one
for which they felt compelled to seek a solution.

Reactions to Violence

There is now a voluminous literature on the predicament and
responses of women who suffer violence at the hands of an intimate

partner (for an account see Campbell & Humphreys, 1993; Dobash & Dobash, 1992; Hague & Malos, 1993; Mullender, 1996; Pahl, 1985). Prior to the "discovery" of the problem of battered women in the early 1970s, psychoanalytic notions characterized women victims of violence in the home as masochistic or provocative. Accounts from the 1970s and 1980s emerging from the battered women's movement based on direct and pragmatic contact with abused women and the growing body of research did not find women to be masochistic or passive recipients of violence. Instead, the evidence showed women to be actively engaged in trying to deal with violent men through various means from private negotiation to public help-seeking (Dobash & Dobash, 1979; Hoff, 1990). The evidence suggested that women were engaged in active efforts to mobilize support from relatives; friends; and professionals, particularly doctors and social workers. Instead of being masochistic or accepting violence, women were found to be struggling to end violence in their relationship or to leave violent men.

At the same time, other explanations depicted abused women as suffering from unique biographies or psychological traits that made them vulnerable to abuse and unable to escape. According to these accounts, women suffered from "learned helplessness" and "battered woman syndrome" (Walker, 1984). These notions echoed the earlier psychoanalytic ideas and were in the ascendancy in the United States in the 1980s. We and others have been critical of these ideas because they misrepresent the predicament of women and characterize them as colluding with violent men and thereby contributing to their own victimization (Dobash & Dobash, 1992). The accounts of learned helplessness are at variance with a wide range of research that shows women to be actively engaged in a struggle to end the violence or to escape violent men (e.g., Bowker, 1983; Dobash, Dobash, & Cavanagh, 1985; Dutton, 1996; Gondolf 1988a; Jacobson, Gottman, Gortner, Bern, & Nushortt, 1996).

The women in this study were also found to be actively engaged in trying to deal with violence and seeking outside assistance with these efforts. These women were neither helpless nor hopeless. While they did speak of the negative effects of living with violence, most had considerable strengths and held many positive views about themselves despite the harm and denigration they had suffered (see also, Goldner, Penn, Sheinberg, & Walker, 1990). Women's efforts to "manage" violent men and their difficulty in escaping violence must be understood in the wider context of a moral climate that places responsibility for family problems on women and their own ambivalence about the man and their relationship with him and in a world of financial dependence and other factors that make it difficult for women to leave and live an independent existence. In addition, the lack of effective intervention to stop violent men, along with men's refusal to change, add further difficulties for women seeking a life free of violence. It is necessary to place women's reactions in this broader context without which their inability to leave a violent man may appear irrational or inexplicable.

Avoiding and Managing Violence

The women told us they tried a range of tactics to alter the violent and coercive behaviors of their partners. Sometimes this involved evasive action prior to what they believed would become a violent incident.

> I used to lock myself in the toilet but he kicked the door in. *Did you ever do anything else [to avoid violence]?* Often I tried [to leave the room] but he used to nip my head [harass, nag] and he used to follow me from room to room. (Woman, Men's Program: 1126)

> *Have you done anything to try and stop him hitting you?* Running out of the house. (Woman, Other CJ: 1062)

Immediate, spontaneous efforts were often followed by negotiations aimed at discussing the violence or attempting to pacify the man into behaving more reasonably. At some point in their relationship, the majority of the women attempted to avoid violence by altering their own behavior in a variety of ways, such as withdrawing from arguments, leaving the room, agreeing with the man, and restricting their own activities. Only a few (7%) typically tried to use violence in defense or retaliation.

> Sometimes I'd say to myself—"Right, we'll do it his way." (Woman, Other CJ: 1160)

> *Have you done anything to try and stop him being violent to you?* Talking.

> *Has talking to him ever helped? Has it ever stopped him?* It has. *How has that worked?* I don't know. I just try to explain to him how hurt I feel. I don't know if that makes a difference.

> *Have you ever done the housework or the cooking to stop being hit?* Well, I've tried to make a bigger effort, like maybe the next day, to save friction and arguments. (Woman, Other CJ: 1055)

> *Did you ever try and calm the situation down and discuss things?* All the time. Like sometimes if we were sitting on the couch I would hold his hands or just touch him, let him know that I was there. I would

touch him, touch his face. That used to help sometimes. It used to be quite good, I'd go over and sit beside him and I'd cuddle into him and tell him I loved him even if I hated him. I'd tell him that I loved him and that would sort of calm him down. A few times he would just get up and shove me off. (Woman, Men's Program: 1064)

[her tactics to stop his violence] Make tea or coffee or just basically try anything, keep him in a good mood. *Does it work?* Rarely, if that's him started. (Woman, Men's Program: 1144)

Did you ever try and do anything to stop him being violent to you? I'd try to speak to him and left the room quite often. *Did these things work?* Talking didn't. (Woman, Other CJ: 1123)

These accounts show women making concerted decisions to alter their own behavior to avoid conflict. They sometimes consoled, appeased, or cajoled the men to manage the conflict and avoid violence. A few tried to bring others into the relationship to provide surveillance, protection, or intervention.

I'll maybe try and get somebody to come up and sit with me. (Woman, Men's Program: 1144)

What have I done to stop him being violent? Like if I know he's ready to start, I'd say, "Look, if you're going to start something then I'm going to get up [and leave]." . . . But if he's wanting to start it, then I'll challenge him or I'll say, "Look, do you want me to go and phone John or Joe [friends/family] to come down here if you're going to start shouting?" *So you just try to calm him down?* Yes, like, "Look, is this going to be worth it?" (Woman, Men's Program: 1082)

Contrary to popular belief and the notions associated with the concept of learned helplessness, these women often left the man in an attempt to avoid violence and change the relationship. Two thirds of the women left at least once during the relationship and many had left more frequently (25% left more than five times). The women usually left for only a few days (40% for 1 to 2 days and 24% for 3 to 6 days), although one third stayed away for 1 month on at least one occasion and two fifths left for a period of 3 to 12 months. The women said that the men viewed their leaving as a serious transgression and it usually delivered a salutary shock. The men concurred.

I came in at night and she had left me. I couldn't understand it. That was the worst time ever. I was really depressed then because I knew I'd blown it. I lost my wife and my kids and everything that I wanted. (Man, Men's Program: 038)

> Oh, I was lost without her. I wasn't cooking or eating or nothing. I
> was lost. (Man, Other CJ: 123)

While about half of the women said that leaving had no effect on
the man or his violence, two fifths told us the relationship improved
and one third reported a reduction in the violence after they returned.
The woman's departure off-balanced some men, even if only temporarily, making them more willing to discuss the violence or renegotiate
the relationship. For some men, the act of leaving makes an impact
where the woman's words about harm and fear do not.

The women returned for a variety of reasons, including the social
and economic factors mentioned earlier as well as notions about the
welfare of the children that relate to the ideal of an intact family. They
also returned because of continued threats to themselves, the children,
and those who provide assistance.

> The reason I went back all the other times was the kids, crying for him
> at night and "Oh, he might be lying dead, he might have been sick,"
> you know. And they just wanted to go back to him, so I let the kids put
> a lot of pressure on me. (Woman, Other CJ: 1089)

The men also apologized and sought forgiveness. They pursued their
partner and attempted to cajole her into returning, promising that they
would reform.

> He used to send letters through the letterbox, phone calls from down
> at my mum's house and he would tell everybody that he loved me so
> that they would come and tell me to try and stop it. The last time ... I
> got three letters from him and another time he kept phoning my mum
> and kept going to my pal's and watching the house. Sitting over there
> telling her that he loved me. (Woman, Other CJ: 1082)
>
> *Why did you go back after leaving?* Oh he'd come over and get me
> with all his soft patter and send me letters. I went back because I
> wanted it to work out. (Woman, Other CJ: 1027)

Such promises rarely last for long, and the women were often
engaged in continuous efforts to alter the men's behavior. The women
reported that occasionally their partner also tried to change. According
to the women, three quarters of the men tried to change their violent
behavior (on at least one occasion) by practicing better self-control,
reducing alcohol consumption, or leaving the room or the house during an argument. A quarter of the men never tried to stop their violence
or seek help in eliminating their violence; "He said that he would go

for help but he never ever did" (Woman, Other CJ: 1160). A small
minority of the men (13%) voluntarily left for a brief period of time
and about half of the women succeeded in persuading the man to leave
on at least one occasion. The women did describe a few attempts by
men to reduce their violence.

> *Has he ever tried to stop being violent to you?* He'd walk out the room
> or go for a walk. *Did these things help?* Yes. (Woman, Other CJ:
> 1123)

> *Has he ever tried to stop being violent to you?* Yes, I think he has. I
> think so. *What has he done?* He's thrown something or done other
> things to avoid hitting me because I know that's really what he wants
> to do. He feels like hitting me because he's so wound up. It's come to
> that—he'll even admit it. I've said, "You feel like that, don't you? You
> feel like belting me one, don't you." "Yes I do, but I won't." (Woman,
> Other CJ: 1056)

The women were generally pessimistic about the men's efforts to
change.

> *Has he ever tried to stop being violent?* That's hard to answer. I don't
> know if it has [ever] stopped because it has continued for 14 years.
> (Woman, Men's Program: 1116)

> I don't know, probably self-restraint really. But, as I say, suddenly it's
> all blown over and everything's swept under the carpet and forgot-
> ten. *And when he does try to exercise self-restraint, does it work? Can
> he stop it?* He can but when he does take a brainstorm, nothing stops
> him. (Woman, Other CJ: 1055)

> If he's gonna do it he's gonna do it. (Woman, Men's Program: 1144)

According to the women, the men's behavior seemed intractable
and the men rarely attempted to change through their own initiative or
voluntarily seek help. More commonly, the women actively engaged in
trying to alter the man's violent behavior, usually through discussion,
but most men refused to talk about the problem.

> *Generally, how often would you talk about what was happening
> between you?* After it? We would probably try and sit down and talk
> about it. She would want to talk about it. I'd be the one who'd rather
> forget it. It happened and that was it. (Man, Men's Program: 117)

> Not very often, you never talk about it, you try to put it to the back of
> your mind hoping it will never happen again. . . . Trying to forget

what happened, trying to shut it away. . . . I do not want to talk about it because it was my fault. (Man, Men's Program: 116)

[after the first assault] He started crying and saying he was sorry? *What did you do?* I just put my arms around him. *Did you talk about what had happened?* No, he wouldn't talk about it. (Woman, Other CJ: 1123)

Some women's attempts to open dialogue or negotiate about the violence increased the risk of more violence, as the men defined this as nagging or confrontational.

I think she realized from that I can only take so much [discussion]. (Man, Other CJ: 056)

If I stood up and went, "Will you shut up," she doesn't understand that when I say that I mean it. (Man, Men's Program: 144)

I tell her to shut up but she doesn't. I feel it building up inside me and I tell her, "Shut up or just take what comes." (Man, Men's Program: 062)

The women were usually unsuccessful in their efforts to manage partners, to persuade them to talk about the violence and its consequences, and to think about their actions and emotions. Eventually—or sometimes very early in the relationship—the women came to the realization that outside help was needed in their efforts to eliminate violence from their relationships.

Contacts With Others

Relatives and Friends

The literature shows that the vast majority of abused women eventually seek help, initially from friends and relatives and later from more formal sources (Dobash & Dobash 1979; Hoff, 1990; Johnson, 1998). Informal networks of relations and friends as well as more formal agencies such as police and health care and social services are generally contacted in women's efforts to deal with violent partners. In the Violent Men Study, only one quarter of the women said they had never told anyone about their partner's violence and almost all said that others knew about the violence through other sources.

Have you ever been to anybody for help about his violent behavior?
No. I just don't know where to go. (Woman, Other CJ: 1055)

No, but at that time that's what we intended to do, we just never did
it. We should go to some sort of marriage guidance but you never do
it when things settle down. (Woman, Other CJ: 1056)

No. There was nowhere I could go because my family just, they were
just fed up with the lot of it. I never bothered anybody. (Woman,
Other CJ: 1058)

No. It was nobody's business. (Woman, Other CJ: 1089)

Unlike the women quoted above, most of the women did tell someone, usually their close relations, parents and siblings. The women who
discussed the violence with others were much more likely to tell mothers and sisters than fathers and brothers. The response of relatives and
close friends was usually positive and supportive of the woman (60%)
and a few also directed their attention at the man. Twelve percent of
those told of the violence expressed their anger about the man's violence to the woman but not directly to her partner. The same percentage said he was to blame and 10% confronted him, but most did not.
The women said that while these efforts were sometimes helpful they
were usually short-lived. Basically, most responses tended to reinforce
the notion that protecting herself and changing the man was the
woman's responsibility.

Social Services and Health Care

Many women also tried to use social services and health care in
their efforts to obtain assistance or to end the violence. In the Violent
Men Study, medical doctors were consulted at least once by about half
of the women and they generally treated injuries and sometimes
offered advice or referrals. Social workers assisted 17% of the women
in various ways, offering counseling and support and information concerning accommodation. Women's groups were not generally used by
this sample of women (only 6% had ever contacted Women's Aid).
Solicitors (lawyers), health visitors, and marriage guidance counselors
were also not likely to have been contacted by these women.

Seeking help from others was almost always undertaken in a context of apprehension concerning the possibility of negative responses
or disapproval from others and against a background of intimidation
and threats from partners. Some women were particularly apprehen-
sive that social services might remove their children.

Why didn't you ever go to the social work department? Well, I didn't go to social work because I'd never like my children to get taken away and I think if you got involved with them and they [think], "Well, if he's hitting her, he's maybe hitting the kids." You hear all these different things. And if they [kids] were fighting and one of them had a bruise they'd maybe think, "That was your dad and we'll take you away." (Woman, Other CJ: 1015)

I don't like involving social workers. They'll say we're arguing and fighting and they'll maybe take the child away from me. (Woman, Other CJ: 1055)

Some women with past experience of psychological professionals were reluctant to seek further assistance because of previous responses that they found unhelpful.

Did you actually go to the psychiatrist? I did go years ago, but I wasn't getting anywhere really. All they seemed to speak about was my sex life. That's what I felt they wanted to know about, "How do you perform and what do you do?" I thought, for God's sake, this was after Irene was born, I took an overdose and they wanted to know. I thought that's got nothing to bloody do with you. And that's when I thought I'm not going back. I felt that all the doctor would do was give me tablets. I was actually feeling like a junky, because I was taking a tablet for this and a tablet for that and I didn't want to take tablets, sitting zombified with silly tablets. *Did the doctor refer you to the psychiatrist because of the postnatal depression or because of the violence?* Both really because they knew that I was getting battered. (Woman, Men's Program: 1021)

They [psychologist] asked us about our marriage and they spoke to him on his own and to me on my own. And she said to me, "Is there somebody else?" I said, "No." She went away and had a conversation with another doctor or somebody and then they took the two of us in again and he said, "We've come to the conclusion that the only thing that is wrong is that you're too much in love." I was like that! Oh, God, I couldn't believe it! A lot of shit. A lot of rubbish. *And what did he think of that?* Oh, he quite agreed with them. Oh, yes! (Woman, Other CJ: 1041)

Intimidation from partners was also an impediment to seeking help. Three quarters of the women reported their partner objected to them contacting others and a quarter said that he strongly objected. The women's reports reveal that help seeking occurs in a context of men's surveillance, condemnation, and possible reprisals.

I spoke to Christine [social worker] and she wanted me to speak to Women's Aid, and I really wanted to speak to Women's Aid but I was frightened. I was frightened to speak to somebody else about it and I think that one phone call could have made an awful lot of difference. I think if I'd maybe made that one phone call he maybe wouldn't have been back. (Woman, Other CJ: 1055)

He had beat me up and it was my head that got it this night and it was that bad I couldn't get me head off the pillow in the morning. And I said to him, "You'll need to phone an ambulance." And he was up like a shot. And he said, "What you gonna say?" He was more worried about himself. I said, "I'll say I fell. Just get an ambulance." I had that severe a concussion that I couldn't think. Doctors up there told him that I had bruising right inside. At that time my neck was all black, all up the side, my ears were double the size they're supposed to be. Once I got in the hospital they said, "We know what's going on. You didn't fall, you weren't in a fight, he's doing this, we're getting the police, we'll get him charged." And I said it wasn't him. *Why did you say that?* Because I was scared of him. (Woman, Other CJ: 1160)

The Justice System

The police had at some time been involved in most of these relationships. Only 18% of the women said that the police had never been involved prior to the specific event that resulted in the charge that led to their inclusion in this study. The police were involved on 5 or more occasions in two thirds of the relationships and over 20 times for a much smaller group (6%). About two thirds of the men had previously been arrested at least once for violence against their partner and about two fifths had five or more arrests. Ten percent of the women said that previous arrests seemed to be related to a reduction in the violence while 62% said arrest appeared to have no effect and 17% felt it resulted in more violence. When asked if their partner's arrest affected the relationship, 7% said it had improved the relationship, 60% indicated it made no difference, and 32% said it made it worse. While arrest generally brings immediate, short-term assistance and relief, the women thought that arrest alone would not permanently stop the man's violence.

I felt happier. I felt safer when they [the police] were there. I felt safe, the fact that they took him away and I knew he was locked up for the whole weekend, and I knew I was safe that whole weekend. (Woman, Other CJ: 1159)

When they arrested him, I knew for a fact that I could sleep all night, get my head down and then when he comes back in the morning everything will be different. [If they didn't come] he would just go ranting and raving all night. (Woman, Men's Program: 1058)

Some women had long-term objectives associated with the use of the justice system. Their accounts suggest that involving the police and pursuing a charge against their partner was motivated by the desire to deter or to secure some form of rehabilitation.

> He needs a reminder now and again that he can't do things like that. (Woman, Other CJ: 1060)

> Well, my husband and his brother both hit their wives and I know for a fact that his father used to hit his mother. And I don't want my kids to grow up [thinking], "Oh, you hit a woman." When I took him to court I thought, the kids are big, they understand now. See him going to court, they know it's wrong. So I did it for all of our sakes: for him, to teach him a lesson; for me just for the peace of mind, because I was fed up; [for the kids] to teach them that it's wrong. (Woman, Other CJ: 1015)

> I think there should be special policemen, like you have special police to deal with rape cases, why not for domestic violence? I mean, I would appreciate that if there was somebody there to deal with domestic violence like after the court case, a follow-up. . . . I need somebody to talk to the two of us to find out why this problem is arising, why he's being violent, because I know there are other ways of dealing with things. You don't have to be violent. (Woman, Other CJ: 1091)

The women were quite negative about the court if there were no sanctions or the particular sanction was deemed inconsequential or did not appear to work.

> I suppose it would make him worse if he's getting off with it all the time. He'll get worse and worse because he knows he's going to get off with it. (Woman, Men's Program: 1082)

> *How do you feel regarding the whole court business?* Pure and utter waste of time. He's getting us to go to court. . . . I mean that hurts us every time we have to go to court. We're having to go there, he's making us go there and making our lives a misery by standing there and forcing us to be there. And the judge just goes, "You're a bad boy, here's a fine.". . . Another thing, he gets us to go to court and every time he goes to court at the last second, he pleads guilty so we're not needed. He knows that. He knows what he's doing. I think that's pretty wrong. (Woman, Other CJ: 1014)

The women were often ambivalent about using the full force of the law. Most expressed a need for the immediate assistance police can provide, but many expressed concern about the potential impact this might have on the children or their partner, and some feared retaliation.

> I was relieved to get out. Even as I got to the phone box, I was in two minds, because I knew he had outstanding fines and I didn't want to be the one to like get the police involved, for him to get put away for his fines. But I never had a choice. I couldn't have come back here if I hadn't got the police. (Woman, Other CJ: 1055)

> In a way I was wanting him put away, and in another way I wasn't. The reason I didn't want him put away is that I need him to help with the kids when I go into hospital [to have their baby]. That's the only reason. And I didn't really want my kids going into care. I felt that would be too much. They've been through a lot as it is. (Woman, Other CJ: 1159)

> I didn't want Gordon [son] to go to court. I thought he was too young, he's only 10. I think that is too young. And to go against his dad. There was going be a bad atmosphere. There would have been a bad atmosphere. There would have been because he would have [thought], "Oh, I didn't like my dad." (Woman, Other CJ: 1015)

About half the women attempted to use the civil law in search of relief and protection. Orders of protection, also referred to as injunctions and interdicts, are now widely used in Britain and elsewhere (Lewis, Dobash, Dobash, & Cavanagh, in press; Stubbs & Egger, 1993). As noted earlier, research conducted in England shows that women have found them unhelpful (see Barron, 1990) while some studies in the United States indicate that they seem to work under certain circumstances (Chaudhuri & Daly, 1992; Finn & Colson, 1990; Keilitz et al., 1996). Of the women in this study who tried to use protection orders, two thirds said that they felt safer for a period of time and just over one half said such orders had temporarily reduced intimidation and violence.

> *How did you feel regarding the interdict [order of protection]?* Great because it gave me the power to say, "Yes, you can come in" or "No, I don't want to see you." Or, "If you don't go I can use it." (Woman, Men's Program: 1066)

> *Why did he stay away so long [6 months] that time?* Because I had an interdict [order of protection] and if he came anywhere near me he was getting arrested. (Woman, Other CJ: 1089)

> *Did you feel safer because you had the interdict [order of protection]?* Yes, it sounds daft to be relying on a bit of paper, but yeah. (Woman, Men's Program: 1082)

The women said that the men often responded negatively to the use of orders of protection. In the interviews, the men told us that they were unnecessary or that they were not bothered by an order of protection. While only a few men said that the orders made them angry, the women told us that two thirds of the men expressed anger at their use. Despite the men's responses, many women felt that a protection order could be used as a tool, lever, or threat in the ongoing process of trying to manage a violent man.

The Violent Event Leading to Conviction and Inclusion in the Study

Whatever the utility of orders of protection, none of the previous efforts of the women in this study had resulted in the permanent cessation of violence. While temporary relief may have been achieved at various points in time, the men did not cease their violent behavior. As a consequence, all of the men in the Violent Men Study were processed through the justice system because of a violent event against their woman partner. This act of violence brought them into this study. The history of violence and the inability of various forms of intervention to bring about a permanent cessation forms the backdrop to the court-mandated men's programs under study here.

The specific violent event that brought men and women into this study did not differ from others that had occurred in the relationships in terms of the nature of the violence, although on this occasion the men were arrested and most were detained for at least one night and charged with assault or other offenses. All of the men were subsequently found guilty of at least one of the offenses for which they were charged (usually assault) and received some type of court sanction.

The violence in these specific incidents was similar to that occurring throughout the relationship. More than three quarters of the women reported being pushed or grabbed. Around one half said their partner restrained them, threatened to hit them with his fists, slapped their face or body, and kicked or punched them on the body and face. In about one third of the incidents, the men threatened to kill the woman, threw objects at her, or used an object as a weapon. Some women (20% to 30%) had their arms twisted and were threatened with a weapon or an object during the assault that brought their partner to court. Very few said their partner demanded or forced them to have sex during these incidents, and only 3% were pregnant and punched or kicked in the stomach. About two thirds reported bruising of the face, body, and limbs as a consequence of the violence and approximately one third suffered a black eye, bleeding face, or a loss of hair on this occasion. There were very few reports of fractures and none of the women said they suffered a miscarriage because of the violence. Other serious injuries—being knocked unconscious, cuts to body or face, and broken facial bones—occurred in about one in eight of these specific incidents. When asked to judge the seriousness of this specific incident, almost nine tenths of the women defined it as either serious or very serious. By comparison, only three quarters of the men said it was serious and one third said the incident was not at all or not very serious.

The evidence presented here indicates that the relationships included in the Violent Men Study were usually plagued by violence and other intimidating and coercive forms of behavior. Consequently, the women were engaged in near-continuous efforts to deal with the violence by negotiating with their partner and seeking assistance from others, including family, friends, and formal agencies. For the vast majority, the particular violent event that led to arrest and prosecution and inclusion in this study was one in a long line of similar incidents. All the men in this study were subsequently sentenced to a range of sanctions including fines, conventional probation, and one of the court-mandated abuser programs. In the following chapters, we compare the effects of these interventions on subsequent behavior, beliefs, and orientations.

6

Can Violent Men Change?

The question, "Can violent men change?" might simply be answered yes or no, depending on one's ideological orientation to this issue. Examples of individual cases could be provided in support of either answer. Such simplicity, however, provides little assistance in the overall transformative process of seeking change with respect to this form of violence, and it offers no help in considering what forms of intervention might deliver the most change among the perpetrators of this violence. So let us address this question seriously and with some care. Here, we turn our attention to the effectiveness of court-mandated abuser programs in eliminating subsequent violence, controlling behaviors, and supporting beliefs and to the fundamental issue of personal change that is central to the transformative process.

Program Integrity and Evaluative Criteria

Before reaching the more general question of the transformative process, it is necessary to ask if those men who have been processed through an abuser program designed to deliver a particular intervention have, in fact, received the stated intervention. The answer involves two elements, program integrity and program completion. That is, did the abuser programs deliver the intervention according to the stated principles, aims, and goals (program integrity) and did the men involved in the study actually complete the program to which they were sentenced. In this study, program integrity was assessed through continuous monitoring of program materials, formal focused group interviews with staff, and information from program participants.[1] On the basis of this analysis, the two abuser programs delivered the program content as intended. In addition, the majority of the men sentenced to the abuser programs did complete them. While the problem of attrition—failure to start or complete—plagues many North American programs (Edleson & Syers, 1991), this was not a significant element of the two programs considered here. In the subsequent analysis, only those men who completed the abuser programs are included in the Men's Program group.[2]

Another important issue concerns the evaluative criteria used to assess success. For a number of years, there have been debates about the appropriate methods for assessing the efficacy of abuser programs. Some commentators argue that evaluations that consider only reductions in rather than the complete elimination of violence are inadequate and maintain that nothing less than a complete cessation of violence should be defined as success (Gondolf, 1987; Hart, 1988). Those concerned about existing evaluations note the failure adequately to assess other acts associated with the violence, such as intimidation and threats (Edleson, 1996). In addition, the issue of women's safety has been the source of criticism with respect to all forms of research as well as to all forms of intervention, including abuser programs and other responses of the justice system. We have attempted to address many of these issues in the process of conducting this multidimensional assessment of the impact of criminal justice interventions. In the following analysis, successful change over the 12-month period of follow-up is defined as a total cessation of violence, a significant reduction in controlling and coercive behavior, and a significant improvement in the quality of life for the women and for the men.

Investigating Selection Bias—
Comparisons of the Groups

The central part of any evaluation is the assessment of the effect of the intervention on the outcome and consideration of other factors that might have contributed to that outcome. These factors include the possibility of selection bias. In this study, selection bias might have been introduced by the courts or through sampling procedures. Here, we consider potential selection bias (the possibility that the two groups might have been different at the start of the research) by comparing the two groups of men at Time 1 in their backgrounds, levels of violence, injuries inflicted, and controlling behavior. The chi square statistic is used to assess differences between the two groups, and only statistically significant results are noted.

Individual and Background Characteristics

The intensive information gathered at Time 1 allowed for an extensive comparison of the men in the two groups on a range of social and demographic characteristics. To consider selection bias, the men's reports were used to make a number of comparisons between the two groups in four broad areas: personal characteristics, the nature of the current relationship, violence in the family of origin, and previous contact with the criminal justice system. Of the nearly 30 comparisons made, only two produced statistically significant differences at or above the .05 level (see Appendix B, Table B.1, for list of comparisons).

Personal Characteristics

The average age of the men in both groups was 32. Long-term unemployment was a feature of the lives of many, and the difference between the two groups was statistically significant, with 52% in the Men's Program group and 73% in the Other CJ group unemployed at the time of intervention. The majority of the unemployed men in both groups had been out of work for 2 years or less, though a considerable number had been unemployed for a much longer period. About half left school with no qualifications at the ages of 15 or 16; only 25% of the men in the Men's Program group and 17% in the Other CJ group had obtained some sort of educational qualification. As to their families of origin, most grew up in households with both natural parents present and a father who was a skilled manual worker.

Relationships

There were few differences between the two groups in the nature of their relationships, and the reports of the men parallel those of the women presented in Chapter 5. Most of the men were in a long-term relationship with the woman they assaulted. They had children living with them, and the men generally described the relationship in a positive way, as "okay," "good," or "very good." There was a statistically significant difference between the two groups in the legal status of the relationship, with more Men's Program men living in state-sanctioned marriages (62%) compared to men in the Other CJ group (36%).

Violence in Family of Origin

There were no statistically significant differences between the two groups on a range of variables about violence in their family of origin. Men in both groups reported a fair amount of physical chastisement of themselves as children: 52% of Men's Program and 72% of the Other CJ men reported experiencing physical chastisement from fathers when growing up, and about one quarter of these men reported fairly persistent chastisement. Forty-four percent of the Men's Program men and 47% of the Other CJ men described this chastisement as "serious" or "very serious," and about one quarter in both groups said they were often hit "too much" and "unfairly." It should be noted that most men identified important distinctions between what they defined as appropriate parental chastisement and physically violent abuse. Very few men reported significant levels of physical chastisement or violence at the hands of mothers. According to the men's reports, when serious violence did occur, it was inflicted by fathers. In addition, the two groups were broadly similar in their reports of what they defined as chastisement or physically abusive behavior from fathers. Sexual abuse as a child was not reported in either group of men.

About the same proportion of men in both groups (40% Men's Program/52% Other CJ) grew up in a family in which their mother was subjected to physical violence at the hands of their father. The majority of these men (79% Men's Program/62% Other CJ) judged the violence used against their mother as "serious" or "very serious," although a much higher proportion of Men's Program men defined such violence as "very serious."

Previous Contact With Criminal Justice

The men in the two groups were compared on several dimensions regarding previous experiences of the justice system, including the number and nature of previous convictions for all offenses, the number of police interventions for domestic violence, and the number of arrests for domestic violence. There were no statistically significant differences for any of these comparisons. It is important to note that only two men in the entire sample had no previous arrest or conviction for any type of offense. Eight out of ten men in both groups had experienced some form of police intervention in connection with violence directed at the present partner. Men in the Men's Program group were more likely to have a record for crimes involving violence, including domestic violence, while men in the Other CJ group were more likely to have a greater number of previous convictions for offenses of all types, including public order offenses that did not involve violence. Overall, the men in both groups were not strangers to the criminal justice process and most had been arrested, charged, and prosecuted on at least one previous occasion.

Violence, Injuries, and Controlling Behavior: The Constellation of Violence

As noted earlier, when the men were asked to respond to open-ended, qualitative questions about their violence and controlling behaviors, most narratives were thin and impoverished. Much more detail was obtained from the men using the lists contained in the three indices, the VAI, IAI, and CBI. The indices were used to make a number of comparisons of violence, injuries, and controlling behavior concerning the *prevalence* and *frequent use* of various acts and consequences. Comparisons were made of the percentage of men in the two groups who reported perpetrating at least one incidence of a particular act (prevalence) and of those who reported the perpetration of five or more such acts (frequent use) in a typical year of the relationship. Comparisons of the men's reports of violence, injuries, and controlling behaviors at Time 1 yielded no statistically significant differences between the two groups (details of these comparisons are reported in Dobash et al., 1996, 1998), thus providing no evidence of selection bias on these criterion behaviors. For example, comparisons of the two groups at Time 1 on the prevalence and frequent use of the long list of violent acts in the VAI shows a very strong similarity between the two groups of men at the point at which the research began.

These percentage comparisons provide a rich source of information and are essential in describing the nature of the phenomenon of violence. What is also needed is a summary indicator of this vast array of vital detail to provide a "snapshot" that can be used to make overall comparisons of individuals and groups. While snapshots, or summary indicators, may be composed of only one or two items from a list, the most common approach is to create a summary score for each individual across a longer list of items and to use these summary scores to compare individuals or groups on a range of other variables.

Creating Summary Scores—Three Indices

To create these parsimonious measures, the results of the VAI, IAI, and CBI were converted into summary scores for each index. This facilitated direct comparisons between the two groups across the three time periods. Before using a set of items in this manner, it is necessary to determine their reliability by assessing their internal consistency. Various statistical tests may be used for this purpose. In this study, Cronbach's alpha was used to assess the internal consistency of each index (Carmines & Zeller, 1979). Using the responses of both men and women, this analysis revealed strong internal consistency of each index with alphas of .93 for the VAI, .90 for the IAI, and .90 for the CBI (for details, see Appendix B, Tables B.2 to B.4). Each index was further refined using established procedures, and a specific assessment was made for each respondent by averaging the number of items he or she responded to on each of the indices. Two scale scores were calculated for each index: one for the prevalence of the acts (at least once) and the other for the frequent occurrence (five or more times) of these acts. These scores were calculated for the relationship prior to the beginning of the research and for the two follow-up periods (Time 2 and Time 3). For example, a man scoring .70 for prevalence on the VAI at Time 1 would have reported perpetrating 70% of the acts included in the VAI at least once during the relationship prior to the start of the research. If at Time 3 he scored .35 for frequent violence on the VAI, he would have reported inflicting 35% of the acts in the index five or more times during that time period. Using these individual scale scores, comparisons between the two groups were calculated based on the averages for each group on a range of dimensions.

The Reports of the Men and the Reports of the Women

While the reports of the men have been used to compare the two groups on the variables relating to their own backgrounds, it seems prudent to ask whether the men's reports should be relied on when considering changes in their violence and controlling behaviors. For a host of reasons, many of which will become clear in the presentation of

Table 6.1 Comparison of Men's and Women's Scores at Time 1 on Three Indices (prevalence and frequent use)

Index	Prevalence Score		Frequent Use Score	
	Men	Women	Men	Women
VAI	.54	.69***	.11	.33***
IAI	.40	.61***	.05	.23***
CBI	.68	.76***	.27	.45***

NOTES: Ns = 122 men, 134 women.
***$p < .001$.

the findings, it is important to reflect on the veracity of the men's accounts of changes in these behaviors. Researchers and those with experience of working with abusers note a strong tendency among these men to deny or minimize their use of violence and its consequences (Dutton & Hemphill, 1992; Pence & Paymar, 1993). One way of examining this is to compare the men's accounts with those of the women who they victimized.

Detailed comparisons of percentage differences in the reports of the men and women in the Violent Men Study have been reported elsewhere (Dobash et al., 1996, 1998). In brief, the men's and women's accounts of violence and injuries reveal many strong, distinct, and statistically significant differences between them. The differences between the men and women are particularly marked for some of the more serious forms of injury and for the frequent use of violence, with women reporting more violence and injuries and men reporting much less (see Appendix A, Figures A.4 and A.5). There were also significant differences between the men and women in average scores for each index at Time 1. Table 6.1 reveals important differences in the scores of men and women on the prevalence and frequent occurrence of violence, injuries, and controlling behaviors reported at Time 1. All of the comparisons between the men and women on all three indices yielded much higher scores for the women and all reached high levels of statistical significance.

Evidence reported elsewhere suggests that women's reports of men's violence constitute more valid indicators than those of men (for a discussion, see Dobash et al., 1998). Given that women's reports constitute a more valid indicator of men's violence and are a more conservative and stringent test of changes in that behavior, the subsequent

Table 6.2 Comparison of Men's Program Group and Other CJ
            Group at Time 1 on Three Indices (prevalence and
            frequent use) (women's reports)

| | Prevalence Score | | Frequent Use Score | |
Index	Men's Program	Other CJ	Men's Program	Other CJ
VAI	.73	.72	.39	.39
IAI	.65	.60	.22	.24
CBI	.71	.75	.22	.24

NOTES: Ns = Men's Program group, 47; Other CJ group, 87.

analysis relies primarily on the women's accounts of the men's
violence.

Using the Women's Scale Scores at
Time 1 to Assess Selection Bias

To further consider the possibility of selection bias at Time 1, the
women's scale scores were compared for the two groups (Men's Program and Other CJ). Table 6.2 shows that the prevalence and frequent
use scores at Time 1 were almost identical on the three indices. Based
on the women's reports of the men's behavior, the average scale score
for prevalence on the VAI at Time 1 was almost identical for the Men's
Program group (.73) and the Other CJ group (.72). Similarly, there was
very little difference in scores on the IAI and the CBI.

Similar patterns are apparent in the average scale scores for the
two groups using the women's reports of the men's perpetration of frequent violence and controlling behavior and the frequent infliction of
a range of injuries. Using the women's reports of the men's frequent
perpetration of violence, the average scores are identical for the Men's
Program group (.39) and the Other CJ group (.39). The women's
scores for the men's perpetration of frequent controlling behaviors
and frequent injuries differ hardly at all.

In summary, the results of the various comparisons of the backgrounds; criminal justice experiences; relationships; and levels of violence, injuries, and controlling behaviors of the men in the two groups
yielded few significant differences at Time 1. In the behaviors of main

concern of abuser programs—violence, controlling behavior, and injuries—the average scale scores of the two groups were very similar at
Time 1. These findings suggest that there was no selection bias on the
criterion behavior. The main differences between the two groups at
Time 1 were that men in the Other CJ group were more likely to be
unemployed and to be in non-state-sanctioned, cohabiting relationships. Research on crime has shown that unemployment is a risk factor
for offending, and emerging evidence from research on intimate violence indicates a greater risk of violence in cohabiting rather than
state-sanctioned relationships (Wilson, Johnson, & Daly, 1995).
Unemployment and the nature of the relationship are not trivial factors
and we should be attuned to the possible effects of these on observed
outcomes. We will return to these issues after considering whether
criminal justice interventions can change violent men.

Do Violent Men Change?

The central question of the Violent Men Study is whether men
change their violent and controlling behaviors as a result of different
types of criminal justice intervention. The specific focus is a comparison of the effect of abuser programs with other forms of intervention
on violence and controlling behavior. First, we consider violence itself;
then controlling behavior; and, finally, the relationship between the
two.

Changes in violent behavior for each group were investigated
using two methods: court reports of prosecutions during the follow-up
periods and women's reports of the men's violence during the same
periods. Changes in controlling behavior were examined using
women's reports of subsequent incidents of this behavior. The possible
relationship between violence and controlling behavior is examined to
consider how the one might be related to the other regardless of the
type of intervention. Finally, we consider the possible effect on these
outcomes of all of the factors previously discussed, including personal
characteristics, nature of relationship, previous contact with criminal
justice, and the specific interventions to examine the effects of each on
the outcome. The overall task is to consider whether court-mandated
abuser programs are more effective than other forms of criminal justice
intervention at eliminating the behaviors that make up the constellation of violence.

Court Records and Subsequent Prosecutions

Existing research and collective experience have shown that criminal justice records and the statistics based on them often fail to reflect the actual incidence of crime, and this is particularly true for violence against intimates (Maguire, 1995). While such records can provide valuable information about the activities of various aspects of the justice system, rearrests by police, sanctions by courts, and so on, they cannot be used as a reliable indicator of the true incidence of subsequent behavior by offenders, since most offenses never come to the attention of the justice system. In the Violent Men Study, court records were continuously monitored throughout the life of the research for incidents of subsequent prosecutions of the men who were in the study. Based on information from these court records, only 3 of the 42 Men's Program men (7%) and 8 of the 80 Other CJ men (10%) were prosecuted for a repeat incident involving violence against their partner during the 12-month follow-up.

It can easily be seen that using court reports at follow-up might lead to three false conclusions: that after one year 93% of men on the abuser programs and 90% of men receiving other sanctions did not commit a subsequent act of violence against their woman partner; that all types of sanctions have an extraordinary impact on subsequent incidents of violence; and that abuser programs are only slightly more successful in reducing violence than other criminal justice sanctions. That is, everything works and there is little difference in outcome between one intervention and another. The conclusion based on court records of subsequent prosecutions that "everything works" and that all interventions are equally successful is, however, not reflected in the data from the follow-up questionnaires with men and women. These data tell a very different story and cast considerable doubt on the use of criminal justice records as an indicator of subsequent acts of violence.

The Women's Reports of the Men's Violence at Follow-Up

The general aim of the abuser programs evaluated in the Violent Men Study was to help men eliminate violence and other controlling and intimidating behavior. If such programs are effective, there should be a significant difference between the Men's Program group and the Other CJ group in the incidence of these behaviors at follow-up. Again, the women's reports were used as the more conservative indicator of changes in the men's behavior. Three months after interview (Time 2),

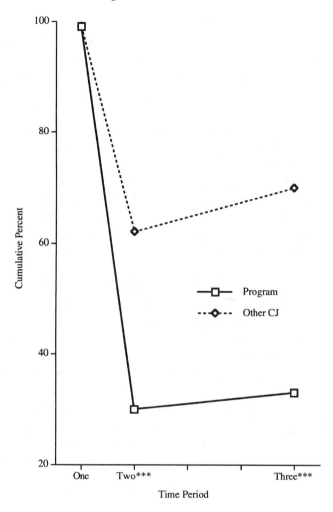

Figure 6.1. Prevalence of Violence (at least one incident) at Three Time Periods, Women's Reports (Program, *n* = 27; Other CJ, *n* = 59) ***p < .001.

62% of women in the Other CJ group but only 30% in the Men's Program group reported a repeat incidence of violence (a statistically significant difference). The findings presented in Figure 6.1 suggest that almost three quarters of the women in the Men's Program group were not subjected to a violent assault 3 months after interview, whereas around two fifths of the women in the Other CJ group had not experienced a violent incident.

A crucial question for the evaluation is the sustainability of these changes. The findings suggest that men in the Men's Program group

are much more likely than men in the Other CJ group to remain violence free over an additional 9-month period. One year after interview
(Time 3), men who completed the court-mandated abuser programs
were much less likely to have committed a subsequent act of violence
(33%) than men sanctioned in other ways (70%), and this difference
was statistically significant.

It is important to note that the vast majority of the subsequent violent acts occurred during the first 3 months of the follow-up period.
There was also a statistically significant difference between the two
groups in the perpetration of frequent violence at follow-up (Figure
6.2). Although there was some disparity between the two groups at
Time 1 in the proportion of women who reported frequent violence by
the man in the year preceding intervention (31% in the Other CJ group
and 26% in the Men's Program group), these differences were not pro-
nounced or statistically significant at that stage. But one year after
interview (Time 3), the women's reports of the men's subsequent perpetration of frequent acts of violence revealed a statistically significant
difference between the two groups, with 37% of the Other CJ group
and 7% of the Men's Program group reporting five or more subsequent
incidents of violence during follow-up. At both points of follow-up,
the proportional differences in the two groups on prevalence and frequent violence are highly statistically significant. This strongly suggests that abuser programs are much more successful than other forms
of criminal justice intervention in eliminating violent behavior. Comparisons of subsequent injuries are not presented here because the differences between the two groups reflect the changes shown for violent
behavior.

Controlling Behavior Reported by
Women at Follow-Up

If, as these findings suggest, abuser programs are more successful
than other types of criminal justice intervention in eliminating subsequent acts of violence, one might also ask if there is any effect on other
factors such as coercion and intimidation. Our initial theoretical statements regarding the constellation of violence posited an association
between violence and other nonviolent forms of behavior such as coercion and intimidation. This, however, is best treated as an empirical
question rather than left as a theoretical assumption. This question
bears on a popular statement so frequently made that it has almost
become a truism despite the fact that we know of no evidence given in
its support—that men in abuser programs who successfully end their

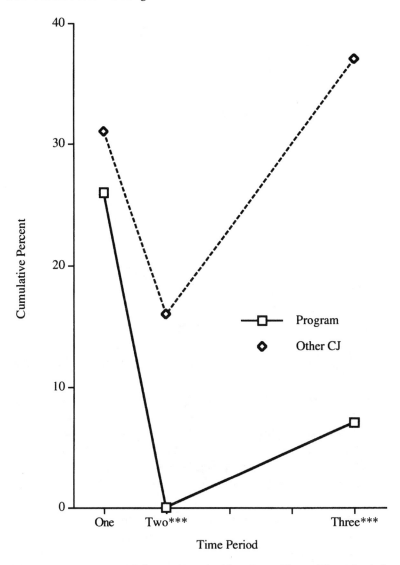

Figure 6.2. Frequent Violence (5+ incidents) at Three Time Periods, Women's Reports (Program, $n = 27$; Other CJ, $n = 59$)
***$p < .001$.

violent behavior simply replace physical acts of violence with various nonviolent forms of intimidation and terror. If the usual outcome of abuser programs is simply to convert men's acts of physical violence into acts of mental or emotional terror, this is obviously a matter of grave concern. Evidence on controlling and intimidating acts collected in the Violent Men Study does not support the notion that men who have completed a men's program are turned into domestic terrorists.

Table 6.3 Average Scores on the Controlling Behavior Index
(prevalence and frequent use) at Three Time Periods
(women's reports)

	CBI-Prevalence		CBI-Frequent Use	
	Men's Program	Other CJ	Men's Program	Other CJ
Time 1	.70	.75	.38	.48
Time 2	.52*	.68	.22	.33
Time 3	.53*	.71	.20*	.36

NOTES: Ns = Men's Program group, 21; Other CJ group, 44 (includes only cases where women
returned questionnaires and completed the CBI at Time 3).

$*p < .05$.

As discussed in the chapter on interventions, the two programs
identify other forms of intimidating behavior as integral elements of
the constellation of violence and seek to change them. Abuser programs help men to identify such behavior and define it as part of their
overall repertoire and to show how such actions can be highly intimidating. This is often a novel insight for men who may be accustomed to
defining only the extremes of physical violence as matters of concern
or in need of change. Because of the focus of abuser programs on wider
attitudes and orientations, men who have completed such programs
would be expected to be more successful at reducing or eliminating
controlling and intimidating behaviors than men who have not been
exposed to such ideas. In ascertaining changes in controlling behaviors, only women who returned their questionnaire at Time 3 were
included in the analysis as it was only for this group that complete evidence for all three time periods was available concerning this issue. In
short, one year after the intervention, the women reported that men in
the abuser programs were more likely to have reduced their controlling
and intimidating acts. Table 6.3 presents the average prevalence and
frequent use scores on the CBI for the two groups at all time periods
based on the reports of the women who returned questionnaires at
Time 3.

Of the men reported on at Time 3, those in the Other CJ group had
reduced only marginally their prevalence scores on the CBI across the
12-month period from .75 at Time 1 to .71 at Time 3. While men in the
Men's Program group who were reported on at Time 3 began with

somewhat lower average scores at Time 1 (.70) than men in the Other CJ group, their average scores were reduced significantly by Time 3 (.53). A similar pattern is apparent when considering the differences between the two groups in scores for the frequent occurrence of controlling acts over the three time periods. Here, the scores for men in the Other CJ group show a marginal reduction over one year (.48 at Time 1 to .36 at Time 3) compared with scores of the Men's Program group. While the average score at Time 1 is somewhat lower for the Men's Program group than the Other CJ group, this difference is not significantly different, and by Time 3 there is a statistically significant reduction in CBI scores for men in the Men's Program group (.38 at Time 1 to .20 at Time 3).

Overall, the findings indicate that while the men in both groups reduced the prevalence and frequent use of controlling behaviors after one year, men in the Men's Program group were more successful than the others. At Time 3, reports of the Other CJ group indicated that the average score for prevalence was reduced by 4% and the average score for frequent controlling behavior by 10%, whereas for the Men's Program group, prevalence scores were reduced by 17% and frequent use scores by 18%. While both groups show reductions, the Men's Program men show much greater reductions and the average scores remain low over the two follow-up periods, while by Time 3 the average scores for the Other CJ men have begun to rise. While men in the Men's Program group had not completely stopped using controlling behavior, the incidence of these acts had been reduced and the acts were occurring on a less frequent basis.

The Relationship Between Violence and Controlling Behavior

These findings show a significant drop in incidents of violence and reductions in controlling behavior after participation in an abuser program. This raises the possibility of a direct relationship between violence and controlling behavior despite the intervention. To examine this, we compared the CBI scores with the prevalence of violence at the three time periods. The possible relationship between violence and controlling behavior was examined regardless of the type of intervention received by the men. Again, the women's reports of the men's behavior were used and only those who remained in the study at Time 3 were compared across the three time periods.

Table 6.4 reveals a significant relationship between subsequent reduction in violence and the prevalence and frequent use of control-

Table 6.4 Average Scores on the Controlling Behavior Index
(prevalence and frequent use) at Three Time Periods and
Men's Violence at Follow-Up (women's reports)

	CBI-Prevalence		CBI-Frequent Use	
Violent at Follow-up	Yes	No	Yes	No
Time 1	.78	.65*	.48	.35
Time 2	.78	.39**	.43	.06**
Time 3	.78	.46**	.44	.10**

NOTES: Ns = Men's Program group, 21; Other CJ group, 44 (includes only those cases where
women returned questionnaires and completed the CBI at Time 3).

$*p < .05, **p < .01.$

ling behavior at all time periods. For those men who eventually fail by
perpetrating a subsequent act of violence at follow-up, their CBI scores
remain the same across all three time periods (.78). By contrast, the
men who had not committed a subsequent violent act at follow-up
began with a somewhat lower CBI score at Time 1 (.65) but ended with
a substantially lower score at Time 3 (.46). A similar pattern can be seen
for the frequent use of controlling behavior. Men who subsequently
used violence at follow-up showed little change in the frequent use of
controlling behavior across the three time periods (.48 at Time 1 to .44
at Time 3) while men who did not use violence at follow-up showed a
significant reduction in the frequent use of these acts from Time 1 (.35)
to Time 3 (.10).

These findings suggest two conclusions: (a) strong support is given
to the theoretical argument that men's violence toward intimate partners is usually associated with other forms of controlling and intimidating behavior; and (b) predictably, whatever the means of violence
reduction, program participation or other avenues, it will be associated
with a concurrent reduction in other coercive and controlling acts.
Given the integral relationship between these two sets of behaviors, it
is difficult to judge whether a reduction in violence leads to a reduction
in controlling behavior or vice versa. Concurrent reduction seems
most likely but this issue needs further study. These findings reveal an
important relationship between violence and controlling behavior and
a reduction in both, particularly among the Men's Program men.
While the effect was observed in both groups, it should be noted that it
was much more likely among the Men's Program group.

Other Factors That May Affect Violence and Controlling Behavior

In light of the differences between the two groups identified at Time 1, it is important to consider what, if any, effect these differences might have on observed outcomes. The question to ask is if the observed changes in each group and the differences between the two groups are solely the result of the criminal justice intervention or are also associated with differences in the characteristics of the two groups prior to intervention. Among the factors that might have had an independent effect on the observed outcome, only two (employment and marital status) were found to have any significant effect on subsequent acts of violence and none appear to be related to subsequent levels of controlling behavior.

In both groups, men in cohabiting or non-state-sanctioned relationships were about one third more likely than men in state-sanctioned marriages to have perpetrated a violent act at follow-up and, as discussed earlier, the men in the Other CJ group were more likely to be cohabiting. Unemployment also appears to be associated with the commission of violence at follow-up, although this association was not statistically significant. Unemployed men in both groups were about 25% more likely than employed men to have perpetrated a violent act by Time 3. The men in both groups who were still in the study at Time 3 were fairly similar in their levels of unemployment (59% in Other CJ and 45% in the Men's Program group). Importantly, however, unemployed Men's Program men were much less likely to fail (56%) by committing a subsequent violent act than similarly unemployed men in the Other CJ group (84%). Criminal justice experiences in the backgrounds of the men in both groups, such as previous arrests, did not appear to be associated with perpetration of subsequent acts of violence. Background characteristics, nature of the relationship, and men's previous experiences with criminal justice did not appear to have any effect on subsequent levels of controlling behavior.

The analysis presented so far has established that stopping violence and reducing the incidence and frequent use of controlling behavior appears to be linked to program participation. The men who completed the abuser programs were significantly more likely to reduce these acts than men sanctioned in other ways. In addition, violence and controlling behaviors appear to be directly related to one another, regardless of the form of intervention, as men who reduce

controlling behavior are more likely than those who do not to eliminate subsequent violence. Various sociodemographic characteristics
(cohabitation and unemployment) also appear to be associated with a
cessation in violence 12 months after the initial assessment, but they do
not appear to be associated with levels of controlling behavior.

Overall Effects

What this analysis cannot tell us is the overall effect of these factors
when considered together. Numerous questions may be asked, such as
what is the relative importance of living in a state-sanctioned marriage
in comparison to program participation? Does the effect of program
participation disappear when other potentially important variables are
considered? Is there an independent program effect once these other
variables have been considered? The usual approach to such questions
is to use a multivariate statistical analysis to assess differential effects.
In light of the data configuration achieved in this study, the best statistical method for addressing these questions is logistic regression
(Hosmer & Lemeshow, 1989). We did in fact use logistic regression,
but the numbers achieved at Time 3 were such that the results of the
regression analysis are unstable. Despite these problems, we consider
the results to be suggestive and useful and, as such, the general findings
are considered here.[3]

The variables selected for inclusion in this multivariate analysis
were those found to be statistically or theoretically significant in the
analysis conducted up to this point, for example, program participation, marital status, employment status, and criminal career. The
analysis involved four models of potential effects: (a) Model 1—program participation on its own; (b) Model 2—program participation
and background and relationship variables; (c) Model 3—program
participation, background/relationship, and criminal justice variables;
and (d) Model 4—program participation, background/relationship
and criminal justice variables, and controlling behavior scale scores. As
expected, Model 1 shows that program participation is associated with
a statistically significant absence of the perpetration of violence at
follow-up. In Model 2, the addition of background and relationship
variables indicates that while program participation still has a statistically significant effect, there is also a significant relationship between
cohabitation and relationships with four children and the perpetration
of violence at follow-up. In Model 3, the addition of criminal justice
variables, specifically an arrest record for any type of offense and previous police interventions for violence against a partner, does not yield

statistically significant results. Thus, previous criminal justice variables seem to have little effect on perpetration of violence at follow-up, although program participation and cohabitation remain significant. In Model 4, the addition of a score designating changes in the prevalence of controlling behaviors shows a statistically significant effect, with a reduction in controlling behavior associated with a reduction in violence, suggesting that when violence ceases, controlling behaviors do not increase in order to replace violence but are also reduced. Cohabitation and the number of children continue to have a statistically significant effect in this model. Program participation, while still important in Model 4, barely failed to reach statistical significance at the .05 level. Overall, however, the findings from the four models combined with the other analysis discussed here suggest that the elimination of violence and reduction in controlling behavior are associated with participation in an abuser program. They also suggest that men with certain characteristics may be more amenable to change than others. Thus, future research might productively focus on the question of which men seem to be most amenable to change as a consequence of this form of intervention.

In addition to considering the effects of such interventions on ending these negative behaviors, it is also relevant to consider any possible effects on more positive factors such as women's sense of safety and well-being. We now turn to these and other factors associated with the quality of life.

Notes

1. We considered the possibility of carrying out observations of program sessions, but staff hesitance and the demands of the research made this impossible. The staff concerns, while possibly regrettable, are perfectly understandable given that both programs had been operating for a very short period of time.

2. Nine men were excluded from the Men's Program group because they did not participate in CHANGE or the LDVPP. With one exception, these men either failed to start because, for example, their employment interfered with participation, or they attended only one or two sessions. One of the men who was sentenced to the program committed another assault prior to participation and was sent to prison. All of these men were considered not to have participated in a program and were therefore assigned to the Other CJ group. Only five of these men were still in the study at Time 3 and, importantly, they did not contribute disproportionately to the levels of failure in the Other CJ group at follow-up.

It should also be noted that the data for both groups at Times 2 and 3 only include reports of those relationships in which women could be considered at risk during the period of follow-up. Women who had no further contact with their partner after Time 1 because of, for example, separation or divorce, were not considered at risk and their questionnaire results were not included in the analysis.

3. The statistical details of this analysis can be obtained from the authors.

7

Changes in
Quality of Life

Men perpetrate violence not just through blows and kicks, with the resulting bruises, cuts, and breaks, but also through threats and intimidation, and as already indicated this overall constellation of violence is important for understanding not only the emergence of violence but also its subsequent continuation or cessation. If, as these findings indicate, violence is a part of a constellation, then changes in violent behavior should be accompanied by a reversal in a whole set of attitudes, orientations, and patterns of communication as lived by the man and the woman. Apart from the violence per se, the relationship may be more or less characterized by intimidation and degradation of the woman. If violence has a negative effect on the individuals concerned and on the relationship between them, then its elimination would be expected to bring some improvement both in the relationship and in the quality of life of both partners. And if, as this evidence suggests, abuser programs are more successful than other criminal justice sanctions in reducing or eliminating violence and other forms of coercive and controlling behaviors, we would also expect differences between these groups in the perceived quality of life of the men and women concerned and in the relationships of these couples. Here, we reflect on these questions using the men's and the women's accounts of the quality of their lives one year after intervention.

Assessing the Quality of Life

Using the Quality of Life Index (QLI) and written comments on the follow-up postal questionnaires, the men and women reflected on changes in the quality of their lives and their relationships. The wealth of written comments illustrate improvements and deterioration and reveal differences between those who successfully completed abuser programs and those who received some other form of criminal justice intervention. While the main objective of any form of intervention is the cessation of violence, and changes in personal well-being or improvements in the relationship may not be the focus or the goal, it may, nonetheless, be speculated that an improvement in one might be accompanied by an improvement in the other, although the relationship between them might not be straightforward or immediate. This shall be considered as we examine the quality of life and end with a word of caution. Summary information from responses to the QLI show the patterns of such change, and the qualitative comments illustrate their content.

Using the QLI (see Chapter 4), the men and the women were asked to give their views on changes in themselves, their partner, and their relationship in terms of whether their life had improved, worsened, or stayed the same in the 12-month period following an intervention. The QLI items are divided into five broad groupings, including women's reports of changes in men's orientations to violence, changes in men's related behaviors and emotional well-being, changes in men's associated attitudes and orientations to their woman partner, women's sense of well-being, and women's assessment of the relationship. The analysis focuses on change one year after the intervention, with things remaining the same, becoming worse, or improving.

Overall, there are consistent patterns in these findings (see Appendix B, Table B.5). The results from the QLI for women show that a reasonable proportion of women in both groups report improvements, although these were experienced by a larger proportion of the women in the Men's Program group than in the Other CJ group. There was a consistent and sometimes considerable proportion of women in the Other CJ group who indicated that there has been a marked deterioration in the man's behavior and orientations, in their own sense of personal well-being, and in their relationship. Conversely, very few women in the Men's Program group reported a reduction in their quality of life. The qualitative comments of both the men and the women confirm these differences. The Men's Program men felt better about themselves and were more likely to report improved relationships than the men in the Other CJ group, and the reports of the women generally confirm these observations, albeit in a more cautious fashion.

Changes in Men's Orientations to Violence

While men may express a desire to change their violent behavior, few make efforts to do so except at points of crisis involving some cost to themselves, such as the woman leaving or intervention by police and courts, and such motivations rarely last once the crisis has passed. Yet, it is at these points that the man might realistically reflect on the current and future costs to himself and others of the continued use of violence and thereby consider personal change. Moments of crisis provoking reflection are useful junctures for intervention. If extended and exploited, they may provide opportunities for more meaningful reflection, enhanced motivation to change, expanded insight into the cost to others rather than just to oneself, and the learning of new attitudes and skills that can be put into practice in fostering and maintaining new behavior.

To assess changes in the men's orientations, the women were asked if they thought their partner was more or less likely to use violence, to see it as a solution to problems, and to want to stop using violence. While women in both groups indicated some improvements in the men's orientations, the men in the Men's Program group were less likely than the men in the other group to see violence as a solution to problems and more likely to want to stop (Appendix B, Table B.5, sec. 1). For example, 71% of the women in the Men's Program group and 49% of those in the Other CJ group thought that their partner was more likely than in the past to want to stop using violence. On the negative side, 20% of the women in the Other CJ group assessed their partner as more likely to use violence against them in the future although only 5% of the Men's Program group were so assessed. The comments of the women and men reflect these changes in men's orientations to the use of violence:

Wants to stop violence (positive change)

> He never wants to be violent again. (Woman, Men's Program: 1075)

> I want to change for myself. (Man, Men's Program: 042)

See violence as solution to problems (positive change)

> Violence gets you nowhere. (Man, Men's Program: 073)

[The Men's Program] makes you realise violence is not the answer. (Man, Men's Program: 118)

I now know violence doesn't solve anything. (Man, Men's Program: 114)

Likely to use violence against her (positive change)

How much has your partner being on the [Men's] Program affected you? Some. Made me feel confident that he won't hit me. (Woman, Men's Program: 1122)

I am just very confident he will never be violent again. (Woman, Men's Program: 1114)

No more violence. I'm wanting my new partner to be happy not miserable. (Man, Men's Program: 064)

Uses violence against her (positive change)

How well are you and your partner getting on? Okay. He isn't violent anymore. (Woman, Men's Program: 1073)

It has been a worthwhile project for us and could help others if they were willing to try and change. (Woman, Men's Program: 1114)

He is not as violent towards me. (Woman, Other CJ: 1094)

While some experienced no change, others reported change for the worse (Appendix B, Table B.5, sec. 1). The men who got worse were more likely to have experienced other forms of criminal justice intervention than to have been in an abuser program.

Wants to stop violence (negative change—the same or worse)

He does not want to stop. (Woman, Other CJ: 1029)

In the last six months, has he done anything to stop being violent to you? No. Thinks he's okay/normal. (Woman, Other CJ: 1072)

Sees violence as a solution to problems (negative change— the same or worse)

A man knows how a woman will react and knows when they will harm them. It's like a game hitting something not strong enough to hit back! (Woman, Other CJ: 1105)

Please name something which he does differently as a result of being on Probation? [He] is maybe a little more careful not to be "caught." . . . [He] Will not mark me. . . . *[Comment]* These questionnaires have helped me recognise the problem—they have aggravated John and made him more resentful towards me. They make me feel it will never change. . . . Sadly for me I don't think there is an answer—just being alone. (Woman, Other CJ: 1120)

Uses violence against her (negative change—the same or worse)

He is still violent but seems to want to hurt me more. *Do you think his violence can be stopped?* He does not want to stop. He can't have me so he wants me to suffer, and I am. (Woman, Other CJ: 1029)

Every week, about three times or more, myself and the kids are put through hours of mental violence, verbal threats and have had to leave the house on numerous occasions in our night-clothes. (Woman, Other CJ: 1126)

Nothing. When he hits me now, he hits me as if I am anybody. (Woman, Other CJ: 1007)

Taking Responsibility for His Violent Behavior

Targeting the offending behavior is an important aspect of abuser program efforts to eliminate violence and its web of supports. An integral aspect of this focus is to encourage men to accept responsibility for their violent and controlling behaviors. While accepting responsibility for one's behavior is considered a fundamental aspect of change in the abuser programs, as we have shown, this is not readily acknowledged by men. The lessons are difficult to learn and difficult to maintain. The programs also focus on the attitudes and behaviors associated with the use of violence against women and men's sense of justification. Program purposes include, among others, efforts to shift the highly egocentric focus of violent men on themselves to a greater awareness of others and relationships with them, particularly those with women and children. Men are encouraged to learn to understand that women also have their own concerns, feelings, and points of view. Without a clear focus on issues such as responsibility, egocentric orientations, and empathy for others, it is unlikely that men will accidentally stumble across them or identify them as issues that need to be addressed in their process of reformation. Yet they are integral aspects of the constellation of violence and are in need of change if violence is to be eliminated. They also have important implications for the quality of life experienced by men, their women partners, and the children who may witness the violence.

The QLI reveals strong and usually statistically significant differences between the orientations of the Men's Program men, who are likely to have had clear and explicit exposure to these issues, and men in the Other CJ group, who have not. For example, the women partners reported that 55% of Men's Program men took responsibility for their violence while only 25% of the Other CJ group did so. In fact, 34% of the Other CJ group were judged to be worse at taking responsibility for their violence than they had been when the women were first interviewed (Appendix B, Table B.5, sec. 1). The comments of the women and men show the strength of this position.

Takes responsibility for his violence (positive change)

Please name something which he does differently as a result of being on the Men's Program.

[He] Tends to think more about the consequences of being violent. (Woman, Men's Program: 1114)

[He] Looks inwardly at himself (more) although this can sometimes make him moody because he feels guilty for what he has done in the past. . . . He now understands that he nearly killed me and the consequences of his violence. (Woman, Men's Program: 1122)

I had no right to use violence at all. (Man, Men's Program: 064)

I have been made to realise I must take responsibility for my own actions. (Man, Men's Program: 142)

I do not use violence now because I think it is wrong. It makes matters worse, not better. (Man, Men's Program: 039)

[He] Is less violent and more likely to discuss a situation. . . . He has realised what he was doing. (Woman, Other CJ: 1113)

Man takes responsibility for his violence (negative change)

Looking to the future, do you think that the court outcome [a fine] will prevent you being abusive to your partner again?

No. Not as long as she's still vindictive and nasty. (Man, Other CJ: 115)

[Comment] You seem to think my court appearance and being put on Probation was due to me being violent towards my ex-wife. I was put on Probation for smashing a window at my ex-wife's house where I hurt myself more than anything else. If you would like to hear the full reason for my appearance at her house and the window being smashed I would be only too happy to talk to you [this is from a man who destroyed the inside of his partner's house, terrorised her and used violence against her on several occasions. (Man, Other CJ: 047)

He doesn't think he has done anything wrong. (Woman, Other CJ: 1129)

In the last nine months, have you talked to any of these people about your violent behaviour? No. I don't have a violent behaviour. *[Comment]* I have had no word from her since I got out of jail apart from when I was at court about my boys. We didn't say anything. No I don't give a toss about her now but if anything happens to my boys and I don't know about it she (and her other half) will pay. (Man, Other CJ: 129)

Changes in Men's Related Behaviors and Emotional Well-Being

The man's happiness, selfishness, and ability to control his temper and reduce his drinking are four indicators used to illustrate changes in men's related behaviors and emotional well-being. Where excessive drinking is perceived as a problem, bringing it under control may form a vital part of the solution to violence. Overall, the pattern is clear: The women in the Men's Program group reported consistent improvement in related behaviors and the emotional state of their partner and very few reported a deterioration. The opposite is true for women in the Other CJ group: Only small proportions of these women reported improvements in the men while fairly substantial proportions saw a deterioration (Appendix B, Table B.5, sec. 2).

On the positive side, the women partners reported that 48% of the Men's Program men and 28% of the Other CJ men made positive changes with problem drinking in the 12-month follow-up period, while 10% of the Men's Program men and 39% of the Other CJ men got worse at controlling their drinking during that period. The women's reports of changes in the men's drinking show a strong and statistically significant difference between the Men's Program group and the Other CJ group as do those for his happiness and his selfishness. Men's Program men were reported by their women partners as happier (52%), more likely to control their temper (71%), and less selfish (52%) than prior to participation in one of the abuser programs and only a few thought they had become worse. The reports of women in the Other CJ group reflect important and statistically significant differences in most of these comparisons. The women in the Other CJ group reported either no change or a worsening of the men's related behaviors and sense of well-being, with 34% less happy, 42% more selfish, and 39% less likely to control their temper. In comparison to the Men's Program group, much smaller proportions of women in the Other CJ group reported improvements in their partner (Appendix B, Table B.5, sec. 2). The comments of the men and women reflect the nature of positive and negative changes and illustrate how these can affect the quality of life for women, men, and their children:

Controls drinking (positive change)

I look at things from [my] wife's point of view and drink less. (Man, Men's Programs: 039)

He drinks less and he thinks about things first and he listens to what I have to say. (Woman, Men's Program: 1009)

Sobriety has come into his life—no alcohol now. (Woman, Other CJ: 1023)

He's cut his drinking down and stays in more and has been working at his job for six months. (Woman, Other CJ: 1119)

Man controls temper (positive change)

His temper is nowhere near as bad as it was. (Woman, Men's Program: 1009)

He just controls his temper. (Woman, Men's Program: 1073)

[We] do have arguments but now I am trying to control my temper and it seems to be working. (Man, Men's Program: 008)

Man's happiness (positive change)

Thinks more [positively] of himself and sees our relationship different[ly]. He can trust [others] more; also he is totally different, better in himself. (Woman, Men's Program: 1038)

He is very pleasant to us all. (Woman, Men's Program: 1075)

He's not hard any more. (Woman, Men's Program: 1040)

My husband has changed so much. . . . He has a better understanding of himself. (Woman, Men's Program: 1039)

[I] Got my self respect back. (Man, Men's Program: 038)

[The program] helps you to relax. . . . I am more settled than before. (Man, Men's Program: 075)

[I have more] Self esteem and confidence in my emotions. (Man, Men's Program: 044)

Those experiencing no change or a change for the worse expressed themselves as follows:

Controls drinking (negative change—the same or worse)

If [he] is drunk, nothing will stop him. (Woman, Other CJ: 1120)

Speaking for our problems; he would have to change completely. How do I stop him drinking? He has been drinking since his teens. (Woman, Other CJ: 1129)

Man controls temper (negative change—the same or worse)

[The program has] Helped his violent behaviour but not his temper. (Woman, Men's Program: 1053)

Man's happiness (negative change—the same or worse)

I think now he really feels he has lost everything. (Woman, Other CJ: 1072)

Selfish (negative—the same or worse)

Likes to get his own way. (Woman, Other CJ: 1077)

What do you think has brought about this change for the better in your relationship? Because [she] let's me get on with what I want to do. *Do you think that this violence can be stopped?* If she just shuts up and accepts what I say and do. (Man, Other CJ: 091)

Changes in Men's Orientations to Their Woman Partner

The women in the Men's Program group reported a number of positive changes among the men, who were more likely than at the time of the interviews to see their point of view (57%), to be aware of their feelings (57%), and to respect them (50%). An overwhelming majority of the women in the Men's Program group (80%) also reported that their partner was less likely to restrict their life. Only small proportions of the Men's Program women wrote that their partner was now less likely to be aware of their feelings (10%), to see their point of view (19%), to respect them (25%), or to restrict their life (5%) (Appendix B, Table B.5, sec. 3).

The women's reports about the men in the Other CJ group are generally in the opposite direction, with these men less likely to see things from the women's point of view (57%), to be aware of their feelings (35%), or to respect them (49%) (Appendix B, Table B.5, sec. 3). Certainly there are some encouraging signs for the women in the Other CJ group, with a reasonable proportion (57%) reporting that the men were less likely to restrict their life. The pattern, however, is usually more negative than positive. Considering a range of measures, the Men's Program men were likely to be more sympathetic toward their woman partner and less self-centered and to take greater responsibility for their violence. For these men, the lessons of the abuser programs seem to have made a difference. These, of course, are elements that form part of the content of abuser programs and are generally missing from other forms of criminal justice interventions. The comments of the women and men reflect improvement or deterioration in these associated attitudes and orientation to women partners one year after the initial interview:

Man aware of women's feelings (positive change)

> *What has changed?* [Him] realising what he was doing. (Woman, Men's Programs: 1009)

Man sees things from partner's point of view (positive change)

> *How much has the Men's Program affected your life?* A lot. It made him see things from my point of view. (Woman, Men's Program: 1008)

> *Have you felt safer since your partner was put on the Program?* Yes because it made him see things from my side of view. (Woman, Men's Program: 1009)

> It [program] makes them see things in a different way. (Woman, Men's Program: 1073)

> Before I always assumed I was right, now I look at an argument from both points of view. (Man, Men's Program: 039)

> You become more aware of other people's feelings. (Man, Men's Program: 053)

> *Do you think she should have gone to others for help?* Yes. She had two young kids in the house. It was about 5 o'clock in the morning and she must have been frightened. (Man, Other CJ: 072)

Man understands woman (positive change)

> *How much has your partner being on the Program affected you?* A lot.
> I know I can talk to a person who understands. (Woman, Men's Program: 1036)

> *How much has being on the Program affected you?* A lot. I try and understand myself and my partner. (Man, Men's Program: 042)

Man respects woman (positive change)

> [He] Respects me more and is more understanding. (Woman, Men's Program: 1039)

> There is no right for a man to hit a woman. (Man, Men's Program: 039)

> [He] Gives me more respect, and others. (Woman, Other CJ: 1023)

Those experiencing no change or a change for the worse in their predicament express this as follows:

Man aware of woman's feelings (negative change—the same or worse)

> He never listens. I feel it's a waste of time. (Woman, Other CJ: 1129)

> Me and my family are all upset and he just laughs at us. (Woman, Other CJ: 1014)

> His drinking has got so much worse and if he gains access to the home [he] will continue to threaten and be violent as he seems to gain some kind of pleasure hurting and frightening both myself and the children. (Woman, Other CJ: 1095)

Man sees things from partner's point of view (negative change—the same or worse)

> *Is there something she could have done to stop you being violent to her?* Yes. Shut up. *Did you feel that you were right to be violent to her?* Yes. She was being cheeky. (Man, Other CJ: 007)

Man restricts woman's life (negative change—the same or worse)

> He is very possessive towards me and does not like me having friends. (Woman, Men's Program: 1154)

> If she's cheeky and is drunk, I'll hit her. And if she's been unfaithful while I've been away, I'll hit her. (Man, Other CJ: 007)

Women feel they have to make up lies to say where they have been because men just don't believe us or like to rule us. It's one set of rules for them. We are just here for their wishes. We give in just to save a hiding or [to get] peace. (Woman, Other CJ: 1091)

Changes in Women's Quality of Life and Sense of Well-Being

It would be expected that men's orientations toward and general treatment of their woman partner would have consequences for the quality of life of the women concerned. Men who remain the same or become worse in the year after intervention offer little or no hope for the woman seeking a life free of violence. On the other hand, the efforts of those who make strides toward changing these related behaviors and orientations hold out a promise, albeit not a guarantee, of a better future.

To assess changes in the women's sense of well-being and quality of life one year after intervention, they were asked whether things were worse, the same, or improved in terms of their feeling happy, relaxed, and frightened. They were also asked about changes in their sense of self-respect. The bundle of indicators used in this assessment show a consistent pattern. While a reasonable proportion of women in both groups noted improvements, those whose partners completed the Men's Program were more likely to report improvements and less likely to report deterioration (Appendix B, Table B.5, sec. 4).

In improvements in the quality of life, comparisons between the two groups show positive change for a substantial proportion of both groups, with somewhat more among the Men's Program group: The women noted improvements in feeling happy (55% Other CJ, 71% Men's Program) and relaxed (50% Other CJ, 62% Men's Program). Improvements in feelings of self-respect were fairly similar for both groups (58% Other CJ, 55% Men's Program) as were feelings of being frightened (50% Other CJ, 45% Men's Program). A worsening of these factors after one year was noted by some women in both groups, but deterioration across these factors was much more likely among the Other CJ group, with up to 32% of Other CJ women reporting that things got worse on these four factors while only 10% or less of the Men's Program women noted a deterioration (Appendix B, Table B.5, sec. 4). The comments of the women reveal changes in their quality of life. They also provide insight into the nature of improved conditions as well as those conditions that remained the same or worsened during the year after intervention.

Woman's happiness (positive change)

Now my kids are happy and so am I and my partner. (Woman, Men's Program: 1082)

[He] has finally sorted himself out. . . . I can now relax and say I'm happy for the first time in awhile. And I now can say I honestly love him where before he was killing my love with his drinking. (Woman, Other CJ: 1119)

Woman feels relaxed (positive change)

I'm a lot more relaxed. (Woman, Men's Program: 1053)

I don't have to worry about him coming home drunk all the time. (Woman, Other CJ: 1121)

Woman's self-respect (positive change)

It [program] opens your mind up. It makes you realise that there is a lot more to life than being beaten up and terrorising children. (Woman, Men's Program: 1082)

I have more confidence in my responsibilities to myself and family . . . power to have him removed. (Woman, Other CJ: 1023)

The women who experienced no change and the smaller proportion who experienced a change for the worse expressed themselves in strong terms:

Woman's happiness (negative change—the same or worse)

How much did your partners appearing in court affect you? A lot. Suffering from depression and very nervous. . . . [He] has always blamed me for having to attend the Program. (Woman, Men's Program: 1126)

He can't have me so he wants me to suffer and I am. (Woman, Other CJ: 1029)

I wanted to die then I could leave all this behind. If it wasn't for the kids, I would have. (Woman, Other CJ: 1159)

Woman feels relaxed (negative change—the same or worse)

These days I'm bad with my nerves. I can't think straight because he loses his temper with me if there is not enough food or we run out of something like milk, or if there is no fags, that's when he really starts ordering me to go and borrow money. If I can't get any he goes mad, that's when the threats start and the hitting me. (Woman, Men's Program: 1017)

[He] Just constantly causes trouble about anything and everything. . . . [I] just feel like no-one cares what's happening to me and the kids. (Woman, Other CJ: 1072)

Woman's self-respect (negative change—the same or worse)

I would rather get battered than have to listen to the things he says to me. (Woman, Other CJ: 1129)

[He] Makes me feel I am not a woman. (Woman, Other CJ: 1070)

Changes in the Relationship

A number of indicators from the QLI as well as some additional items were used to assess changes in the relationships during the 12-month follow-up. Overall, eight indicators were used. From the QLI, men and women indicated whether they were more or less likely to "get on," "have a laugh," "discuss things," "enjoy one another's company," and "spend time together." Additional items evaluated the relationship, how the couple were getting on, and the frequency and seriousness of arguments (Appendix B, Table B.5, sec. 5-6). The women were also asked if they thought their relationship had improved, stayed the same, or worsened in the year since their interview, and they assessed changes in the seriousness and level of conflicts and arguments in the relationships. Here, the general pattern shows marked differences between the two groups, with improvements in the relationships of Men's Program women and a worsening in the relationships of women in the Other CJ group. A number of comparisons were statistically significant (Appendix B, Table B.5, sec. 5-6).

With one exception, over half of the women in the Men's Program group noted improvements in seven of the eight variables, while about one third of the Other CJ women did so. Conversely, one third to one half of the Other CJ women experienced a worsening of the relationship while about 15% to 20% of the Men's Program women did so (see Appendix B, Table B.5, sec. 5-6). The strongest comparisons among these factors show improvements in the Men's Program couples' ability to have a laugh together (57% improved) and enjoy spending time together (52% improved) compared to a worsening of these among Other CJ couples (53% and 64% worsened). In addition, three quarters of the Men's Program women (76%) evaluated their relationship as having changed for the better. By contrast, nearly half the women in the Other CJ group (43%) judged their relationship to have changed for the worse. Similarly, over two thirds of the Men's Program women (69%) saw an improvement around serious arguments while one third of the Other CJ women (32%) saw a worsening (Appendix B, Table B.5, sec. 5-6).

In their own words, the women and the men described the nature of the changes in the quality of their relationship a year after the intervention:

Discuss things, communication (positive change)

He has learned to open up and talk instead of just lashing out. . . . He has stopped his violent behaviour and now talks more openly. . . . [He] Talks to me about how he feels. (Woman, Men's Program: 1108)

I can talk to him more. (Woman, Men's Program: 1082)

What aspects of the Program have been most useful to you? Being able to speak about my feelings. (Man, Men's Program: 042)

I listen to her now. (Man, Men's Program: 040)

We talk more about our problems. (Man, Other CJ: 123)

Relationship (positive change)

How well are you getting on? We understand each other more. *What has brought about the change?* We work things out more and listen to each other more. *What's brought about change in his violence?* He has calmed down a lot and the CHANGE Men's Program worked. (Woman, Men's Program: 1037)

We are more understanding to each other. (Man, Men's Program: 114)

It [the program] helped [us] to overcome a lot of things by talking about them. [He is] More loving towards me. (Woman, Men's Program: 1075)

We have gotten to know each other better. (Woman, Men's Program: 1039)

It is important to point out that improved communication alone will not alter the levels and nature of violence and other controlling behavior or improve women's sense of well-being. Improvements in a man's ability to relate to his partner follow a greater understanding of the impact of violence and coercion and enhanced empathy. While not all these differences between the two groups reached statistically significance, the overall pattern persists across all but one of the 25 indicators of quality of life and across evaluations of the relationship showing more improvement for the Men's Program group than the Other CJ group and a worsening among the Other CJ group compared with the Men's Program group.

Reducing Conflicts

All couples sometimes argue, yet chronic conflict over a wide range of issues is a recurring feature of many of the relationships in the Violent Men Study (see Chapter 5). Seeking to end all conflict and arguments is clearly utopian, but to reduce the number and intensity of these conflicts and to enhance the possibility of arguing without endangering one's personal safety is clearly important. Three items measured changes in conflict after one year: whether the couple were "able to argue," the frequency of arguments, and their seriousness. In general, the findings show slightly under half of both groups experienced no change in being able to argue, with slightly more improvement in the Men's Program group and some worsening in the Other CJ group (Appendix B, Table B.5, sec. 5).

By contrast, the frequency and seriousness of arguments revealed a greater difference between the two groups, with one third worsening in the Other CJ group and two thirds improving in the Men's Program group. There were also improvements in the Other CJ group, but less than reported by the Men's Program women, and there was a statistically significant difference between the two groups in "serious arguments" (Appendix B, Table B.5, sec. 6). It is, of course, serious arguments that would appear to represent a greater risk of subsequent violence.

Women who experience men's violence usually learn that to argue with them, even in a mild form or with considerable justification, can be dangerous and may end with him using violence to stop what he does not want to hear. As reported earlier, many women withdraw or try to avoid arguing or attempt to reduce the intensity of arguments to avoid a violent conclusion. Thus, to increase women's ability to argue with a male partner in a less dangerous atmosphere may constitute a vast improvement on enforced silence or the near certainty of blows following dispute or debate. Increasing the ability to argue safely is probably an important aspect of the overall complex of reducing violence itself.

Able to argue with less danger (positive change)

> We can speak better now, also have arguments together without [me] being afraid. (Woman, Men's Program: 1038)

> As there is no fear of me now. We trust each other. (Man, Men's Program: 038)

> He walks out after an argument as before he would smash [the] house up then beat me up. (Woman, Men's Program: 1082)

Yet for some women, change in their ability to argue safely was not apparent and the pithy responses of two men in the Other CJ group seem to reflect the attitudes linked to frequent and intense forms of conflict and violence:

Able to discuss things; communication (negative change—the same or worse)

> *Is there something she could have done to stop you being abusive to her?* Yes. Shut up. (Man, Other CJ: 007)

> I have no violent behaviour. . . . She knew she deserved it. She does my head in [by arguing][scored out word *violent*]. (Man, Other CJ: 005)

Safety and Anger

It would be wrong to leave a discussion on quality of life without acknowledging the very real anger felt by a woman toward the man who has abused her, the sustained sense of fear of someone who has repeatedly shown himself willing and able to use violence against her, and reservations about his willingness or ability to change. It cannot and should not be assumed that because a man has remained violence free for a year the woman can or should simply forget and forgive the long history of abuse that preceded this change and the many promises so earnestly made and so quickly broken. To forget so easily and quickly is not only unlikely given women's experiences with broken promises but might also be dangerous if they leave themselves without escape plans or lose the ability to detect signs of danger. It would, of course, be most beneficial if men would change and the change became permanent, thus allowing women to safely begin to put the injuries and dangers in the past and for both to move toward a more positive future. That is the ideal, and it may indeed be reached, but it would be irresponsible of others to expect women to throw caution to the winds in what might become a precipitant move toward the positive in the face of the possibility that the man may cease to improve or even revert to his previous violent behavior.

Care must be taken with this prospect of change: care not to lose the moment to move forward to positive change and care not to lose the ability to detect the risk of violence should change not take place. For the most part, women have learned from the past that it is wise to keep a watching brief with respect to the future and this is true of the women in both groups Several women illustrate this stance in their comments about their feelings of safety:

Have you felt safer since your partner received the sanction?

[I] Still fear that he could resort sometimes to violence if he lost control, but [I] feel safe most of the time. (Woman, Men's Program: 1122)

To a certain extent, but I will always be scared. It just never leaves you. Violence is a thing not easily forgotten. I think the wives should maybe be counselled as well. (Woman, Men's Program: 1114)

No. I still fear him. (Woman, Men's Program: 1021)

No. I still think he is capable of being violent towards me and I'm still frightened of him. [*Comment*] I've answered the questions the best I can as I'm now divorced [and] the only time I see him is a Saturday which usually ends up in an argument about one thing or another. (Woman, Men's Program: 1126)

I never feel totally safe with [him]. (Woman, Other CJ: 1120)

I don't feel safe at all. (Woman, Other CJ: 1072)

No. He could get me any time he wanted. (Woman, Other CJ: 1011)

It would also be wrong to deny women an expression of legitimate anger and to allow men to avoid the opportunity to recognize one of the very real consequences of that which they have inflicted. This is not an argument for the unbridled release of women's anger or purely retributive responses but rather for a recognition that anger may well be a part of the process of change and one that women may feel free to express only after men have become less dangerous and do not expect to stop arguments with blows. The comments of the women seem to indicate that those who are now less likely to anticipate violent responses feel safer to engage in disagreements and arguments, even to express anger:

> I feel anger about all the years I had to put up with it and couldn't do anything about it. Now he knows our daughters can give a statement to police. (Woman, Other CJ: 1077)

> Although the visits and, therefore, the violence has become less, the only way I feel I will be really safe is if I move house and don't tell my neighbours where I am going so he can't find me. At the moment he is refusing to sign over the house as he is demanding capital. It makes me feel bitter as my children and I are having to uproot our lives just to feel safe and have peace of mind. (Woman, Other CJ: 1095)

Summary

The evidence on violence, controlling behaviors, and quality of life show that criminal justice sanctions can make a difference, particularly for men who successfully complete a court-mandated abuser program. Women partners who report improvements in the behavior and orientations of the men are more likely to experience positive changes in their own quality of life. While various indicators suggest that men can change, it is prudent to ask if these improvements can be maintained beyond one year. More confidence might be placed in the possibility of sustained improvement among men who have changed in a number of ways by, for example, engaging in nonviolent approaches to conflict resolution, reducing and taking responsibility for their violence and controlling behavior, improving their empathy and understanding of their partner, enhancing and improving their own self-respect, and reducing alcohol consumption.

For some, the positive changes in the quality of life represent an overall change in the nature of their daily life from one marked by violence to one free of violence. For others, there is little change or even a worsening of their quality of life as the constellation of violence remains intact or worsens. The findings show that men who have successfully completed an abuser program are more likely to have changed across the wider spectrum of the complex of factors contained in the constellation of violence, and this appears to be associated with positive improvements in the quality of life for both women and men as well as an improvement in the relationship of these couples. Let us now consider the processes whereby such change might be achieved.

8

Why Men Change

The evidence presented earlier indicates that men who have used violence against a woman partner can change both the behaviors and the orientations associated with this violence and that these changes can have an important impact on their partner's quality of life. Here, we consider the process associated with such changes. The comments of the men who have passed through the justice system and of their women partners provide some insights into the nature of the transformative process. The men and the women provided numerous comments on changes, for better and for worse, and on the prospects of a future without violence. Their written comments on the postal questionnaires reflect outcomes ranging from the complete failure of the men to eliminate their violence to the total cessation of violence. They show variation in the beliefs and attitudes associated with the use of violence, ranging from men who cannot or will not change to those who have altered both behavior and beliefs.

Overall, the data show that while all forms of intervention from the justice system have some impact on subsequent violence in the short term, those men who successfully complete an abuser program are much more likely than those who receive some other intervention from the justice system to change subsequent behavior and modify associated beliefs and, importantly, that such changes are much more likely to be sustained over a period of one year. Why might this be so? While the effect has been observed, what processes might be associated with this outcome? In addressing this question, we use the comments

provided by the men and their women partners at follow-up to construct a model of the processes of change. While based on empirical
evidence from the follow-up questionnaires, this eight-part model
must nonetheless be seen as an initial effort to conceptualize the
process of change rather than a definitive statement. While this empirically informed conceptual, or theoretical, model is developed only to
the extent that these data will allow, it has also been informed by the
work of others who have also examined the detailed processes of personal change. In turn, this model of the transformative process may
stimulate others to further investigate this process of personal change.

While the Violent Men Study suggests that sanctions seem to have
at least some short-term effect on abusive men, the reasons for this outcome and its sustainability need to be addressed as a part of providing
an explanation of the move away from violence. There may be various
reasons for changing personal behaviors and beliefs: because any form
of sanction instills fear of greater sanctions and escalating costs for the
continued use of violence; because some forms of intervention provide
an opportunity for personal reflection that may lead to personal transformation; or because they offer an environment focused on and con-
ducive to personal change. The men and women in this study reflect on
the various interventions the men received and on changes in behavior
and beliefs and the possible reasons for them. While noting that most
interventions by the justice system seemed to have at least some short-
term effect on the abusers in this study and that abuser programs seem
to have a more positive effect sustained for a longer period of time, it is
nonetheless important to stress that some men do not change whatever
the intervention and a few appear to continue in their preexisting
upward trajectory of increasing use of violence or an escalation in its
severity.

Spontaneous Reflections About Change

The men and their women partners were asked at follow-up if the
men had changed, remained the same, or become worse. They were
also asked to comment on why that might be so, and space was provided for written comments. Over 700 comments were received.[1]
Some have already been used to illustrate changes in the men's and
women's quality of life. Here, they are used to illustrate the dynamic
and multifaceted process of personal change experienced by some men
and the absence of change in others. The follow-up questions "Why?"
"How?" and "Comment" facilitated spontaneous and unique personal

Table 8.1 Positive and Negative Comments From Postal
            Questionnaires About Change Following a Criminal
            Justice Intervention

	Men's Program		Other CJ	
	Men	Women	Men	Women
Positive comments	94%	59%	29%	20%
Negative comments	6%	41%	71%	80%
TOTAL	100%	100%	100%	100%
Average number comments per person	4.8	4.4	3.8	3.6

input without the preconceived categorization of questions with a closed answer format. While it was not necessary for the men and women to provide such comments to complete the questionnaires, nonetheless hundreds of spontaneous comments were offered. On average, three to five comments were made per person, with the greatest number from men on the Men's Programs and the lowest number from women partners of men who experienced another form of intervention from the justice system. In addition to using the comments to provide specific insights into the process of personal change, we have also analyzed the comments quantitatively to show the general direction of the spontaneous statements indicating positive or negative expectations, orientations, and outcomes (see Table 8.1).

The spontaneous comments of men in the abuser programs overwhelmingly reflected a positive view that change had been achieved and a belief that it would be sustained. Ninety-four percent thought positive change had been made and were confident it would be maintained. The content of the spontaneous comments also reflected the view that changes were the result of what was learned in the men's programs and achieved through putting the lessons into practice. For this group, positive outcomes were attributed to learning rather than fear of sanctions. The comments reveal that the content of what was learned includes new attitudes; new behaviors; and a new appreciation for partners, children, and family life, as well as a transformed view of the costs and rewards of using violence. Men's Program men repeatedly reiterated the notion of personal transformation and were the most vociferous of all the groups in expressing their views, averaging 4.8 comments per person. More so than any other group, Men's Program men reflected a sense of achievement, of learning, of change, and of sustainability. While a few indicated that they had not changed and did not expect to, there were far fewer of them than among the men who experienced other criminal justice sanctions.

Comments from the women partners of Men's Program men were more mixed—with 59% spontaneously expressing positive views. The content of their comments included enthusiastic confirmations of changes in men's behavior and attitudes as well as expressions of hope for the best while maintaining a more cautious, watching orientation lest promises were broken or changes did not persist. Some partners of Men's Program men noted an absence of change in the men and a few were critical of the programs they had hoped or expected would effect this transformation. Most women, however, expressed support for such programs either because they believed them to have played an important role in changing their own partner or because they believed that such programs would help others. The majority of Men's Program women who experienced changes in a man's violent behavior also commented on changes in his use of intimidation and other forms of controlling behavior and in his more general attitudes toward women, wives, family life, and the costs of using violence. The nature of comments made by Men's Program men and by their partners were broadly similar in content. The men's comments were overwhelmingly confident about change, however, while the women's comments were divided almost evenly between those that were positive and those that were negative or expressed cautious optimism. But in general, the picture from those in the Men's Program group was more positive than negative.

In stark contrast, the spontaneous comments from men and women in the Other CJ group were overwhelmingly negative and, again, the women were even more pessimistic than the men. Of the spontaneous comments about change made by men receiving other sanctions, 71% were negative, while 80% of those made by women partners were negative. Among those who reported some form of reduction in violent behavior, both men and women usually attributed this to the threat of personal costs to the man. No mention was made of new behavior, new beliefs, new orientations, or a new life. Instead, both men and women partners commented on the lack of change and in some cases even an escalation in violence. For those in the Other CJ group reporting a reduction in violence, this was often attributed to an external threat of punishment or to the possibility of surveillance of the man's behavior backed by a belief that a price would be paid for a return to violence. That is, for those in the Other CJ group who reported some type of positive change, usually contained in the first few months after intervention but not maintained thereafter, this was attributed to various external constraints such as surveillance, costs, and punishment rather than to any type of controls brought about by the learning of new attitudes and behaviors.

Three Stories of Change

The comments of the men and women reflect three stories of change:

- Men who cannot or will not change despite the nature of intervention
- Men who engage in limited and temporary change maintained under the watchful eye of the enforcers of law and the threat of sanctions
- Men who change their violent behavior and associated attitudes and begin to regulate their own behavior

These patterns are indicative of the overall process of personal transformation and are best characterized by the comments of the men and women.

Men Who Cannot or Will Not Change

Little or No Prospect of Change

> *Do you think that this violence can be stopped?*

> I think if a man hits a woman, no matter what help they've had, I think a man who's hit a woman once will certainly do it again. (Woman, Men's Program: 1126)

> It is in the male ego and make-up. It has gone on since time began and it will go on forever more, just like wars, famine and cruelty. (Woman, Other CJ: 1130)

> No. He won't change, he doesn't want help. (Woman, Other CJ: 1072)

> No. Human relationships [are like that]. (Man, Other CJ: 060)

> No, because men are men and women are women. (Man, Other CJ: 090)

> Men think they can hit their wives to keep them in control. (Man, Other CJ: 007)

No. Not when women have the law on their side all the time and the men are always the guilty party. (Man, Other CJ: 115)

No. I think some men will never change; they are just too aggressive. (Man, Men's Program: 039)

What would prevent you [from being violent]?

Nothing. (Man, Other CJ: 007)

My death. (Man, Other CJ: 115)

A Prospect of Change Given a Different Intervention?

Can violence be stopped? No. Pressure of the life we live in and with the way our government has us living in poverty and unemployment all the time. *[Comment]* Thank you for talking to me. I feel it helped a lot. I think the court should maybe make offenders get counselling from [specific programs] or someone like you. (Man, Other CJ: 130)

Men Who Curtail Violence Only Under Surveillance or Threat (External Constraints)

Law doesn't seem to bother [him]. They would need to sentence him. *What would prevent him?* Giving him a sentence of six months. (Woman, Other CJ: 1105)

What would prevent you from being violent? Six months [in prison]. [I have] Too many charges, don't want to go to jail. (Man, Other CJ: 063)

Do not fancy the idea of prison. (Man, Other CJ: 022)

[Fines] Cost too much. (Man, Other CJ: 015)

Have you felt safer since the court outcome?

Yes, because he can't afford to be [arrested] again. (Woman, Other CJ: 1094)

I think he got a fright. (Woman, Other CJ: 1096)

Men Learning to Eliminate Their Violent Behavior (Internal Controls)

Those Who Experience Change

Do you think that this violence can be stopped? How?

[Yes] If the partners learn to love and trust each other. (Man, Men's Program: 046)

[Yes] By getting on with each other. (Man, Men's Program: 075)

[Yes] Better education on men/women's issues. (Man, Men's Program: 053)

[Yes] Education and more domestic violence groups. (Man, Men's Program: 122)

[Yes] By [men] admitting their past actions and forcing them to face up to them. (Man, Men's Program: 114)

Women Remain Cautiously Optimistic

Looking to the future, do you think that being on the Program will prevent him being violent to you again? Yes. He thinks more. Before he just blew up then thought after. *Have you felt safer since your partner was put on the Program?* Yes, because I know he won't do anything like that again. [*Comment*] [He] has changed a lot but is still drinking. I don't one hundred percent trust him yet as he still tells little lies often. He is still jealous of my friends so I don't know if that will ever change. (Woman, Men's Program: 1082)

Growing Confidence Combined With Cautious Optimism

Will the Program help prevent future violence? [Yes] Because he can't hit me. I now stand up to him. I'm not scared any more. *Have you felt safer since the Program?* Not really because if he wanted to use violence he probably would. . . . Things are not too bad in this house any more. We have seemed to sort most things out now. Well, I'll keep my fingers crossed. [The same woman comments again at Time Three, one year after interview] *Have you felt safer since your partner was put on the Program?* He's not hard any more. . . . This household is doing alright just now. Every day is a blessing that all this "carry-on" is passed with. (Woman, Men's Program: 1040)

The Process of Change

Based on the findings of the Violent Men Study, we have developed a framework for delineating the elements and processes that appear to be associated with personal change. While it is important to remember that there are those who seem to be unwilling or unable to change regardless of the nature of the intervention, it is equally important to examine more closely those who do demonstrate some form of change to better to understand this process. We theorize that the transformative process is multifaceted and unfolding and progresses loosely through stages beginning with the recognition that change is possible through learning specific techniques that can be put into practice in becoming nonviolent. Of course, others have worked on the notion of a process of personal change associated with a variety of behaviors, including alcohol abuse, gambling, smoking, and others (DiClemente & Prochaska, 1982; Prochaska & DiClemente, 1983, on stages of change for those addicted to smoking). In this respect, the concept of stages of change is not unfamiliar. While the transformative process presented here does have a starting point and involves some stages that would be expected to precede other stages, it is not a linear process with each step following the other but rather one that involves several facets that may be progressing at the same time and may, in turn, be mutually reinforcing. The transformative process for violent men is presented in Table 8.2.

Overall, the elements of personal change reflect new ways of thinking, speaking, and acting. They are the product of learning that which is new and replacing that which was previously commonplace. In delineating this process of personal change, we discuss each of the elements in turn and further reflect on them using comments of the men and women in the Violent Men Study.

1. Change Is Possible: *Shifting attitudes away from the position that change is neither possible nor desirable to considering the idea of change as a real prospect*

Individuals cannot even begin the process of personal change unless and until they come to see it as a real prospect. This necessary first step may, in fact, be one of the most difficult steps of all as it involves a profound shift in orientation from a position that previously may have been taken for granted. Of course, the realization that personal change is possible does not automatically ensure that the person proceeds through the transformative process or that it is completed successfully. It is, however, impossible for the process to begin unless this initial shift in orientation occurs. The comments used to illustrate the three stories of change show how some men and their women partners view change as an impossibility and a few men indicate that nothing can effect change except death itself. Contrary to this, others view change as possible but believe it can occur only under a changed set of circumstances or under constant surveillance (external constraints) or with crucial changes in the man himself (internal controls).

Table 8.2 The Transformative Process

---

1. CHANGE IS POSSIBLE. Thinking what was previously unthinkable.

2 MOTIVATION TO CHANGE. Desiring that which was previously unwanted.

3. WHY CHANGE? Reevaluating the costs and benefits of violence to self and others.

4. WHAT CHANGES? Transforming the self from "object" to "subject."

5. GENERAL MECHANISMS OF CHANGE. Shifting the regulation of behavior from external constraints to internal controls.

6. THE DISCOURSE. Replacing old ideas and words that support and justify violence to new ones that reject violence and acknowledge harm done to others.

7. THE MEDIUM OF CHANGE. Talking and listening; thinking and learning; practicing.

8. SPECIFIC ELEMENTS OF CHANGE. New skills and orientations.

---

2. Motivation to Change: *Individuals must be motivated to change and become ready for that process*

It is not sufficient simply to perceive personal change as possible; it is also necessary to be motivated to undertake the process of personal transformation. If any intervention is to have a real or lasting effect, the man must be motivated to change. Short of constant surveillance or permanent incarceration, it is impossible to imagine how or why a man might eliminate his violent behavior unless he is personally motivated to do so. The comments of the men and women reflect this notion:

Men With Little or No Motivation to Change

> *In the last six months, have you wanted to stop being violent to her?* No. She's my wife. (Man, Other CJ: 063)

> *Do you think that this violence can be stopped?* No, because every man thinks it's okay to hit a woman, but until he admits he has a problem himself he will carry on being violent. Then and only then will he get help. *What would prevent him from being abusive?* Admitting to himself he has a problem. No matter what anyone does, a man like mine will always feel they have the right to hit women as they feel you

are their property and they can do what they want to you. I really do
think a violent man will never change, he'll get worse. But there are
good men too—but where? (Woman, Other CJ: 1098)

[He] Won't change. (Woman, Other CJ: 1077)

Positive Motivation

[*Comment*] I think some men would benefit from the CHANGE Program more than others. It would be better than sending them all to
prison when there is a chance to change some of them. (Man, Men's
Program: 039)

[The Program] makes me try harder. (Man, Men's Program: 126)

Each time I fill in this [questionnaire] I remember what I *was* like and
how lucky I am now. You can change if you personally want to. (Man,
Men's Program: 038)

A Prospect of Change Given a Different Intervention?

Do you think that this violence can be stopped? Yes. I try by restraining myself but it is sometimes hard. There must be something medi-
cally that can be done. (Man, Other CJ: 062)

I hate any man to hit a woman but I do it myself and I don't know why
I do it. I am always sorry afterwards. (Man, Other CJ: 072)

Programs for violent men may have different effects at different
stages in the man's development or location in the transformative
process. Abuser programs may assist in the transformation of the attitudes, behaviors, and orientations of men who are ready to change.
They may bring those who are not yet ready to change deeds and words
to a stage where they begin to shift to a prestage of readiness for
change. For those completely resistant to change, any form of intervention is unlikely to have an effect. In such instances, the only form of
deterrence would seem to be the complete removal of the man from the
household, incarceration in prison, or some form of constant surveillance. Currently, there seem to be differing opinions about what proportion of abusers fall into the category of those with no prospect of
change. Some express the view that most men have little prospect of
change and only incarceration can stop the violence. Others are less
pessimistic about the possibility of personal change with respect to
this behavior and see well-designed and well-managed cognitive-
behavioral programs as a part of efforts to end the violence.

When do men become ready to change? What, if anything, can be done to help them bring themselves to this point? Edleson (1996), Miller and Rollnick (1991), and others have commented on the notion of a stage of preparation in advance of beginning the process of individual change. Based on the comments of the men and women in the Violent Men Study, the first point of readiness rarely comes from some form of personal enlightenment or awareness but rather from a personal crisis bearing the potential of costs to the man (e.g., arrest, the woman leaving, inflicting an injury of such severity that he might be punished) or because of a recognition of the effect on the woman of the injuries inflicted or the fear instilled in her or the children.

> I was crying because when I was told that [she] was in hospital, I thought I'd just about killed her and I was afraid in case she died because I'd get done for murder. (Man, Men's Programs: 038)

> *Was there any particular incident or discussion which really helped you to change your behavior or attitudes to the violence? What was it?* Yes. When I was charged [by the police]. (Man, Men's Program: 126)

> *What's brought about change in violence?* He knows now that I would leave him and take his kids away too. (Woman, Men's Program: 1082)

> *Have you felt safer since your partner was put on the program?* Yes. He knows if he continues to be violent sometimes it's a custodial sentence and he wouldn't see his kids. (Woman, Men's Program: 1042)

Earlier intervention might be useful before violence becomes habituated and the man becomes insensitive to its use and consequences. At this stage, men may feel more ambivalent and guilty about the use of violence, although this effect might be counterbalanced by the greater risk of violence among younger men and those with less commitment to a relationship. Postponing intervention not only allows time for a man to become habituated to the use of violence and accustomed to its benefits but may also provide greater opportunity for him to learn that there may be few costs associated with its use. Once this lesson has been learned, even greater effort may be required to shift him away from violence. Thus, early intervention may offer more prospect of change than a postponed intervention that allows violence to become habituated and the "rewards" to accrue to such an extent that they overshadow other reasons for giving it up.

If you think that your violence has changed in any way, what, in your opinion, has brought about this change? I'm too old. (Man, Men's Program: 089)

3. What Changes? *Shifting the schedule of costs and benefits and moving beyond the self to include the other*

Getting ready for change would seem to require a shift in awareness away from the potential benefits of violence to the costs of its continued use. While the costs are both to the man and to others, particularly the woman and their children, he begins first with a focus on himself. A change in the schedule of costs and benefits to the man himself seems to be necessary to tip the balance toward an increase in motivation to begin the process of change. For some, this may come too late or the violence may simply be too rewarding and the perceived costs too few to effect any change in the man's orientation toward its use. Past motivations to change, like New Year's resolutions, may have long been forgotten and become too distant to revive. Recent resolutions, similarly, may all too easily be broken. In addition to the perceived costs and benefits to oneself of the continued use of violence, the process of personal transformation also requires an expansion or alteration of one's concerns beyond the narrow parameters of the self to include others and the costs to them of the continued use of violence. The most obvious of these is the woman but also the children and others. It is important not only that the man recognizes that others exist and that they are important to him and are harmed by his violence but also that he is genuinely concerned to eliminate that harm.

Men who had embarked on the process of change seemed more likely to recognize that violence did have costs for others (e.g., women and their children) and that it might also have long-term costs for themselves (e.g., loss of partner and children or sanctions from the justice system or other sources). Both those in one of the abuser programs and those receiving other sanctions commented on the costs of violence but did so in different ways. Men's Program men were more likely to expand their balance sheet beyond possible costs to themselves to include harm done to others and to the possible loss of a newly revalued partner or family life. These new acknowledgments may provide important vehicles to motivate personal efforts to eliminate violence and intensify a commitment to change. This would seem to constitute an important move beyond the narrow perimeter of self-interest to a wider world that includes the well-being of others.

Benefits of Using Violence (primary focus on self)

> *What did you want to get by using violence?*
>
> To be treated right and live at home. (Man, Other CJ: 024)
>
> Silence. (Man, Other CJ: 094)
>
> I go out when I want. (Man, Other CJ: 063)
>
> [To] get on with what I want to do. (Man, Other CJ: 091)

A different view expressed primarily by men who participated in one of the abuser programs reflected the costs rather than the benefits of violence and saw costs of inflicting pain on others and costs incurred by the man himself:

Costs of Using Violence (expanding from costs to self to costs to others; developing empathy)

> I learned a lot from the Domestic Violence [Program], how to understand my partner's feelings. (Man, Men's Program: 064)
>
> *Was there any particular incident or discussion which really helped you to change your behavior or attitudes to violence?* [Learning] What it must be like for a woman living in fear. (Man, Men's Program: 122)
>
> *Looking to the future, do you think that being on the Program will prevent you being abusive to your partner again?* Yes. Put myself in [her] position. (Man, Men's Program: 117)
>
> *What would prevent future violence?* Because I know that a woman is to be respected and not abused. (Man, Men's Program: 154)
>
> *What in your opinion has brought about this change?* Seeing the heartbreak and pain for partner and family. (Man, Men's Program: 118)
>
> After being on the Program it helps you to look back at what you have done not only to your partner but others. (Man, Men's Program: 046)
>
> *Looking to the future, do you think that being on the Program will prevent you begin abusive?* Yes, because I [now] recognise the relationship we have and would not like to ever lose it again. (Man, Men's Program: 174)

Williams and Hawkins (1989) have investigated why men might change given the hypothetical possibility of arrest for domestic violence. Their survey study of a sample of the general population appears to show that when asked to speculate about the impact of an arrest and its potential deterrent effect, male respondents were most concerned about the "social stigma of one's own image," followed by family stigma and social disapproval. The least effective deterrent would be jail time and loss of job (both deemed unlikely to occur). The loss of partner had some weak effect, but the authors indicate that this may not serve as a strong deterrent because the men believe that their relationships are sufficiently robust to be sustained beyond a violent incident. The authors believe their findings have implications for an expanded version of the notion of deterrence.

By contrast, the results of the Violent Men Study show a considerable concern about criminal justice sanctions (including arrest, fines, and jail) and about the loss of a partner or children among men who have actually perpetrated violence and experienced subsequent consequences. The lived experiences of these men seem to result in reports that are at variance with those of men without such experience who are asked to speculate about potential costs. In contrast to men interviewed in Williams and Hawkins's (1989) survey, men in this study were not much concerned about stigma and the loss of one's self-image (this occurred both at interview and in the follow-up questionnaires). While both studies may help provide a more complex understanding of the notion of deterrence, they may also suggest the effects of different approaches to research questions. Although differences in the results of the two studies may reflect different sample populations—one includes a broad-based sample of men while the other includes those convicted of a violent act—the difference may arise because in the Williams and Hawkins study the men simply engaged in speculation about the hypothetical impact of arrest and potential deterrent effects while in the Violent Men Study the calculation of cost was situated in the context of the lived experiences of violent men who have actually been arrested and prosecuted and who may have lost their partner (even if only for a short period of time). While Williams and Hawkins are very careful to note that their findings are based on the speculations of the respondents, there may be a more general lesson here for others who would use such findings as though they reflected lived experience rather than a speculation about such experience.

4. What Changes? *From object to subject*

For men who manage to make positive changes, a shift appears to occur from seeing themselves as objects acted on by external events and by others to seeing themselves as subjects, making choices and taking decisions, including decisions about the use of violence. Shifting from viewing one's self as an *object* to viewing one's self as a *subject,* combined with an imagery of self expanded to include others, may constitute the difference between a man who views himself as a person creating events through purposeful action and one who is simply acted on by others. Violent men often see women as the "cause" of their violence. Such men may also view their own behavior as controlled solely by others rather than by themselves. In this case, judges, probation officers, police officers, and prison officers become the necessary vehicles of observation, surveillance, and control imposing costs for the continued use of violence. The man himself is the author of neither his violence nor its cessation. Both are deemed to be generated and sustained by others, first by the woman and then by the officials. For his part, the man views himself simply as a reacting object rather than as a decision-making subject. This provides the justifications for continued violence and offers little possibility for change that might be sustained for any length of time or outside the nexus of external surveillance and control.

Seeing Self as an Object (others responsible for the violence and for changes in one's behavior)

> *Is there something she could have done to stop you being abusive to her?* Doing things I don't want her to. (Man, Other CJ: 062)

> Yes. Stopped screaming insults at me. (Man, Other CJ: 094)

> Yes, stop being sarcastic. (Man, Other CJ: 115)

> Yes. Stop nagging. (Man, Other CJ: 058)

Acting as a Subject (responsible for one's own violence and for changes in one's behavior)

Acting as a subject requires taking charge of one's personal behavior and its transformation. Men must "own" their own behavior, including their violence. They must see their violence as a result of choices they made and options they chose and recognize that while they do, in fact, benefit from using violence it also exacts costs for themselves and others. The process of acting as a subject rather than an object requires that a man claim responsibility for his own actions rather than attributing them to others, to life's present circumstances, or to some distant and unchangeable past. The process of personal transformation requires that men recognize that they are the authors of their behavior and of any future transformation. This does not mean that the task must be undertaken alone or without assistance but that their actions are their own and the process of personal transformation cannot be obtained by others or without the man's own involvement as central. In this respect, men's programs can only assist in this transformative project. The single most important focus must, of necessity, be on the man himself as he becomes the owner of his own behavior and the author of his own fate.

> *How has the Program affected you?* A lot. Made me more responsible for my actions. (Man, Men's Program: 119)

> *Was there any particular incident or discussion which really helped you to change your behavior or attitude to the violence?* Yes. Make yourself responsible for what you do—i.e. stop saying she made me do it. (Man, Men's Program: 118)

> I now realise I am totally responsible for my own actions. (Man, Men's Program: 142)

> I know what I did was wrong and I know it won't happen again. (Man, Men's Program: 053)

The content of the men's programs evaluated in this study was structured to help men shift from seeing themselves as objects to seeing themselves as subjects—from being without responsibility for their own actions, out of control, and beyond any and all efforts to effect change to making choices, being responsible for and in control of their actions, and gaining or losing from those choices. These changes were seen a crucial part of the process of eliminating violence and affecting patterns of behavior that had the possibility of being sustained over time.

5. General Mechanisms of Change:
External constraints or internal controls?

Moving from external constraints to internal controls reflects a move from change through surveillance and control by others to change governed by the individual himself. While this involves other factors in the transformative process (the shift from benefits to costs and the move from object to subject), it is not reduced to them alone. The men in the two groups responded very differently to questions about changes they might have made as a consequence of the intervention they received from the justice system. The men in the Other CJ group noted changes in their techniques for avoiding arrest or incurring increased sanctions while the Men's Program men said they had learned new attitudes and behaviors they could use to try to avoid using violence. The men who acted relative to external constraints showed less orientation to eliminating their violent behavior and had acquired no new techniques for this task while the men who acted relative to internal controls seemed to have progressed toward new and different orientations and had acquired new techniques for achieving personal change.

Men Responding to External Constraints

> Looking to the future, do you think that the court outcome will prevent you being abusive to your partner again? Yes. Do not fancy the idea of prison. (Man, Other CJ: 065)

> *Have you felt safer since the court outcome?* Yes. He knows if he is violent to me [or the] children the Sheriff [judge] will come down hard—possible imprisonment next time. (Woman, Other CJ: 1023)

Some men did not fear sanctions nor did they see them as a deterrent:

> *Looking to the future, do you think that the court outcome will prevent you being abusive to your partner again?*

> No. The court did nothing to punish me. (Man, Other CJ: 010)

> No. Courts are not strict enough. (Man, Other CJ: 062)

> It [Fine] only has to be paid once. (Man, Other CJ: 059)

> No. I've been here [prison] before, no fears. (Man, Other CJ: 127)

Men Responding With Internal Controls

> *What aspects of the Program have been most useful to you?*

> Knowing the different forms of controlling your partner and learning how to stop. (Man, Men's Program: 108)

> Overall, it helps to change the way you think. (Man, Men's Program: 146)

External constraints and internal controls are two different routes to behavioral change. The first depends on constant vigilance and periodic displays of external authority and thus is a more tenuous and contingent route to personal change, requiring the imposition of costs in the form of punishment or feared forms of intervention to have an effect. By contrast, internal controls depend on changes within the individual (his attitudes, behaviors, orientations to others, and forms and style of communication). These changes also require serious reflections about one's self and the use of violence against others. Such changes are difficult to achieve, are inevitably painful if they are to be achieved, and must be nurtured if they are to be sustained. Such a transformative process is, nonetheless, based on a self-generated nexus of control from within the individual and, as such, is much less likely to require forms of external compulsion and constraint along with surveillance and management by others, whether from the justice system, the abused women, or kin and community. Once achieved, such changes are thus much more likely to be sustained after the police and others have gone away and the memory of the court has faded. The costs to the man of arriving at this position must inevitably involve the personal pain of realizing the true extent of the harm he has done to others, and this can never be easy, but the benefits of the successful completion of this transformative process involve an end of the behaviors that caused such harm. Transferring the locus of control from external controls to internal constraints offers the best prospect of achieving change in violence and controlling behaviors and of sustaining such change over time.

6. The Discourse

Long-held and unquestioned notions about the right to use violence against a woman partner along with the language of denying responsibility, blaming others, and minimizing the harm done constitute the fundamental elements of the discourse used by men when they talk about the violence. These need to be replaced by new notions of thinking about relationships between men and women; new notions about expectations, rights, and responsibilities; and a changed sense of self-other relationships. This involves a language describing new forms of action, understandings, and rationales.

What seems clear from the Violent Men Study is that those men who did not participate in one of the abuser programs were unlikely to adopt new ways of thinking about *their* violence, *their* responsibility, *their* notions of their partner's blameworthiness, or *their* need to change their beliefs and behavior. While a few of the men in the Other CJ group did seem to modify their violent behavior as a consequence of fear of greater sanctions, they did not change the thinking that had originally underpinned the use of violence and its rationalization. Instead, they continued to use an exculpatory language in the spontaneous comments written one year after the initial intervention. The discourse used in these later comments mirrors almost identically the words and tone of language used in the first interview. Virtually nothing in this language reflected a change in the sentiments that form the essential building blocks of the constellation of violence. The language often reflects anger and aggression and implies the potential to do harm.

Violence Is Right and the Victim Is to Blame

In the Violent Men Study, several questions elicited responses reflecting the notion that violence was right, acceptable, or justifiable, particularly under certain circumstances in which the woman was viewed by the man as causing his violence and, in a general sense, when a wife "deserved" such treatment in relation to some behavior he deemed inappropriate. Items in the follow-up questionnaires included the following: "On these occasions did you feel that you were right to be violent to her?" "Is there something *she* could have done to stop you being violent to her?" "Why were you violent to her?" "What will stop this violence?" The language of some men's responses bears all the hallmarks of justification, minimization, denial, and blame. The following man provided a text that read a bit like an automatic rifle, repeating over and over again the volleys of a discourse of violence:

> She was looking for it. . . . She needed it. . . . She nags me all the time, won't let me go out. . . . Stop nagging. . . . Keep her mouth shut. . . . She won't shut up. . . . She's my wife. . . . Stop them from nagging. . . . Let you go out more. (Man, Other CJ: 063)

Another provided the curious but not unfamiliar paradox of denying he was violent and then claiming his partner deserved his violence:

> I have no violent behavior. . . . She knew she deserved it. . . . (Man, Other CJ: 005)

Other men simply cite the verbal behavior of a woman or their attempts to negotiate as the causes of and justifications for violence.

Minimization and Denial

Much of the content of men's programs focuses on the "language of violence" in an attempt to transform these discourses and the sentiments they reflect. Such a transformation is unlikely to occur solely on the basis of a single, discrete criminal justice intervention (such as arrest). Arrest on its own does have some immediate impact and conveys a symbolical message that such behavior is viewed as wrong by one of the social institutions deemed to be responsible for conveying notions of the acceptability of various forms of behavior. It is not sufficient, however, to transform a set of personal notions and behaviors that are securely anchored in custom, belief, and habit. Even after having been arrested, charged, found guilty, and sanctioned for violence against their partner, the following men were still able to deny that violence had ever happened:

> I am not and never have been physically abusive to [her]. We only argue. (Man, Other CJ: 139)

> This was the only time I have been sent to prison for hitting a woman. I have never done it before. I have a lot of lady friends who know that I am a really nice bloke. (Man, Other CJ: 092)

Such tenacity in the face of all evidence to the contrary should not be taken as a reason that such men should simply be ignored because the quick and instant fix of an arrest alone does not bring reformation but, rather, as a clear indicator that for many men such an intervention is unlikely to have a lasting effect and something more is required. Findings from the Violent Men Study indicate that this needs to include transformations in the language of violence.

While exculpatory language was common among many men in both groups at Time 1, it had almost disappeared among Men's Program men by the point of the follow-up and had, instead, been replaced by comments reflecting new thinking about women, partners, themselves, and their violence. The new discourse reflects orientations that violence is wrong and a new and different sense of rights and responsibilities. It also includes an acknowledgment of the use of violence in the past, which forms part of the process of moving away from its use in the future. A new language develops that shows an alteration in thinking that includes more reflection by the men on their past, present, and future and provides a foundation for the beginning of new and different behavior.

New Rights, Responsibilities, and Respect

> [I now] Reflect on gains and losses [learned through the] CHANGE
> Program. (Man, Men's Program: 118)
>
> *What, in your opinion, has brought about this change?* To respect my-
> self and my wife and family. (Man, Men's Program: 038)
>
> *Please name something you do differently as a result of being on the
> Program?* Don't jump off the handle so quick, listen to partner. (Man,
> Men's Program: 151)
>
> *How much has being on the Program affected you?* It makes you re-
> spect women. (Man, Men's Program: 170)

7. The Medium(s) of Change: *Talking and listening; thinking and learning*

The process of personal transformation is effected through learning, and men have a lifetime of learning attitudes, general behaviors,
and specific techniques prior to the intervention of the justice system
and their participation in an abuser program. The sites of learning
include a variety of settings: the family, the community, education,
male culture, and the popular media. The lessons learned are varied
and often contradictory, but in the case of men who use violence the
lessons seem to form a web of orientations and reactions linked to and
used in violent events. If such behaviors and orientations can be
learned, then it seems reasonable to assume that others can also be
learned, but it would be naive to believe that this can be done easily.
What has come to seem natural, unproblematic behavior must be
rethought and redefined as problematic and recast as purposeful
action. Cognitive restructuring seems to involve explicit and self-
conscious reflections on thoughts and actions that have become so routinized that they cease to be the topic of reflection. Routinized behavior involves action requiring little thinking and even less reflection.
Redefining such actions involves raising to the level of explicit awareness thoughts and actions that have been submerged in the context of
the natural, usual, ordinary, and insignificant. Based on the comments
of the men who have successfully completed the men's programs, this
process of relearning seems to be achieved through the mediums of
talking, listening, reflecting, and practicing with the explicit intent of
replacing the old actions and orientations with those newly learned.

Men's programs undertake to educate in the familiar pedagogic
forms of lessons, interactive learning, and homework. They do not

involve one-way forms of communication from teacher to pupil or those of Sunday sermons in church, nor do they follow the unstructured free association of therapist and patient. Instead, they tread the style of focused, interactive engagement of individual men and the group in clearly delineated tasks focused on the problem and approaches to its solution. The abuser programs evaluated in the Violent Men Study, like those in the model program of Duluth and others, operated adult forms of learning based on participatory discussion and interaction in a group context where there are explicit lessons to be learned and clear goals to be achieved. The men repeatedly commented on the importance of talking to others and reflected on what they had learned, identifying new orientations, skills, and behaviors.

Learning these new lessons seems to be done through the medium of talking explicitly about the violence, controlling behaviors, and orientations to women and women partners. Men who resist changing these orientations and behaviors initially resist talking about these issues. They strongly resist any and all forms of communication about the violence and supporting beliefs. In addition, they do not want their women partner to discuss these topics with others and treat it as an offense against the man and their relationship should she break the silence he has imposed on her and on himself. Those who would change must first think the thoughts of change and then they must talk. Men who would not enter the transformative process were clear on the point of silence:

> *In the last six months, have you talked to any of these people about your violent behavior?*
>
> No. Nothing to do with them. (Man, Other CJ: 007)
>
> No, because they can't help and I don't want to talk to them. (Man, Other CJ: 127)

By contrast, the men who engaged in the transformative process came to value discussions about their violence, no matter how difficult or painful, and came to value the ability to communicate with other men in the group and with their partner. They were also less likely to try to prohibit their partner from speaking with others about the violence or to resent her doing so. While some men valued the opportunity just to talk with others, others clearly articulated the value of talking explicitly about the violence. Men in the programs were much more likely than those receiving other forms of intervention to have the opportunity to talk with others about the violence, and they valued being able to talk about the violence with other men and being able to talk about it with their partner. Asked what aspects of the program had been most useful, many men mentioned talking in the group:

> Talking openly about violent abuse. . . . Describing the violence. (Man, Men's Program: 073)

> Talking about it. (Man, Men's Program: 075)

> Talking about my behavior. (Man, Men's Program: 126)

Working in groups was particularly important and provided a context in which the violence could be discussed with other men and with group workers. Groups provided the setting where the violence could be named and the focus could be clearly directed at the offending behavior and supporting beliefs with a view to moving away from them and toward new, nonviolent orientations and behavior. Many men listed talking with other men as the aspect of the program that had been most useful to them:

> Just having someone to talk to. (Man, Other CJ: 090)

> When we had to discuss what we had done. . . . Talking with others about everyone's problems. (Man, Men's Program: 170)

> Being with other men in the same boat and being able to discuss things openly. (Man, Men's Program: 114)

Finally, and most important, they learned to talk with their partner and they recognized the value of this new or newly rediscovered form of communication:

> *What do you think has brought about this change?*

> Talking more to each other about the way we feel. (Man, Men's Program: 042)

> I like doing things with [her], e.g. even just talking. (Man, Men's Program: 038)

> I talk out problems without bottling things up now. (Man, Men's Program: 053)

For many men, the act of talking about such topics with anyone was novel and considerable value was attached to this part of the transformative process. Of course, it is not important simply to talk—without listening—or simply to talk in the old language of minimization, denial, and blame. Of importance is not simply the act of talking but also what is said, for it has the potential to enter into the dynamics of the continuation or cessation of men's violence and of increasing or decreasing women's sense of isolation or support. These men also learned to listen:

> *If you think that your violence has changed in any way, what, in your opinion, has brought about this change?* Sharing problems, listening to both sides. (Man, Men's Program: 019)

> *Please name something which you do differently as a result of being on the Program.* Listen to my partner. (Man, Men's Program: 170)

The fact of learning new values and new behaviors was both recognized and valued by those men who entered the process of personal change. They were clearly aware that they were unlikely to have been able to enter the transformative process without the assistance of others. They articulated the notion that it was they who must do the learning but were also aware that getting to the point of learning was something they were unlikely to achieve on their own.

> *Looking to the future, do you think that being on the Program will prevent you being abusive to your partner again?*

> I owe it all to the CHANGE Project. They helped me then I learned to help myself. (Man, Men's Program: 038)

> I understand my partner's views and I respect my partner more, so I must thank the Domestic Violence Program for what they have taught me. I will put it to good use. (Man, Men's Program: 064)

> Overall, it helps to change the way you think. (Man, Men's Program: 146)

> By learning new ways to cope. (Man, Men's Program: 064)

Learning to think before acting was another one of the outcomes that warranted comment by the men as a necessary part of the transformative process. In addition to forming a part of new behavior associated with the immediate act of violence, self-reflection, thinking, or self-examination may also be put to the task of examining wider issues about the relationship itself or the impact of violence on others, which should, in turn, feed back into the overall process of personal change.

> *Do you think that this violence can be stopped?* Yes. Stop drinking, start thinking. (Man, Men's Program: 089)

I now think things over more and I talk to my wife and discuss things all the time. (Man, Men's Program: 114)

[I] Think a lot more. (Man, Men's Program: 151)

I am thinking now before going into moods. (Man, Men's Program: 073)

I tend to think before action. (Man, Men's Program: 040)

8. Specific Elements of Change: *Behavioral skills and new orientations*

Talking Program Talk

The men in the Violent Men Study reflected on their newly learned attitudes and skills in various ways. Some remembered terms identified with specific techniques, such as taking time out or notions about power and control. Others modified their language, adopted new terms, and learned to call their partner by her name rather than identify her with a label such as "the wife" or a disparaging term such as "that cow, bitch, or ****." When asked to identify specific aspects of the abuser program that were most useful in helping them to change their behavior, they spontaneously mentioned substantive discussions remembered from the group sessions and listed specific activities and techniques that were taught. They noted discussions about minimization and denial and attitudes toward women and partners. The specific techniques identified as most useful included the group discussions and techniques that helped them recognize the patterns of their violence and the triggers they associated with aggression and violence. Videos, homework, and the practicing of skills were also identified as useful.

It would be fair to ask if the men in the programs have learned new attitudes and skills or if they have simply learned to use "program-speak" and to reproduce it in their comments about personal change. Two observations are of relevance here: First, while some men did remember program language, others used different terms to express what they had learned and these reflected the basic ideas and concepts that formed the core concepts of program materials; and, second, the women partners also reflected the nature of the changes in the men's behavior and orientations but, obviously, could not do so in program-speak as they had not been in one of the abuser programs and thus had no opportunity to learn a language or a set of ideas that could simply be reproduced for the researcher. Scores of written comments made at follow-up reflect the specific lessons learned in the programs. Some show new understandings and others reflect the learning of new skills. Few reflect programspeak reiterated by rote but, instead, take the form of new lessons incorporated into the everyday language and thinking of the speaker.

> *How much has being on the Program affected you? In what way?*
>
> Understanding jealousy and control. . . . I realised I was a dick head. (Man, Men's Program: 049)
>
> A lot. Made me realise I was violent. (Man, Men's Program: 126)
>
> A lot. To help you understand things. (Man, Men's Program: 075)
>
> Realising I was being emotionally violent. (Man, Men's Program: 009)
>
> Learning how violence can be interpreted. (Man, Men's Program: 174)
>
> Learning the danger signs and about time-outs. (Man, Men's Program: 146)
>
> Helps address issues and warning signs towards violence. . . . Examination of minimisation, intimidation, denial. (Man, Men's Program: 142)

The problem of excessive abuse of alcohol can be a compounding factor and can be so severe that comprehension of program content is severely hindered and thus attendance at the programs cannot be sustained. Where this was clearly a problem, the abuser programs recommended that help be sought before the man could productively engage with the material presented in the programs. A distinct focus on alcohol abuse was deemed necessary to ensure that the problem of violence was clearly addressed by the abuser program rather than simply assumed to be solved by addressing alcohol abuse. Nonetheless, the problem of alcohol abuse still needed to be addressed in the content of the programs to the extent that it compounds the problem of violence.

> *Please name something which you do differently as a result of the court outcome.* Cut down drinking, control temper, try and talk about differences. (Man, Other CJ: 115)
>
> My husband seems to be unable to deal with any pressure of any sort without lashing out verbally on whoever is around. Dealing with that pressure without alcohol seems to be the main problem. (Woman, Men's Program: 1174)

The Sustainability of Change

In the short term, men may cease or reduce their violent behavior because of costs to themselves (such as the loss of a woman or children) or fear of external constraints and punishments that might be inflicted on them by others, especially by the justice system. Or men may change because of an increase of internal controls relating to changes in attitudes about the acceptability of using violence, notions of who is responsible, an increase in empathy with the victim, and an awareness of the cost to others. But will short-term expedients become long-term changes? In terms of what is known about changes in personal behavior, those most likely to persist over the long term are those generated from internal controls rather than imposed by external constraints. This is vital for constructing the forms of intervention likely to lead to more long-term or permanent changes in violent men. As part of the process, men must be prepared to look back on past behavior as an integral element in the process of "respectful retribution." This concept is adapted from Martin Luther King, Jr.'s ideas about how one should respond to those who committed racist violence. Our adaptation is as follows: The person should be treated with respect, but the acts must be acknowledged, remembered, and condemned in the effort to ensure that they are not repeated.

Respectful Retribution (reflecting on the past to avoid its repetition in the future)

> I have learned how wrong I've been in the past. (Man, Men's Program: 053)

> The Program made me realise my faults. (Man, Men's Program: 044)

> Seeing the heartbreak and pain for partner and family. . . . Thinking about the consequences. . . . Made me think about life and family. . . . Make yourself responsible for what you do (i.e. stop saying she made me do it). . . . Makes you realise violence is no answer. Respect my partner's opinions. [Program will prevent future abuse?] because violent incidents happen in minutes but pain and heartache lasts a lot longer. (Man, Men's Program: 118)

> *Looking towards the future, do you think that being on the Program will prevent you being abusive to your partner again?* Yes. I just stop and think about my past and what happened. (Man, Men's Program: 046)

What would prevent you from being violent again? I can now remember always what I did to [her], that's enough. I don't want to forget. (Man, Men's Program: 146)

Note

1. The spontaneous comments used here are from the postal questionnaires returned by the men and women at Times 2 and 3; the majority were obtained at Time 3.

9

The Challenge

The challenge is twofold. Seeking an effective and sustainable solution to the problem of men's violence against intimate partners involves recognizing the issue and addressing it is a problem. This cannot be undertaken without including concerted efforts to engage violent men. Seeking a solution must, of necessity, address the source of the problem—men's violence—and the consequence of such acts of violence—harm to women partners. It must also address the wider social conditions in which such behavior emerges and continues.

It is clear from the outset that assistance and support must be provided for women who have been the victims of violence. In modern industrial societies, this involves agencies of the state and community as well as the traditional supports from friends and kin. For over a quarter of a century, such efforts have, for the most part, been undertaken by activists in the women's movement, who have provided refuge or shelter to women escaping from violent men and who have spearheaded what is, in effect, an international movement to recognize and effectively respond to this problem. It is this work that truly began what can now be seen as a new phase in the long history of "wife beating," a phase that has taken the fundamental step of departure away from social tolerance and acceptance to unequivocal rejection. This first, fundamental, and radical step has served as an essential starting point for launching thousands, if not tens of thousands, of local campaigns, plans of action, and support services for abused women. At the same time, creative efforts have been put into the essential task of educating the general public about the nature, extent, and consequences of this form of violence with an eye to ending its toleration in the wider society. In addition, efforts have focused on educating the next generation of young people about relations between the sexes with an eye to fostering nonviolent relationships in their adult lives. There has also been a sustained engagement with various aspects of law and law enforcement, from campaigns to make and change laws to those focused on their enforcement by police and in the courts. These efforts have focused on the treatment of victims of violence who seek assistance through the law and effective responses to those who break the law through the perpetration of violence. All of these efforts form the overall complement of action and activities essential to addressing the complex issue of violence against women.

Violence against women in marriage or marriage-like relationships will not be stopped unless and until the men who use this violence cease to do so. While some women may escape from violent men, it is unlikely, although not impossible, that the man will cease to use violence and enter his next relationship as a changed person posing no threat to his new partner. Instead of an end to violence facilitated through an end to the relationship in which it occurred, it is likely that a new violent relationship will be formed and another woman will be victimized. In short, no serious effort to stop domestic violence can be made that does not include concerted efforts to stop it at its source, with the man who is its perpetrator and will very likely continue to be its perpetuator. It is here that the justice system comes into play and has a positive role.

With its focus on acts of violence, on the unacceptability of such acts, and on the perpetrators of such acts, the justice system has a complex and vital role to play both in real and in symbolic terms not only for the individuals directly concerned but also for the society at large. In many, if not most, societies, law and law enforcement play an important role in the daily lives of some individuals and in the overall fabric of the entire society. In general, theoretical or symbolic terms, the law represents what a given society has deemed to be right or wrong, good or bad, acceptable or unacceptable. Overall, its operation illustrates to the society as a whole which behaviors will or will not be treated seriously and will or will not be tolerated by the institution that adjudicates the social rules of tolerable behavior. If an institution charged with this symbolic role acts in such a fashion as to illustrate to everyone that while many forms of violence are deemed to be wrong and will be treated accordingly, the violent abuse of a wife or intimate partner is not so defined or treated, then we have all received a pragmatic lesson in what really counts and what is truly valued. In this sense, the justice system forms an important part of the overall context in which this form of violence is deemed important or unimportant and is, in effect, tolerated or condoned. The symbolic lessons for the public at large and for the next generation may be a continuation of the long, historical legacy of social and legal acceptance or tolerance of the use of violence against wives or the lessons may constitute a clear break with that legacy and form a vital part of the unequivocal rejection of this form of violence. Either way, it cannot be argued that the actions of law and law enforcement have no wider place or meaning beyond affecting those directly subject to its interventions.

Obviously, law and law enforcement have a direct effect on those who are processed through its various systems. Here, the very real, material effects of such interventions have an impact, for better or for worse, on the lives of the men who perpetrate this violence, on the women who are abused, on the children who live in this environment and may witness both the violence and the interventions of the police and courts. They also have a material effect, albeit less direct, on relatives, neighbors, and the immediate community. For those most directly involved, the role of law and law enforcement is both real and material in nature as well as symbolic and educative. There are consequences and lessons for all as a result of the intervention of the justice system. The man who uses violence may feel more or less justified in its use and more or less confident about its subsequent use with respect to possible costs to himself. The woman who has been abused may feel more or less vulnerable to future attack and more or less confident in her belief that this behavior is wrong and should not occur, and that someone will assist with putting an end to it. The children watch and learn. They may learn the negative lessons embodied in the past acceptance by those in authority of the abuse of a wife or they may learn the more positive lessons embodied in the radical departure from that past, with clear and complete rejection of the use of violence against a woman partner.

In both material and symbolic terms, the justice system plays a crucial role in the continuation or cessation of this form of violence. Its interventions embody the symbolic messages of right and wrong and contain the potential for the real or material effects of surveillance, management, and control with the implication of some form of costs to the perpetrator for the continued use of violence. Responses from the justice system have varied, ranging from a legacy of almost complete indifference and inaction to singular forms of intervention, such as arrest on its own with no subsequent action, incorporating an implicit belief that this act alone would somehow solve the problem. More recently, new reactions have involved the justice system accepting greater responsibility for its role in responding to men who use violence against an intimate partner, including clear and proactive policies of arrest and improved responses to the victims who report violence and thereby seek their assistance. In some locations, this has been further augmented with sentencing for violent abuse expanded to include programs for abusers specifically designed to reflect the nature of the problem based on a foundation of knowledge about this particular form of violence.

The state of knowledge about this phenomenon, whether the age-old problem of "wife beating" or the modern concept of "woman abuse," is by no means complete but has grown alongside, and sometimes within, the wider social movement seeking recognition and rectification of this problem. Much has been learned from the scholarship that began in the 1970s and continues today. While much remains to be learned, some important points can be made about the nature and extent of this form of violence and about the dynamics of how it emerges and continues. Knowledge about the phenomenon comes from a wide variety of sources, including national and local victim surveys, police and court records, homicide data, and numerous qualitative studies. Both quantitative and qualitative data have been used to provide fuller knowledge about the nature and extent of the violence and to examine in detail the nature of violent events and the various contexts in which they occur.

This wider body of knowledge, as well as the findings from the Violent Men Study, show that violence between intimate partners is asymmetrical in nature, with men as the usual perpetrators and women the usual victims. The sources of conflict that most commonly lead to arguments and violent events revolve around the more general, recurring themes of jealousy and possessiveness, domestic work and service, and male authority along with specific issues relating to money, children, sex, and alcohol. Notions of the man's sense of ownership and control of his woman, his expectations of domestic and sexual service from her, and his authority over her constitute the foundations of a relationship in which he has authority over her and becomes the adjudicator of the work and routines of her daily life. It is in these capacities that he judges her labors and controls her behavior in the domestic arena. Violations, real or perceived, are, from his perspective, justly punished in a variety of ways, including the use of violence. Traditional concepts about the proper role and behavior of a wife in relation to her husband serve as a backdrop to a complex of behaviors and orientations that give rise to the conditions in which violence is used. Deprivation, poverty, and unemployment often intensify conflicts of interests between partners, and the excessive use of alcohol exacerbates such situations and appears to be a factor in some violent outcomes. Rationalizations of and justifications for violence are an integral part of the problem. Men habitually blame women for their use of violence against them and thereby justify the use of violence against someone who "deserved" it. They minimize the nature of the violence used and the consequences of the pain and injuries inflicted. They selectively forget or fail to recognize much of what occurs, and men's and women's differential accounts of violent events attest to these differences.

The findings of the Violent Men Study extend this body of knowledge by examining in detail the orientations and attitudes of men who use violence and by comparing the accounts of perpetrators of violence and women who have been abused. In the Violent Men Study, we have identified a constellation of violence that includes not only violent acts and injuries but also other forms of controlling and intimidating behaviors. The findings from this study show that acts of physical violence along with other forms of controlling behavior and intimidation form integral and inseparable parts of a constellation, and this has implications for how we define and theorize the phenomenon of violence against women and, thus, how we address the question of its elimination. These findings show that changes in one part of the constellation necessarily involve changes in the other, with a strong connection between violent acts and controlling and intimidating acts forming a complex or cluster of behaviors that are used in conjunction with one another as a part of the overall pattern of abuse. In turn, these behaviors also decline together, suggesting that when violence ceases, controlling and intimidating acts decline, although they are not completely eliminated. This finding seriously challenges the popular although unstudied notion that men who cease to use physical violence simply replace it with other acts of intimidation and terror. Instead, the obverse was found, and this would seem to provide further insight into the phenomenon of this form of violence and implications for how we theorize about its nature and dynamics. This finding also challenges the popular notion that the violence is merely a product of generalized stressful situations leading to outbursts of anger and violence that will be resolved simply by relieving the source of stress or learning to manage anger. While stress and anger may be a part of some violent relationships or events, they are neither the sole source nor the solution to this particular problem.

Abuser programs have been operating in the United States for over two decades. In the beginning, many were inspired by and linked to the shelter movement through overlapping ideals and sometimes through organizational structures. The knowledge and achievements of the battered women's movement fueled the development of efforts to confront violent men. In their most developed form, men's programs are embedded in a wider network of community and government action. The program in Duluth, Minnesota, has served as an influential and successful model of such an approach, with agencies of the state (police, courts, and social services), women's groups, and men's programs working toward agreed-on goals aimed at providing support and protection for women while holding men responsible for their violence and working with them to bring it to an end. The overall aim is not just the transformation of individuals but also the transformation of the institutional, organizational, and community frameworks of response.

Many of these programs, like the two considered in the Violent Men Study, are profeminist in their ideals and educational in their format. Instead of a traditional therapist-client relationship, the approach is closer to that of teacher-pupil, with a pedagogical format, albeit one that is augmented with many of the techniques of counseling. These programs include group work and role playing meant to be two way, with program workers communicating disapproval of the violence while at the same time providing a generally supportive context in which abusive men can begin to learn new ways of thinking and acting. For their part, the men are generally mandated to attend such programs. They may be socially mandated by an abused woman, who threatens to leave if the man does not stop beating her, or through the legal system, which mandates attendance for men found guilty of using violence against a woman partner. In the Violent Men Study, all the men were legally mandated. Once in the abuser program, men are urged to talk about their violent behavior and associated beliefs in order to begin the transformative process of taking responsibility for their own behavior and for its elimination. The terms "feminist" or "profeminist" signify that such programs consider violence against women to be an issue of gender power and domination. While some abuser programs are run on different principles and by those with little knowledge of the gendered nature of this form of violence, it is our contention that an understanding of the gendered nature of this form of violence is essential to the design and development of programs that are likely to fit the phenomenon and therefore offer interventions with greater prospects of change and of change that is sustainable over time.

The Violent Men Study was designed to consider the effect of various forms of criminal justice interventions on the behavior of men found guilty of using violence against their woman partner, specifically court-mandated abuser programs and other more traditional sanctions. To do this, it was necessary to design a study that provided the best possible "fit" between the phenomenon of violence that is the topic or goal or focus of change, the criminal justice intervention meant to provide a vehicle or means of change, and the research meant to evaluate the impact of the various forms of intervention. This requires a fit between all three. That is, the research must be both theoretically informed and embedded in empirical evidence about the phenomenon of violence that is to be changed by the intervention, and in turn it must consider the specific aspects of the intervention as they relate to that phenomenon. For the research to contribute to the transformative project, this three-way fit is essential.

The results of the Violent Men Study strongly suggest that criminal justice-based profeminist, cognitive-behavioral programs are more likely than other types of criminal justice interventions to affect the constellation of violence. The findings show that all forms of criminal justice intervention have some immediate effect on acts of repeat victimization, particularly in the first 3 months after intervention. But the men who have successfully completed an abuser program are more likely to eliminate their violent behavior in the short term, and this change is more likely to be sustained one year after the intervention. One year after intervention, men who participated in one of the abuser programs were significantly more likely than men sanctioned in other ways to have reduced their violence and controlling behaviors. In addition, women partners of men in the abuser programs were more likely to report an improvement in the men's associated beliefs and orientations, in their relationship, and in their own quality of life. Both qualitative and quantitative data were used to provide evidence about the patterning of this violence and about the dynamic processes of its development and progression as well as the process of its elimination. Several indices were developed to measure various facets of the constellation of violence: the Violence Assessment Index (VAI), the Injury Assessment Index (IAI), the Controlling Behavior Index (CBI), and the Quality of Life Index (QLI) for men and for women. These have been validated and provide measurement tools for further studies of the constellation of violence and the quality of life of violent men and the women they abuse.

The study reported in *Changing Violent Men* is part of a growing body of research that points to the utility of cognitive-behavioral programs in the treatment of abusive men. While earlier studies suffered from a number of limitations that led to serious questions about their validity, more recent work in the United States and Canada using quasi-experimental, comparative designs suggests that men's programs can lead to reductions in violent behavior. More broadly, evaluations of cognitive behavioral programs for various types of offenders, including sex offenders, suggest that this approach can have an effect on subsequent offending (Andrews et al., 1990; Gendreau, Cullen, & Bonta, 1994; Marshall & Eccles, 1991). This growing body of evidence indicates that the most effective interventions focus on offending behavior and associated beliefs and attitudes and are delivered in a structured group format. Successful programs, like the ones studied here, aim to improve internal control, develop social skills, increase the critical reasoning associated with the offending behavior, establish reasoned methods for solving problems, and enhance insights into the consequences for victims (empathy). Unstructured programs targeting general mental heath problems such as self-esteem or those narrowly focusing on emotions such as anger appear less likely to bring about sustainable change. Of course, all interventions benefit from the support and dedicated work of energetic staff.

But do abuser programs work equally well for all men? Findings from the Violent Men Study suggest that men who are married and employed are more likely to succeed than men who are younger, unemployed, and in non-state-sanctioned relationships. Curiously, the nature and number of previous convictions did not appear to be related to subsequent success or failure, and many of the men who succeeded were those who could be described as medium to high risk based on their previous criminal justice record. Why might this be so? Intuitively, as we have previously argued, it might be thought that younger men with minimal offending careers would be easier to change. Furthermore, it has been argued that younger men ought to be less habituated to violent reactions and less committed to the other components of the constellation of violence than their older counterparts. While older men may have more convictions for various types of offenses, including violence against their partner, such experiences may eventually begin to create a point of crisis, heightening introspection as these men more seriously contemplate the potential loss of both partner and children and the possibility of an escalation in sanctions. Older men may become more reflective and may have begun the process of contemplating their own behavior and the circumstances they have created for their partner and children. Thus, they may be ready to start the process of personal transformation necessary to end their violence.

Certainly, the general criminological literature suggests that maturation is one of the important pathways out of a career of crime.

In addition to age and maturation, other factors seem to be relevant. Research shows that various forms of social and economic attachments that provide sources of involvement and control may reduce the likelihood of various types of criminal behavior, including domestic violence (Fagan, 1992, 1993; Lackey & Williams, 1995). Following from this, it would be reasonable to speculate that the relatively greater success of men who are employed and married may be associated with these attachments. Thus, it may be that various forms of embeddedness in the family and the wider economy lead to stronger commitments to the relationship and provide additional means of support for the man and the woman as well as various other forms of observation, regulation, and control. This may also mean that men have a greater stake in the relationship, and harm done to it or its loss constitutes a greater cost to them. Employment not only has the potential to embed men in the wider economy and in the family itself, with the potential for greater control, it may also reduce the financial deprivations often associated with conflicts and violence. But the implications of these findings are not that because younger, unemployed men appear to be less amenable to change they should be ignored or simply allowed to continue. Instead, these factors should be defined as indicators of high risk of reoffending and incorporated into responses to them both in the criminal justice system and in abuser programs.

Despite the circumstances or characteristics of individual men and their potential for change, abuser programs cannot have any effect unless men participate in them. This means there must be mechanisms to get men in abuser programs and to continue their participation through the entire program. Accumulating experience and research suggests that while some men may voluntarily start an abuser program, the vast majority are unlikely to continue to participate once the immediate crisis has passed. Research suggests that men who are mandated by the courts are more likely to begin and to complete an abuser program than those who volunteer. In the Violent Men Study, most of the men in the abuser program had not previously sought help for their violent behavior and said that without arrest and prosecution they would not have begun to address this problem.

Efforts to change violent men must incorporate reactions that involve costs for the continued use of violence and place the men in a nexus of control and surveillance while they work to change their behavior. In the most general sense, this policy is also supported by anthropological evidence, which shows that kinship societies with low levels of violence against women are those in which there is a low tolerance of such behavior accompanied by various forms of control of potential perpetrators and costs for the perpetration of such acts. Such societies also contain supports and sanctuaries for women who are abused. In industrial, state societies, these same mechanisms are likely to operate in a somewhat different manner with agencies of the state and the community playing a crucial role in the transformative process (Hanson & Whitman, 1995). Both the justice system and court-mandated abuser programs contribute to this function by bringing men into a system that contains these mechanisms, first through arrest and prosecution and then through weekly attendance in the program, which involves monitoring of behavior in a form of social control and social surveillance. This monitoring occurs at the same time as the men work to change themselves to the end that none of these measures should be needed as they become the monitors of their own behavior.

While abuser programs are a vital part of the overall societal response to violence against women in the home, they certainly cannot be the only part, and numerous other agencies need to be involved in constructing an overall approach to responding effectively to men who already use violence; to the needs of women who are abused; and to the children who make up the next generation of adults, some of whom will become the next group of abusers and abused unless and until concerted efforts are focused clearly on the cessation of this violence. Whether undertaken by agencies of the state, the community, education, the media, or others, all responses should be carefully examined with an eye to considering the extent to which they are simply oriented to tending to the inevitable rather than contributing to the transformative project of ending violence against women in the home.

Appendix A

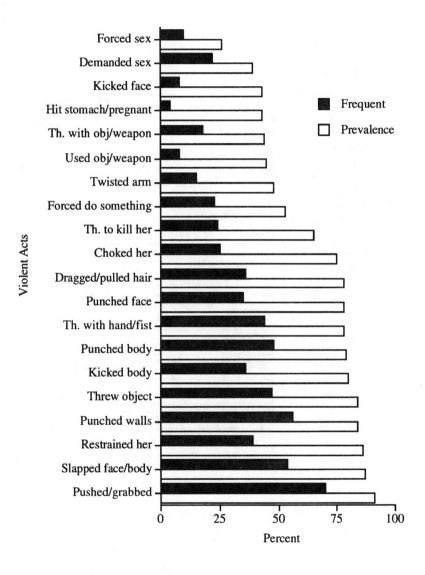

Figure A.1: Prevalence (at least once) and Frequent (more than 5 times in a typical year) Violence (reports of women Time 1)

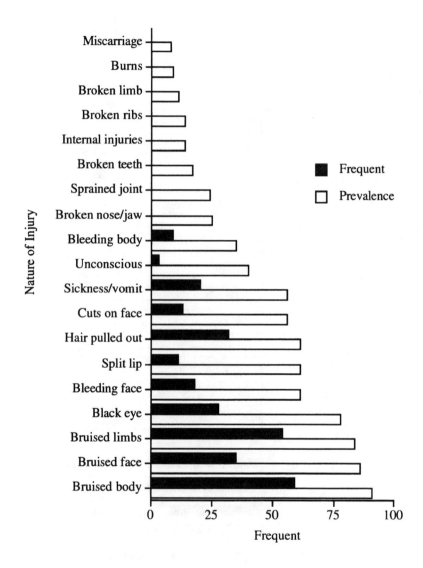

Figure A.2: Prevalence (at least once) and Frequent (more than 5 times in a typical year) Injuries (reports of women Time 1)

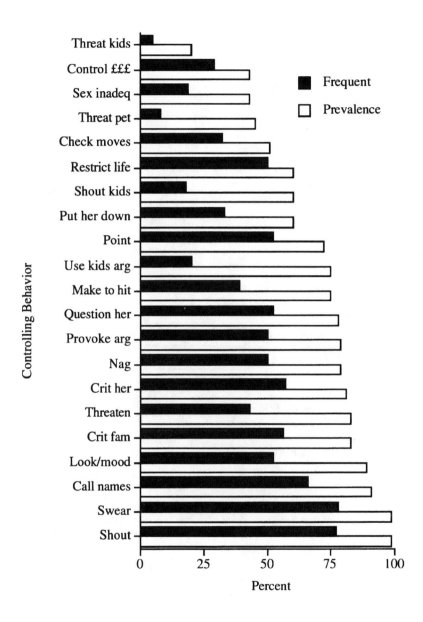

Figure A.3: Prevalence (at least once) and Frequent (more than 5 times in a typical year) Controlling Behaviors (reports of women Time 1)

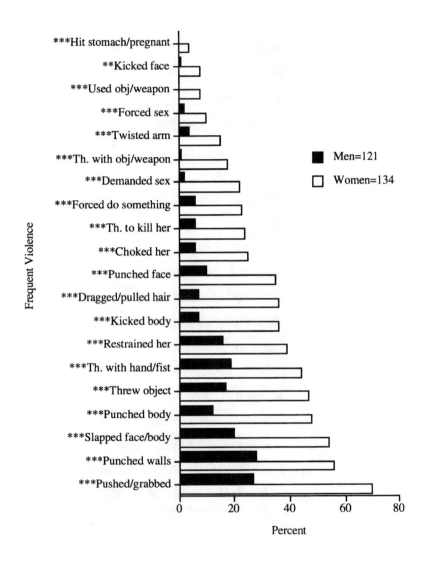

Figure A.4: Reports of Frequent Violence (more than 5 times in a typical year) Compared (men and women)

p<.01, p<*.001.

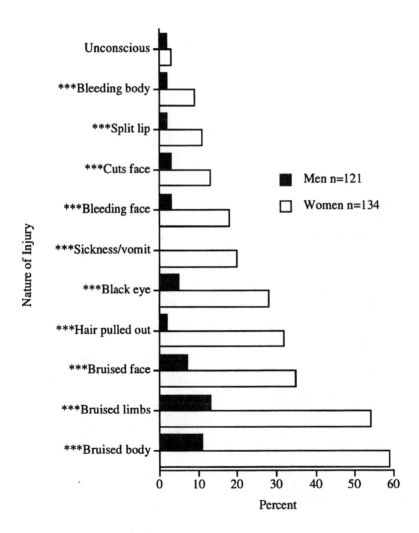

Figure A.5: Reports of Frequent Injuries (more than 5 times in a typical year) Compared (men and women)
***p < .001.

Appendix B

Table B.1 Comparison of Men's Program Group and Other
CJ Group Men on Individual and Background
Characteristics (modal categories and statistically
significant differences)

Personal Characteristics	*Modal Categories*
Caretakers when children	Both natural parents
Average age	32
Education	No qualification
Father's employment	Skilled manual
Employment status**	Unemployed (more evident in Other CJ)
Time unemployed	1 month to 2 years

Current Relationships	
Marital status***	Men's Prog. = Married/ Other CJ = cohabiting
Length of relationship	1 to 5 years
Man's relationship to children	Natural father to all
Number of children	1 to 2
Man's perception of quality of rel.	Good to very good
Man's perception of sex life	Good to very good
Argue	Often

Violence in Family of Origin	
Physical chastisement as a child:	
By father	Sometimes/often
Seriousness	Serious/very serious
By mother	Never
Seriousness	Not at all serious
Hit unfairly as a child	Never
Hit too much when child	Never (one quarter often/always)
Sex abuse as a child	Never

Father's Violence Toward Mother	
Frequency of violence	Never
Seriousness of father's violence	Three quarter Men's Prog. men = very serious/one third Other CJ men = very serious
Witnessed father's violence to m.	Sometimes/often

Previous Contact With Criminal Justice	
Number of previous convictions	2 to 5
Nature of previous convictions	Assault partner 30%, assault others 45%
Number of previous police interventions for domestic violence	1 to 4 incidents
Previous arrests for domestic violence	1 to 4 times

NOTE: **$p < .01$; *** $p < .0001$.

190

Table B.2 Results of Applying Cronbach's Alpha to the Violence Assessment Index (VAI)

Violence Assessment Index Items	Corrected Item-Total Correlation (21 items)	Corrected Item-Total Correlation (17 items)
Punched her on the body, arms or legs	.7634	.7779
Kicked her on the body, arms or legs	.7481	.7540
Pushed, grabbed or shoved her	.7328	.7431
Dragged her or pulled her hair	.7117	.7142
Punched her in the face	.6589	.6595
Restrained her from moving/leaving the room	.6510	.6569
Slapped her on face, body, arms or legs	.6223	.6441
Choked her or held hand over her mouth	.6061	.6092
Tried to strangle, burn or drown her	.6026	.6092
Threw things at her or about room	.5917	.6009
Threatened to kill her	.5885	.5837
Punched or kicked the walls/furniture	.5679	.5851
Twisted her arm	.5572	.5570
Threatened her with an object or weapon	.5517	.5381
Used an object to hurt her	.5238	.5244
Kicked her in the face	.5189	.5182
Forced her to do something against her will	.4747	
Demanded sex when she didn't want it [a]	.4455	
Forced her to have sex[a]	.4453	
Kicked/punched her in stomach when pregnant	.4430	
Number of cases:	251	251
Cronbach's Alpha	.9274[b]	.9272[b]

NOTES: a. It is important to note that the sexual coercion and violence items did not correlate highly with the physical violence items. We will explore the implications of this finding in future publications.

b. Carmines and Zeller (1979, p. 51) suggest that a set of items scoring less than .80 cannot be considered internally consistent and should not be used for summary purposes. Employing this criterion the indices used in this study seem highly consistent, although the larger the number of items the potentially higher the alphas achieved. It is customary to delete items from calculations to conduct a more stringent test of internal reliability. In this study, items were deleted from indices because they either failed to reach our minimum level of specific interitem correlation of .50 or because, in retrospect, they seemed not to fit theoretical criteria for inclusion (see Chapter 4), although this was only the case in the VAI. Nine items were dropped from the initial 26 of the VAI inventory: Four were eliminated because they failed to reach the minimal level of .50 and another five were removed because they involved nonphysical acts—shouted and screamed at her—or aggressive acts directed at others, such as "shouted at or threatened the kids" (this sort of item was initially included to make the inventory more palatable to men during interview). The final VAI index includes 17 items, the derived IAI includes 11 items out of the initial 21, and the final CBI index includes 16 out of the initial 20 items. Deletion of items had almost no affect on the achieved alphas.

Table B.3 Results of Applying Cronbach's Alpha to the Injury
Assessment Index (IAI)

Injury Assessment Index Items	Corrected Item-Total Correlation (21 items)	Corrected Item-Total Correlation (11 items)
Bruises on her body	.7712	.7773
Bruises on her face	.7400	.7523
Bruises on her arms or legs	.7098	.7246
Black eye	.7085	.7091
Bleeding on any part of the face	.6673	.6718
Cuts on her face	.6567	.6523
Hair pulled out	.6536	.6403
Cuts on her arms or legs	.6482	.6636
Bleeding on body, arms or legs	.6285	.6142
Split lip	.6170	.6087
Cuts anywhere on body	.5469	.5576
Sickness or vomiting	.4908	
Blackout or unconsciousness	.4651	
Broken ribs	.3792	
Broken nose, jaw or cheekbone	.3572	
Sprained wrist or ankle	.3549	
Lost or broken teeth	.3251	
Broken arm or leg	.2549	
Internal injury	.2366	
Burns anywhere on face/body	.2339	
Miscarriage	.2250	
Number of cases	250	253
Cronbach's alpha	.9006	.9124

Table B.4 Results of Applying Cronbach's Alpha to the Controlling Behavior Index (CBI)

Controlling Behavior Index Items	Corrected Item-Total Correlation (20 items)	Corrected Item-Total Correlation (16 items)
Try to provoke an argument	.6781	.6804
Have a certain look/mood	.6483	.6260
Restrict her social life	.6394	.6149
Threaten her	.6032	.5810
Criticized her	.6009	.6195
Point at her	.5975	.6140
Call her names	.5810	.5971
Swear at her	.5799	.6116
Make to hit, without doing so	.5793	.5857
Nag her	.5685	.5357
Put her down in front of others	.5467	.5273
Use kids in argument against her	.5304	.5019
Shout at her	.5295	.5543
Make her feel sexually inadequate	.5234	.5157
Question her about her activities	.5199	.5197
Criticized her friends and family	.5174	.5470
Deliberately keep her short of money	.4824	
Check her movements	.4587	
Threaten to hurt the children[a]	.3173	
Shout at the children[a]	.3017	
Number of cases	194	212
Cronbach's alpha	.9030	.9007

NOTES: Ns = 122 men and 134 women.

a. Not only did the items on aggression toward children fail to correlate with other items on the Controlling Behavior Index, but very few women reported that their partner engaged in aggressive acts toward their children.

Table B.5 Changes in Quality of Life and Evaluation of
Relationship: Comparisons of Other CJ and Men's
Program Groups One Year After Interview (women's
assessments in percentages)

Quality of Life Index (QLI)	Change in Behavior/Orientation After One Year					
	Worse		Same		Improved	
	OCJ	Prog.	OCJ	Prog.	OCJ	Prog.
1. Men's Orientation to Violence						
Man likely to use violence	20	5	13	19	67	76
Man threatens woman	18	7	24	27	59	67
Man wants to stop violence	23	5	28	24	49	71
Man responsible for own violence*	34	20	41	25	25	55
2. Related Behaviors and Men's Emotional Well-being						
Man selfish**	42	10	37	38	20	52
Man controls temper	39	10	30	19	32	71
Man controls drinking**	39	10	33	43	28	48
Man happy**	34	5	41	43	24	52
3. Associated Attitudes/Orientations to His Woman Partner						
Man restricts woman	17	5	26	15	57	80
Man understands woman	50	18	20	45	30	36
Man aware of woman's feelings**	35	10	37	33	28	57
Man sees woman's point of view**	57	19	27	22	19	57
Man respects woman**	49	25	38	25	13	50
4. Women's Sense of Well-being						
Woman frightened	20	10	30	45	50	45
Woman feels self-respect	9	5	33	40	58	55
Woman relaxed	32	10	18	29	50	62
Woman happy	24	10	22	19	55	71
5. Relationship						
Couple able to argue	31	19	44	43	24	38
Couple discuss/talk	57	19	14	24	29	57
Couple like time together**	64	29	18	19	18	52
Couple able to have a laugh***	53	14	27	29	20	57
6. Items additional to the QLI						
Frequency of arguments	33	17	14	22	53	61
Serious arguments**	32	6	30	25	39	69
How well getting on*	49	11	22	28	30	61
Evaluate relationship**	43	12	22	12	35	76

NOTE: *p < .05, **p < .01, ***p < .001.

References

Adams, D. (1988). Treatment models for men who batter: A profeminist analysis. In K. Yllö & M. Bogard (Eds.), *Feminist perspectives on wife abuse* (pp. 176-199). Newbury Park, CA: Sage.

Andrews, B., & Brown, G. W. (1988). Marital violence in the community: A biographical approach. *British Journal of Psychiatry, 153,* 305-312.

Andrews, D., Zinger, I., Hoge, R. D., Bonta, J., Gendreau, P., & Cullen, F. T. (1990). Does correctional treatment work? A clinically relevant and psychologically informed meta-analysis. *Criminology, 28,* 369-404.

Barron, J. (1990). *Not worth the paper . . . ?: The effectiveness of legal protection for women and children experiencing domestic violence.* Bristol, UK: Women's Aid Federation England.

Berk, R. A., Campbell, A., Klap, R., & Western, B. (1992, October). The deterrent effect of arrest in incidents of domestic violence: A Bayesian analysis of four field experiments. *American Sociological Review, 57,* 698-708.

Berk, R., & Newton, P. (1985, April). Does arrest really deter wife battery? An effort to replicate the findings of the Minneapolis spouse abuse experiment. *American Sociological Review, 50,* 253-262.

Berk, R., Smyth, G., & Sherman, L. W. (1988). When random assignment fails: Some lessons from the Minneapolis spouse abuse experiment. *Journal of Quantitative Criminology, 4,* 209-223.

Bersani, C., Chen, H. J., & Denton, R. (1988). Spouse abusers and court-mandated treatment. *Crime and Justice, 11,* 43-59.

Bowker, L. H. (1983). *Beating wife beating.* Lexington, MA: Lexington.

Bowling, A. (1995). What things are important in people's lives? A survey of the public's judgements to inform scales of health related quality of life. *Social Science and Medicine, 10,* 1447-1462.

Bowling, A. (1997). *Research methods in health: Investigating health and health services.* Philadelphia: Open University Press.

Buel, S. M. (1988). Mandatory arrest for domestic violence. *Harvard Women's Law Journal, 11,* 213-226.

Burns, N., Meredith, C., & Paquette, C. (1991). *Treatment programs for men who batter: A Review of the evidence of their success.* Ontario: Abt Associates of Canada.

Busch, R. (1994). Don't throw bouquets at me . . . (judges) will say we're in love: An analysis of New Zealand judges' attitudes towards domestic violence. In J. Stubbs (Ed.), *Women, male violence and the law* (Institute of Criminology Monograph Series, No. 6, pp. 104-146). Sydney: Sydney University Law School.

Buzawa, E., & Buzawa, C. (Eds.). (1992). *Domestic violence: The changing criminal justice response.* Westport, CT: Auburn House.

Campbell, J. C. (1989). Women's responses to sexual abuse in intimate relationships. *Health Care for Women International, 10,* 335-346.

Campbell, J. C. (1992). "If I can't have you, no one can": Power and control in homicide of female partners. In J. Radford & D. E. H. Russell (Eds.), *Femicide: The politics of woman killing* (pp. 99-113). New York: Twayne.

Campbell, J. C., & Humphreys, J. C. (1993). *Nursing care for survivors of family violence.* Newbury Park, CA: Sage.

Campbell, J. C., McKenna, L. S., Torres, S., Sheridan, D., & Landburger, K. (1992). Nursing care of abused women. In J. C. Campbell & J. Humphreys (Eds.), *Nursing care of survivors of family violence* (pp. 248-289). Boston: Mosby.

Campbell, D. T., & Stanley, J. C. (1963). *Experimental and quasi-experimental designs for research.* Chicago: Rand McNally.

Cantoni, L. (1981). Clinical issues in domestic violence. *Social Casework, 62,* 3-12.

Carmines, E. G., & Zeller, R. A. (1979). *Reliability and validity assessment* (Quantitative Applications in the Social Sciences, vol. 17). Beverly Hills, CA: Sage.

Chagnon, N. A. (1983). *Yanomamö: The fierce people* (3rd ed.). New York: Holt, Rinehart & Winston.

CHANGE. (1994, March 15-17). *Conference report.* (Available from author, University of Stirling, Stirling FK9 4LA)

CHANGE. (n.d.). *Information leaflet for men.* (Available from author, University of Stirling, Stirling FK9 4LA)

CHANGE. (n.d.). *Information leaflet for women.* (Available from author, University of Stirling, Stirling FK9 4LA)

CHANGE. (n.d.). [Program materials]. (Available from author, University of Stirling, Stirling FK9 4LA)

CHANGE. (n.d.). *Information for women.* (Sheets 1-4). (Available from author, University of Stirling, Stirling FK9 4LA)

CHANGE. (various years). *Annual report.* (Available from author, University of Stirling, Stirling FK9 4LA)

Charlesworth, H., & Chinkin, C. (1994). Violence against women: A global issue. In J. Stubbs (Ed.), *Women, male violence and the law* (Institute of Criminology Monograph Series, No. 6, pp. 13-33). Sydney: Sydney University Law School.

Chaudhuri, M., & Daly, K. (1992). Do restraining orders help? Battered women's experiences with male violence and legal process. In E. Buzawa & C. Buzawa (Eds.), *Domestic violence: The changing criminal justice response.* Westport, CT: Auburn House.

Chen, H. T., Bersani, C., Myers, S. C., & Denton, R. (1989). Evaluating the effectiveness of a court-sponsored abuser treatment programme. *Journal of Family Violence, 4,* 309-322.

Cook, S., & Bessant, J. (Eds.). (1997). *Women's encounters with violence: Australian experiences.* Thousand Oaks, CA. Sage.

Counts, D. A., Brown, J. K., & Campbell, J. (1992). *Sanctions and sanctuary: Cultural perspectives on the beating of wives.* San Francisco: Westview Press.

Daly, M., & Wilson, M. (1988). *Homicide.* New York, Aldine de Gruyter.

Daly, M., & Wilson, M. (1990). Killing the competition: Female/female and male/male homicide. *Human Nature, 1,* 81-107.

Daly, M., & Wilson, M. (1992). Stepparenthood and the evolved psychology of discriminative parental solicitude. In S. Parmigiani, B. Svare, & F. vom Saal (Eds.), *Protection and abuse of infants.* London: Harwood Academic Publishers.

Davis, R., & Taylor, B. (1995, July). *Experimental evaluations in treatment for batterers and victims: A coordinated response to domestic violence.* Paper presented at the 4th International Family Violence Research Conference, New England Center, Durham, NH.

DeMaris, A. (1989). Attrition in batterers counseling: The role of social and demographic factors. *Social Service Review, 63,* 142-154.

Descola, P. (1996). *The spears of twilight: Life and death in the Amazon jungle* (J. Lloyd, Trans.). Glasgow: HarperCollins. (Original work published in French)

DiClemente, C. C., & Prochaska, J. O. (1982). Self-change and therapy change of smoking behavior: A comparison of processes of change in cessation and maintenance. *Addictive Behaviors, 7,* 133-142.

Dillman, D. (1978). *Mail and telephone surveys: The total design method.* New York: John Wiley.

Dobash, R. E., & Dobash, R. P. (1979). *Violence against wives.* New York: Free Press. (Available from Paramount Publishing/ Simon & Schuster, London)

Dobash, R. E., & Dobash, R. P. (1984). The nature and antecedents of violent events. *British Journal of Criminology, 24,* 269-88.

Dobash, R. E., & Dobash, R. P. (1992). *Women, violence and social change.* London & New York: Routledge.

Dobash, R. E., Dobash, R. P., & Cavanagh, K. (1985). The contact between battered women and social and medical agencies. In J. Pahl (Ed.), *Private violence and public policy* (pp. 142-165). London: Routledge.

Dobash, R. P., & Dobash, R. E. (1983). The context specific approach. In D. Finkelhor et al. (Eds.), *The dark side of families* (pp. 261-276). Beverly Hills, CA: Sage.

Dobash, R. P., Dobash, R. E., Wilson, M., & Daly, M. (1992). The myth of sexual symmetry in marital violence. *Social Problems, 39,* 71-91.

Dobash, R. P., Dobash, R. E., Cavanagh, K., & Lewis, R. (1995). Evaluating programmes for violent men: Can violent men change? In R. E. Dobash, R. P. Dobash, & L. Noaks (Eds.), *Gender and crime* (pp. 358-389). Cardiff: University of Wales Press and Concord, MA: Paul.

Dobash, R. P., Dobash, R. E., Cavanagh, K., & Lewis, R. (1996). *Research evaluation of programmes for violent men.* Edinburgh: Her Majesty's Stationery Office.

Dobash, R. P., Dobash, R. E., Cavanagh, K., & Lewis, R. (1998). Separate and intersecting realities: A comparison of men's and women's accounts of violence against women. *Violence Against Women, 4*(4), 382-414.

Dobash, R. P., Dobash, R. E., & Gutteridge, S. (1986). *The imprisonment of women.* Oxford, UK: Basil Blackwell.

Duff, R. A.(1986). *Trials and punishments.* London: Cambridge University Press.

Dutton, D. G. (1986). The outcome of court-mandated treatment for wife assault: A quasi-experimental evaluation. *Violence and Victims, 1,* 163-175.

Dutton, D. G. (1995). *The domestic assault of women: Psychological and criminal justice perspectives.* Vancouver: University of British Columbia Press.

Dutton, D. G., & Hemphill, K. J. (1992) Patterns of socially desirable responding among perpetrators and victims of wife assault. *Violence and Victims, 7*(1), 29-39.

Dutton, M. A. (1996). Battered women's strategic response to violence: The role of context. In J. L. Edelson & Z. C. Eisikovits (Eds.), *Future interventions with battered women and their families* (pp. 105-124). Thousand Oaks, CA: Sage.

Edleson, J. L. (1990). Judging the success of interventions with men who batter. In D. Besharov (Ed.), *Family violence: Research and public policy issues* (pp. 358-389). Washington, DC: AEI Press.

Edleson, J. L. (1996). Controversy and change in batterers' programs. In J. L. Edleson & Z. C. Eisikovits (Eds.), *Future interventions with battered women and their families* (pp. 154-169). Thousand Oaks, CA: Sage.

Edleson, J. L., & Syers, M. (1990, June). Relative effectiveness of group treatments for men who batter. *Social Work Research & Abstracts,* pp. 10-17.

Edleson, J. L., & Syers, M. (1991), The effects of group treatment for men who batter: An 18-month follow-up study. *Research in Social Work Practice, 1,* 227-243.

Edleson, J. L., & Grusznski, R. J. (1988). Treating men who batter: Four years of outcome data from a domestic abuse project. *Journal of Social Service Research, 12,* 3-22.

Edleson, J. L., & Tolman, R. M. (1992). *Intervention for men who batter: An ecological approach.* Newbury Park, CA: Sage.

Eduards, M. (1997). The women's shelter movement. In G. Gustafsson, M. Eduards, & M. Ronnblom (Eds.), *Towards a new democratic order? Women's organizing in Sweden in the 1990s* (pp. 120-168). Stockholm: Publica.

Edwards, S.S.M. (1986, July). Police attitudes and dispositions in domestic disputes: The London study. *Police Journal,* pp. 230-241.

Edwards, S.S.M. (1989). *Policing domestic violence.* London: Sage.

Eisikovits, Z. C., & Edleson, J. L. (1989). Intervening with men who batter: A critical review of the literature. *Social Science Review, 37*(3), 385-414.

Fagan, J. (1992). The social control of spouse assault. In F. Adler & W. Laufer (Eds.), *Advances in criminological theory* (Vol. 4, pp. 187-235). New Brunswick, NJ: Transaction.

Fagan, J. (1993). Social structure and spouse assault. In B. Frost (Ed.), *The socioeconomics of crime and justice* (pp. 209-254). Toronto: M. E. Sharpe.

Faragher, T. (1985). The police response to violence against women in the home. In J. Pahl (Ed.), *Private violence and public policy: The needs of battered women and the response of the public services* (pp. 110-124). London: Routledge.

Fields, M. D. (1994). Criminal justice responses to violence against women. In A. Duff, S. Marshall, R. E. Dobash, & R. P. Dobash (Eds.), *Penal theory and practice: Tradition and innovation in criminal justice* (Fulbright Papers, Proceedings of Colloquia, the Fulbright Commission, pp. 199-215). Manchester, UK: Manchester University Press.

Finkelhor, D., & Yllö, K. (1985). *License to rape.* New York: Free Press.

Finn, P., & Colson, S. (1990). *Civil protection orders: Legislation, current court practice, and enforcement.* Washington DC: National Institute of Justice, U.S. Department of Justice.

Foucault, M. (1977). *Discipline and punish* (A. Sheridan, Trans.). London: Allen Lane. (Original work published in French)

Francis, R. (1995). An overview of community-based intervention programmes for men who are violent or abusive in the home. In R. E. Dobash, R. P. Dobash, & L. Noaks (Eds.), *Gender and crime* (pp. 390-409). Cardiff: University of Wales Press and Concord, MA: Paul.

Garner, J., Fagan, J., & Maxwell, C. (1995). Published findings from the spouse abuse replication project: A critical review. *Journal of Quantitative Criminology, 11,* 3-28.

Gender, P., & Ross, R. R. (1987). Revivification of rehabilitation: Evidence from the 1980s. *Justice Quarterly, 4,* 349-358.

Gendreau, P., Cullen, F. T., & Bonta, J. (1994). Intensive rehabilitation supervision: The next generation in community corrections? *Federal Probation, 58*(1), 72-78.

Goldner, V., Penn, P., Sheinberg, M., & Walker, G. (1990). Law and violence: Gender paradoxes in volatile attachments. *Family Process, 29*(4), 343-364.

Gondolf, E. W. (1987). Changing men who batter: A developmental model of integrated interventions. *Journal of Family Violence, 2,* 345-369.

Gondolf, E. W. (with Fisher, E. R.). (1988a). *Battered women as survivors*. Lexington, MA: Lexington.

Gondolf, E. W. (1988b). The effects of batterer counselling on shelter outcome. *Journal of Interpersonal Violence, 3*, 275-289.

Gondolf, E. W. (1991). A victim-based assessment of court-mandated counseling for batterers. *Criminal Justice Review, 16*, 214-226.

Gondolf, E. W. (1997). Batterer programs: What we know and need to know. *Journal of Interpersonal violence, 12*(1), 63-74.

Gondolf, E. W., & Foster, R. A. (1991). Pre-program attrition in batterer programs. *Journal of Family Violence, 6*, 337-350.

Grace, S. (1995). *Policing domestic violence in the 1990s* (Home Office Research Study, No. 139). London: Her Majesty's Stationery Office.

Grau, J., Fagan, J., & Wexler, S. (1985). Restraining orders for battered women: Issues of access and efficacy. *Women and Politics, 4*(3), 13-28.

Hague, G., & Malos, E. (1993). *Domestic violence, action for change*. Cheltenham, UK: New Clarion Press.

Haj-Yahia, M. M. (1996). Wife abuse in the Arab society in Israel: Challenges for future change. In J. L. Edleson & Z. C. Eisikovits (Eds.), *Future interventions with battered women and their families* (pp. 87-101). Thousand Oaks, CA: Sage.

Hamm, M. S., & Kite, J. C. (1991, Autumn). The role of offender rehabilitation in family violence policy: The batterers anonymous experiment. *Criminal Justice Review, 16*(2), 227-248.

Hanson, R. K., & Whitman, R. (1995). A rural, community action model for the treatment of abusive men. *Canadian Journal of Community Mental Health, 14*(1), 49-59.

Hart, B. (1988). *Safety for women: Monitoring the batterers' programs*. Harrisburg, PA: Pennsylvania Coalition Against Domestic Violence (524 McKnight St., Reading, PA).

Hart, B. (1993). Battered women and the criminal justice system. *American Behavioral Scientist, 36*(5), 624-638.

Heise, L. L. (with Pitanguy, J., & Germain, A.). (1994). *Violence against women: The hidden health burden* (World Bank Discussion Papers). Washington DC: World Bank.

Heise, L. L. (1996). Violence against women: Global organizing for change. In J. L. Edleson & Z. C. Eisikovits (Eds.), *Future interventions with battered women and their families* (pp. 7-33). Thousand Oaks, CA: Sage.

Hey, V. (1986). *Patriarchy and pub violence*. London: Tavistock.

Hoff, L. A. (1990). *Battered women as survivors*. New York: Routledge.

Homer, M., Leonard, A., & Taylor, P. (1985). Refuges and housing for battered women. In J. Pahl (Ed.), *Private violence and public policy: The needs of battered women and the response of the public services* (pp. 166-178). London: Routledge.

Horton, A. L., Simonidis, K. M., & Simonidis, L. L. (1987). Legal remedies for spousal abuse: Victim characteristics, expectations and satisfaction. *Journal of Family Violence 2*(3), 265-279.

Hosmer, D. W., & Lemeshow, S. (1989). *Applied logistic regression*. New York: John Wiley.

Ignatieff, M. (1978). *A just measure of pain: The penitentiary in the industrial revolution, 1750-1850*. London: Macmillan.

Jacobson, N. S., Gottman, J., Gortner, E., Bern, S., & Nushortt, J. (1996). Psychological factors in the longitudinal course of battering: When do the couples split up? When does the abuse decrease? *Violence and Victims, 11*(4), 371-392.

Jaffe, P., Wolfe, D. A., Telford, A., & Austin, G. (1986). The impact of police charges in incidents of wife abuse. *Journal of Family Violence, 1*, 37-49.

Jennings, J. L. (1990). Preventing relapse versus stopping domestic violence: Do we expect too much too soon from battering men? *Journal of Family Violence, 1*(1), 43-60.

Johnson, H. (1996). *Dangerous domains: Violence against women in Canada.* Toronto: Nelson.

Johnson, H. (1998). Rethinking survey research on violence against women. In R. E. Dobash & R. P. Dobash (Eds.), *Rethinking violence against women* (pp. 23-51). Thousand Oaks, CA: Sage.

Johnson, H., & Sacco, V. F. (1995). Researching violence against women: Statistics Canada's national survey. *Canadian Journal of Criminology, 37*(3), 281-304.

Keilitz, S. L., Hannaford, P. L., & Efkeman, H. S. (1996). *Civil protection orders: The benefits and limitations for victims of domestic violence.* Washington DC: National Institute of Justice.

Kelleher, P., Kelleher, C., & O'Conner, M. (1995). *Making the links: Towards an integrated strategy for the elimination of violence against women in intimate relationships with men.* Dublin: Women's Aid.

Kennedy, H. (1992). *Eve was framed: Women and British justice.* London: Chatto & Windus.

Klein, E., Campbell, J., Soler, E., & Ghez, M. (1997). *Ending domestic violence: Changing public perceptions, halting the epidemic.* Thousand Oaks, CA: Sage.

Kurz, D. (1997). Violence against women or family violence: Current debates and future directions. In L. L. O'Toole & J. R. Schiffman (Eds.), *Gender violence: Interdisciplinary perspectives* (pp. 443-453). New York: New York University Press.

Lackey, C., & Williams, K. (1995). Social bonding and the cessation of partner violence across generations. *Journal of Marriage and the Family, 57,* 295-305.

Langan, P., & Innes, C. (1986). *Preventing domestic violence against women* (Special report). Washington DC: Bureau of Justice Statistics, U.S. Department of Justice.

Lees, S. (1998, April 16). A fistful of promises. *The Guardian Newspaper,* p. 4.

Lewis, R., Dobash, R. P., Dobash, R. E., & Cavanagh, K. (in press). Protection, prevention, rehabilitation or justice? Women using the law to challenge domestic violence. *International Review of Victimology.*

Longino, H. E. (1993) Essential tensions—phase two: Feminist, philosophical, and social studies of science. In L. M. Antony & C. Witt (Eds.), *A mind of one's own: Feminist essays on reason and objectivity* (pp. 257-273). Boulder, CO: Westview.

Lothian Domestic Violence Probation Project. (n.d., circa 1994). *Role of the group worker.* Unpublished program materials. (Available from author, Edinburgh, Scotland)

Lothian Domestic Violence Probation Project. (n.d.). [Program materials]. (Available from author, Edinburgh, Scotland)

Maguire, M. (1995). Crime statistics, patterns, and trends: Changing perceptions and their implications. In M. Maguire, R. Morgan, & R. Reiner (Eds.), *The Oxford handbook of criminology* (pp. 233-291). Oxford, UK: Oxford University Press.

Marshall, W. L., & Eccles, A. (1991). Issues in clinical practice with sex offenders. *Journal of Interpersonal Violence, 6*(1), 68-93.

Marshall, W. L., Laws, D. R., & Barbee, H. E. (Eds.). (1990). *Handbook of sexual assault: Issues, theories and treatment of the offender.* New York: Plenum.

Martinson, R. (1974). What works: Questions and answers about prison reform. *The Public Interest, 35,* 22-54.

Masters, G., & Smith, D. (1998). Portia and Persephone revisited: Thinking about feelings in criminal justice. *Theoretical Criminology 12*(1), 5-27.

McFarlane, J., Parker, B., Soeken, K., & Bullock, L. (1992). Assessing for abuse during pregnancy: Frequency and extent of injuries and associated entry into prenatal care. *Journal of the American Medical Association, 267,* 3176-3198.

McGregor, H., & Hopkins, A. (1991). *Working for change: The movement against domestic violence.* Sydney: Allen & Unwin.

McWilliams, M., & McKiernan, J. (1993). *Bringing it out in the open: Domestic violence in Northern Ireland.* Belfast: Her Majesty's Stationery Office.

Miller, W. R., & Rollnick, S. (1991), *Motivational interviewing: Preparing people to change addictive behavior.* New York: Guilford.

Mirrlees-Black, C. (1994). *Estimating the extent of domestic violence: Findings from the 1992 BCS* (Home Office Research Bulletin, No. 37). London: Home Office Research and Statistics Department.

Mooney, J. (1994). *The prevalence and social distribution of domestic violence: An analysis of theory and method.* Unpublished doctoral dissertation, Middlesex University.

Morran, D., & Wilson, M. (1994). Confronting domestic violence: An innovative criminal justice response in Scotland. In A. Duff, S. Marshall, R. E. Dobash, & R. P. Dobash (Eds.), *Penal theory and practice: Tradition and innovation in criminal justice* (Fulbright Papers, Proceedings of Colloquia, the Fulbright Commission, pp. 216-230). Manchester, UK: Manchester University Press.

Morran, D., & Wilson, M. (1997). *Men who are violent to women: A groupwork practice manual.* Lyme Regis, UK: Russell House.

Mullender, A. (1996). *Rethinking domestic violence.* London: Routledge.

Nazroo, J. (1995). Uncovering gender differences in the use of marital violence: The effect of methodology. *Sociology, 29*(3), 475-494.

Pagelow, M. (1985). The "battered husband syndrome": Social problem or much ado about little? In N. Johnson (Ed.), *Marital violence* (pp. 135-150). London, Routledge.

Pahl, J. (Ed.). (1985). *Private violence and public policy: The needs of battered women and the response of the public services.* London: Routledge.

Painter, K., & Farrington, D. (in press). Marital violence in Great Britain and its relationship to marital and non-marital rape. *International Review of Victimology, 5.*

Parliament, House of Commons. (1993, February). *Domestic violence* (Vol. 1: Third report). London: Home Affairs Committee.

Pate, A. M., & Hamilton, E. E. (1992). Formal and informal deterrents to domestic violence: The Dade County spouse assault experiment. *American Sociological Review, 57,* 691-697.

Pawson, R., & Tilly, N. (1997). *Realistic evaluation.* Thousand Oaks, CA: Sage.

Pence, E. (1983). The Duluth domestic abuse intervention project. *Hamline Law Review, 6*(2), 247-275.

Pence, E. (with Duprey, M., Paymar, M., & McDonnell, C.). (1989). *Criminal justice response to domestic assault cases: A guide for policy development* (rev. ed.). Duluth, MN: Domestic Abuse Intervention Project.

Pence, E., & Paymar, M. (1985). *Power and control: Tactics of men who batter. An Educational Curriculum* (rev. ed., 1990). Duluth: Minnesota Program Development (206 West Fourth Street, Duluth, MN 55806).

Pence, E., & Paymar, M. (1993). *Education groups for men who batter.* New York: Springer.

Pence E., & Shepard, M. (1988). Integrating feminist theory and practice: The challenge of the battered women's movement. In K. Ylló & M. Bogard (Eds.), *Feminist perspectives on wife abuse.* Newbury Park, CA: Sage.

Pirog-Good, M. A., & Stets, J. (1986). Programs for abusers: Who drops out and what can be done. *RESPONSE, 9,* 17-19.

Pleck, E. (1987). *Domestic tyranny.* Oxford, UK: Oxford University Press.

Polk, K. (1994). *When men kill: Scenarios of masculine violence.* New York: Cambridge University Press.

Prochaska, J. O., & DiClemente, C. C. (1983). Stages and processes of self-change of smoking: Toward an integrative model of change. *Journal of Consulting and Clinical Psychology, 51,* 390-395.

Ptacek, J. (1988). Why do men batter their wives? In K. Yllö & M. Bogard (Eds.), *Feminist perspectives on wife abuse* (pp. 133-157). Newbury Park, CA: Sage.

Ptacek, J. (1995) *Disorder in the courts: Judicial demeanor and women's experience seeking restraining orders.* Unpublished doctoral dissertation, Brandeis University.

Reiss, A. J., & Roth, J. A. (Eds.). (1993). *Understanding and preventing violence* (especially Chapter 4). Washington, DC: National Academy Press.

Ribisl, K. M., Walton, M. A., Mowbray, C. T., Luke, D. A., Davidson, W. S., & Bootsmiller, B. J. (1996). Minimizing participant attrition in panel studies through the use of effective retention and tracking strategies: Review and recommendations. *Evaluation and Program Planning, 19*(1), 1-25.

Römkens, R. (1997). Prevalence of wife abuse in the Netherlands: Combining quantitative and qualitative methods in a survey. *Journal of Interpersonal Violence, 12,* 99-125.

Russell, D. (1982). *Rape in marriage.* New York: Macmillan.

Saunders, D. G. (1996). Feminist-cognitive-behavioral and process-psychodynamic treatments for men who batter: Interaction of abuser traits and treatment models. *Violence and Victims, 11,* 393-413.

Saunders, D. G., & Azar, S. (1989). Treatment programs for family violence. In L. Ohlin & M. Tonry (Eds.), *Family violence, crime and justice* (Vol. 11, pp. 481-546). Chicago: University of Chicago Press.

Saunders, D. G., & Hanusa, D. (1986). Cognitive-behavioral treatment for men who batter: The short-term effects of group therapy. *Journal of Family Violence, 1,* 357-372.

Schalock, R. L. (1995). *Outcome-based evaluation.* New York: Plenum.

Schechter, S. (1982). *Women and male violence: The visions and struggles of the battered women's movement.* Boston: South End Press.

Schneider, E. (1992a). Particularity and generality: Challenges of feminist theory and practice in work on woman abuse. *New York University Law Review, 67,* 520.

Schneider, E. (1992b). Violence against women and legal education: An essay for Mary Joe Frug. *New England Law Journal, 26,* 843.

Scourfield, J. B., & Dobash, R. P. (1999). Programmes for violent men: Recent developments in the U.K. *The Howard Journal, 38*(2), 128-143.

Seddon, N. (1993). *Domestic violence in Australia: The legal response* (2nd ed.). Sydney: Federation Press.

Sherman, L. W. (1992). *Policing domestic violence: Experiments and dilemmas.* New York: Free Press.

Sherman, L. W., & Berk, B. A. (1984). The specific deterrent effects of arrest for domestic assault. *American Sociological Review, 49,* 261-272.

Sherman, L. W., & Smith, D. A. (1992). Crime, punishment, and stake in conformity: Legal and informal control of domestic violence. *American Sociological Review, 57,* 680-690.

Sinclair, H. (1989). *The MAWS men's program and the issue of male-role violence against women* [Training manual]. San Rafael, CA: Marin Abused Women Services.

Smart, C. (1989). *Feminism and the power of law.* London: Routledge.

Smart, C. (1995). *Law, crime and criminality: Essays in feminism.* London: Sage.

Smith, L. (1989). *Domestic violence: An overview of the literature* (Home Office Research Study, No. 107). London: Her Majesty's Stationery Office.

Snider, L. (1990). The potential of the criminal justice system to promote feminist concerns. *Studies in Law, Politics and Society, 10,* 143-172.

Stanko, E. A. (1985). *Intimate intrusions: Women's experience of male violence.* London: Routledge.

Stanko, E. A. (1989). Missing the mark? Policing battering. In J. Hanmer, J. Radford, & E. A. Stanko (Eds.), *Policing and male violence: International perspectives* (pp. 46-69). London: Routledge.

Stark, E. (1993). Mandatory arrest of batterers. A reply to its critics. *American Behavioral Scientist, 36*(5), 651-680.

Stubbs, J. (Ed.). (1994). *Women, male violence and the law* (Institute of Criminology Monograph Series, No. 6). Sydney: Sydney University Law School.

Stubbs, J., & Egger, S. (1993). *The effectiveness of protection orders in Australian jurisdictions.* Canberra: Australian Government Printing Service.

Sumner, M., & Parker, H.(1995). *Low in alcohol: A review of international research into alcohol's role in crime causation.* London: Portman Group.

Tavuchis, N. (1991). *Mea culpa: A sociology of apology and reconciliation.* Stanford, CA: Stanford University Press.

Tjaden, P., & Thoennes, N. (1997, November). *The prevalence and consequences of intimate partner violence: Findings from the national violence against women survey.* Unpublished paper presented at the 49th annual meeting of the American Society of Criminology, San Diego, CA.

Tolman, R. M., & Bennett, L. W. (1990). A review of quantitative research on men who batter. *Journal of Interpersonal Violence, 5,* 87-118.

United Nations. (1995). *Declaration of elimination of violence against women.* Beijing: Author.

Van Voorhis, P., Cullen, F., & Applegate, B. (1995, June). Evaluating interventions with violent offenders: A guide for practitioners and policy makers. *Federal Probation, 56*(3), 17-27.

Walker, L.E.A (1984). *The battered woman syndrome.* New York: Springer.

Wallace, A. (1986). A typology of homicide. In A. Wallace (Ed.), *Homicide: The social reality* (pp. 83-109). Sydney: New South Wales, Bureau of Crime Statistics and Research.

Waterhouse, L., Dobash, R. P., & Carnie, J. (1994). *Child sexual abusers.* Edinburgh: Scottish Office Central Research Unit.

Weiss, H. B., & Jacobs, F. H. (Eds.). (1988). *Evaluating family programs.* New York: Aldine de Gruyter.

Williams, K. R., & Hawkins, R. (1989). The meaning of arrest for wife assault. *Criminology, 27*(1), 163-181.

Williams, L. M., & Finkelhor, D. (1990). The characteristics of incestuous fathers. In W. L. Marshall, D. R. Laws, & H. E. Barbee (Eds.), *Handbook of sexual assault: Issues, theories and treatment of the offender* (pp. 231-256). New York: Plenum.

Wilson, M., Johnson, H., & Daly, M. (1995) Lethal and nonlethal violence against wives. *Canadian Journal of Criminology, 37*(3), 331-362.

Worrall, A., & Pease, K. (1986). Personal crime against women: Evidence from the 1982 British Crime Survey. *Howard Journal, 25*(2), 118-124.

Wright, S. (1995). The role of the police in combating domestic violence. In R. E. Dobash, R. P. Dobash, & L. Noaks, (Eds.), *Gender and crime* (pp. 410-428). Cardiff: University of Wales Press and Concord, MA: Paul.

Yllö, K. (1993) Through a feminist lens: Gender, power and violence. In R. J. Gelles & D. R. Loseke (Eds.), *Current controversies on family violence* (pp. 47-62). Newbury Park, CA: Sage.

Zorza, J., & Woods, L. (1994). *Mandatory arrest: Problems and possibilities.* New York: National Center on Women and Family Law.

Index

About the Authors

Rebecca Emerson Dobash is Professor of Social Research and Russell P. Dobash is Professor of Criminology in the Department of Social Policy and Social Work at the University of Manchester, U.K.; they are also codirectors of the violence Research Center. they have coauthored several books and numerous government reports and scores of articles in journals and scholarly anthologies. Their books include *Violence Against Wives* (1986), *Women Viewing Violence* (1992), and *Women, Violence and Social Change* (1992). *Violence Against Wives* won the World Congress of Victimology Award; *Women, Violence and Social Change* won the American Society of Criminology's Distinguished book Award for Comparative Research; and they have also been awarded the American Criminological Association's August Vollmer Award. Their most recent coedited book is *Rethinking Violence Against Women* (1998).

They have twice been scholars in residence at the Rockefeller Foundation Study and Conference Centre in Bellagio, Italy, and have held fellowships and/or research grants from the Fulbright Foundation, the Harry Frank Guggenheim Foundation, the Economic and Social Research Council, and several British governmental departments and have been international fellows in criminology at the University of Melbourne.

In more than two decades of research on violence they have collaborated with colleagues in many academic disciplines, worked with women's groups in several countries, and served as research advisors to agencies of the British, Canadian, U.S., and Australian governments. Current research includes work on convicted child sex abusers; an evaluation of criminal justice-based treatment programs for violent men; bodybuilding, steroids and violence; a comparison of men's and women's accounts of violent events; and men's reactions to televised violence. Along with Kate Cavanagh and Ruth Lewis they are currently conducting the first national study of homicide in Britain.

Kate Cavanagh holds a doctorate from the University of Manchester and is a lecturer in social work in the Department of Social Policy and Social Work at Glasgow University, Scotland. She has been involved in the issue of domestic violence for the last 20 years as an activist, practitioner, and researcher. She has also undertaken research on drug takers, disability, and child abuse. She is particularly interested in developing feminist perspectives in social work and is coeditor of *Working With Men: Feminism and Social Work* (1997). Her current research interests include mental health, the social construction of violent relationships, and feminist methods; and with Ruth Lewis she is now assessing interventions for violent men in European countries. Along with the other coauthors of this book she is currently investigating homicide in Britain.

Ruth Lewis received her doctorate from the University of Manchester and is currently a lecturer in the Department of Social Policy at the University of Newcastle, U.K. Her research interests focus on gender, violence, and sociolegal issues. She is engaged in research exploring how survivors and perpetrators of domestic violence experience civil and criminal justice systems, and with Kate Cavanagh she is assessing interventions for violent men in several European countries. Along with the other coauthors of this book she is currently investigating homicide in Britain.